THE OTHER SIDE OF
ISRAEL

THE OTHER SIDE OF

ISRAEL

My Journey Across the Jewish-Arab Divide

SUSAN NATHAN

NAN A. TALESE

DOUBLEDAY

New York   London   Toronto   Sydney   Auckland

PUBLISHED BY NAN A. TALESE
AN IMPRINT OF DOUBLEDAY
a division of Random House, Inc.

DOUBLEDAY is a registered trademark of Random House, Inc.

Library of Congress Cataloging-in-Publication Data
Nathan, Susan.
The other side of Israel: my journey across
the Jewish-Arab divide / Susan Nathan.
p.   cm.
1. Palestinian Arabs—Israel—Tamra—Social conditions.
2. Tamra (Israel)—Social conditions. 3. Israel—Ethnic relations.
4. Pluralism (Social sciences)—Israel.
5. Multiculturalism—Israel. 6. Nathan, Susan—Biography.
I. Title.

DS113.7.N385 2005
305.8'0095694'5—dc22
2005043717

ISBN 0-385-51456-5

PRINTED IN THE UNITED STATES OF AMERICA

October 2005
First published in Great Britain in 2005 by HarperCollins Publishers
First Edition in the United States of America

1   3   5   7   9   10   8   6   4   2

In memory of my parents,
Sam and Maisie Levy,
and for my children,
Daniel and Tanya

CONTENTS

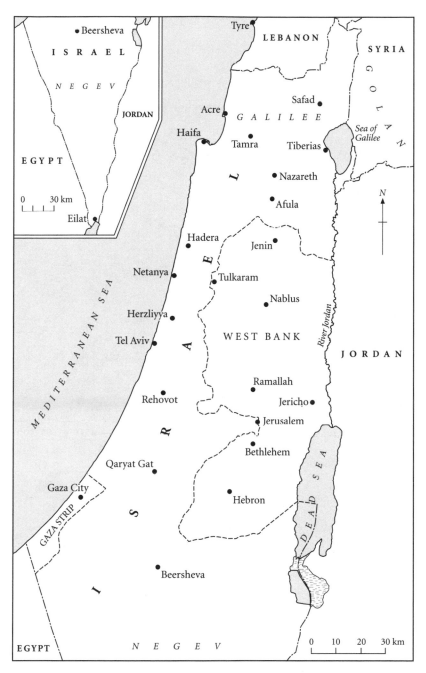

The State of Israel

Northern Israel, including the Galilee

Palestinian towns and villages depopulated during the foundation
of Israel in 1948

ACKNOWLEDGEMENTS

It was a sweltering July night nearly two years ago when friends introduced me to Jonathan Cook, a British reporter based in the Israeli Arab city of Nazareth. The place of our meeting was the Beit al-Falastini (the Palestinian House), a renovated ancient stone building in the city's old market that during the day serves as a coffeehouse and at night is the nearest thing Nazareth has to a pub. We chatted in the dim surroundings of the cavernous interior, barely able to make out each other in the flickering candlelight. But it soon became clear from our conversation that we shared a concern about the direction Israel is taking. For both of us, this was of more than academic interest: I have adopted this country as my new home, and Jonathan has adopted it through his marriage to Sally Azzam, a native Nazarene.

After our first meeting, Jonathan, ever the inquisitive journalist, arranged to come to Tamra to talk to me again. He published the interview in Britain's *Guardian* newspaper on 27 August 2003, under the headline "A Jew Among 25,000 Muslims." That article sparked worldwide interest in my story and brought me to the attention of HarperCollins, who have now encouraged me to publish a much fuller account of my journey from one side of the ethnic divide to the other. My deepest thanks go to Jonathan, who has been a companion on that journey, helping a novice author give expression to her thoughts, experiences and impressions. Without his guidance, I have no doubt this would have been a poorer book. But most of all I want to thank Jonathan for his dedication to reporting the truth and his unwavering commitment to creating a more just and humane society in Israel.

My thanks also go to Sally Azzam Cook, for her patience, suggestions and help to Jonathan; Dr. Asad Ghanem, head of politics at Haifa University, and his wife, Ahlam, for opening their home to me and helping to change the course of my life by teaching me about the reality of theirs; Dr. Uri Davis, for his steadfast friendship and sound advice on a wide variety of subjects and his enormous contribution towards explaining the essence of the conflict; Rabbi Dr. John D. Rayner, for his support and enthusiasm regarding my move to Tamra; Dr. Afif Safieh, the Palestinian delegate to the United Kingdom and the Holy See, for his support, guidance and encouragement; Dr. Mahdi Abdul Hadi, head of the Palestinian Academic Society for the Study of International Affairs (PASSIA), East Jerusalem, for his friendship and support and the use of his wonderful library; Dr. Daphna Golan, director of the Minerva Centre for Human Rights, Hebrew University of Jerusalem, for her friendship, shared concerns and time; Dr. Adel Manna, of the Van Leer Institute, Jerusalem, whose phone call of support was deeply appreciated, for his historical input; Dr. Said Zidanem, associate professor at Al-Quds University, East Jerusalem, for enlightening conversations held in his family's home in Tamra and for his continuing support of my endeavours; Amin Sahli, Tamra's city engineer, for teaching me the difficulties of planning in a town without land; Eitan Bronstein of Zochrot, for his shared vision of what life could be in Israel and for his courage; Harry Finkbeiner of Kibbutz

Harduf, for help with research; the Gaza Community Mental Health Care project, for their guidance of and support for my work for Mahapach, and for their generous invitation to visit Gaza to learn from them; Wehbe Badarni of Sawt al-Amal (Voice of the Labourer) in Nazareth, for teaching me about employ-ment discrimination and for his devotion to his work; Abdullah Barakat, assistant to the governor of Jenin, for helping me meet the people of Jenin; Mayor Adel Abu Hayja and the Municipality of Tamra, for welcoming me into their community; Richard Johnson, my editor, for his determination to see my story in print and for his continuous encouragement; Dr. Carlos Lesmes, anaesthetist, for his ongoing help and support with pain control and his interest in the book. My deepest thanks go to Nan Talese and Doubleday for their belief and constant support of my en-deavours and their determination to publish this book. Dr. Oded Schoenberg for his patience and compassion, and the rest of the team at the Herziliya Medical Centre who have been on my case for the last five years; Arlette Calderon, Dr. Nissim Ohana, Dr. Daniel Kern, and Avi Millstein; Professor Ya'acov Pe'er and the Department of Ophthalmology at Hadassah Hospital, Jerusalem, without whom I would never have got this far; Mahapach, for their unique contribution to Israeli society; and my friends, too numerous to mention individually. Special thanks go to my "fam-ily" in Tamra, for their trust in me and for the remarkable way in which they absorbed me into their circle.

Finally, I have changed the names of some people who appear in the book, including my family in Tamra, for reasons of confi-dentiality and safety.

Susan Nathan
Tamra, Israel
December 2004

THE OTHER SIDE OF
ISRAEL

1

THE ROAD TO TAMRA

The road to the other side of Israel is not signposted. It is a place you rarely read about in your newspapers or hear about from your television sets. It is all but invisible to most Israelis. In the Galilee, Israel's most northerly region, the green signs dotted all over the highways point out the direction of Haifa, Acre and Karmiel, all large Jewish towns, and even much smaller Jewish communities like Shlomi and Misgav. But as my taxi driver, Shaher, and I look for Tamra, we find no signs—or none until we are heading downhill, racing the other traffic along a stretch of dual carriageway. By a turn-off next to a large metal shack selling fruit and vegetables is a white sign pointing rightwards to Tamra, forcing us to make a dangerous last-minute lane change to exit from the main road. Before us, stretching into the distance, is a half-made road, and at the end of it a pale grey mass of concrete squats within a shallow hollow in the rugged Galilean hills. Shaher looks genuinely startled. "My God, it's Tulkaram!" he exclaims, referring to a Palestinian town and refugee camp notorious among Israelis as a hotbed of terrorism.

A few weeks earlier, in November 2002, I had run the removals company in Tel Aviv to warn them well in advance of my move to Tamra, a town of substantial size by Israeli standards, close to the Mediterranean coast between the modern industrial port of Haifa and the ancient Crusader port of Acre. Unlike the communities I had seen well signposted in the Galilee, Tamra is not Jewish; it is an Arab town that is home to twenty-five thousand Muslims. A fact almost unknown outside Israel is that the Jewish state includes a large minority of one million Palestinians who have Israeli citizenship. Making up a fifth of the population, they are popularly, and not a little disparagingly, known as "Israeli Arabs." For a Jew to choose to live among them is unheard of. In fact, it is more than that: it is inconceivable.

When I told my left-wing friends in Tel Aviv of my decision, all of them, without exception, were appalled. First they angrily dismissed my choice, assuming either that it was a sign of my perverse misunderstanding of Middle Eastern realities or that it was a childish attempt to gain attention. But as it became clear that my mind was made up, they resorted to more intimidatory tactics. "You'll be killed," more than one told me. "You know, the Arabs are friendly to start with, but they'll turn on you," advised another. "You'll be raped by the men," said one more. Finally, another friend took me aside and confided darkly, "I have a telephone number for a special unit in the army. They can come in and get you out if you need help. Just let me know."

The woman at the removals company was less perturbed. "Will it be possible for you to move me from Tel Aviv to Tamra?" I asked, concerned that as far as I could discern, no one was living as a Jew inside an Israeli Arab community. I told her that if they had a problem with the move, they should tell me now. "Madam, we will deliver your belongings to anywhere in the state of Israel," she reassured me.

I arranged for Shaher, whom I had used often in Tel Aviv, to collect me from my apartment on the day of the move. On the two-hour journey north we would lead the way in his taxi, with the removal truck following behind. Shaher phoned the day before to reassure me. "I have been looking carefully at the road map and I've devised a route to the Galilee which won't involve passing too many Arab villages," he told me. "But we are heading for an Arab town," I reminded him. "Why on earth would I be worried about the route?" Shaher did not seem to get my point.

We set off early the next day. Shaher was soon announcing, unbidden, his concern over my move to Tamra. What followed was a surreal exchange, the first of many such conversations I would have with taxi drivers and other Jews I met after I started living in Tamra. "So why are you moving there?" he asked several times, apparently not persuaded by my reply each time: "Because I want to." Finally he changed tack: "You know it's an Arab area?" Yes, I said, I think I know that. "So have you got an apartment there?" Yes. "How did you get an apartment?" I rented it, I said, just as I had done in Tel Aviv. Under his breath I could hear him muttering, "But it's an Arab area." Then suddenly, as though it were a vital question he should have asked much earlier, he said, "Do you have a gun?" Why would I need a gun? I asked. "Because they might kill you." I told him he was talking nonsense. Silence separated us until his face changed again. "Ah," he said, "you must be working for the government and I didn't know it." No, I said, I work just for myself. "But it's an Arab area," he said again. It was a cold winter's day, but by the time we reached the road into Tamra I could see Shaher starting to break into a sweat. In a final offer of help, he said, "Susan, you have my telephone numbers. If you need to come back to Tel Aviv, just call me."

We followed the only proper road in Tamra to the central mosque and then negotiated our way up a steeply sloping side street till we reached my new home, hidden down a small alley. I was renting the top-floor apartment in a three-storey property belonging to a family I had already befriended, the Abu Hayjas. Several members of the family came out to greet me, including the matriarch of the house, Hajji, and one of her granddaughters, Omayma. I went into the ground-floor apartment and had been chatting for maybe twenty minutes when Omayma interrupted. "Susan, why don't they get out and start moving your furniture?" I went to the door and looked at the removal truck for the first time since we had entered Tamra. The two young men sitting in the cab looked as if they were afflicted with total paralysis. I turned to Omayma and replied, only half jokingly, "Because they think you are going to eat them."

I went over to the truck, knocked on the closed window, and told them it was time to get to work. They didn't look convinced, and could only be coaxed out when Hajji proved the natives' hospitality by bringing a pot of coffee, two cups and some biscuits and placing them on a table close to the truck. Once out in the street, the removal men opened the back of the truck and did the job in no time, running up and down the stairs with the boxes. Finished, they hurried back into the truck and raced down the steep street towards the mosque and on to freedom. I never saw them again. The reinforced cardboard packing boxes they were supposed to return for a week later remained in my spare room, uncollected, for weeks. Eventually I rang the company. "I'm sorry, but they won't come back to an Arab area just for the boxes," said the woman I spoke to.

It started to dawn on me that I had crossed an ethnic divide in Israel that, although not visible, was as tangible as the concrete walls and razor-wire fences that have been erected around the occupied Palestinian towns of the West Bank and Gaza to separate them from the rest of the country. Nothing was likely to be the same ever again.

I had no intention of hiding from Tamra's twenty-five thousand other inhabitants the fact that I was a Jew. But from the moment I arrived in the town to teach English, I began redefining my identity, as a Jew, as an Israeli and as a human being. The first and most apparent change was that I was joining a new family, the Abu Hayjas, who immediately accepted me as one of their own, as integral to the family's life as any new daughter-in-law. In keeping with Arab tradition, I was soon renamed Umm Daniel (Mother of Daniel), after my son, a status conferred on older, and wiser, parents.

The family I live with is small by Tamra's standards, consisting of only six other members. The eldest is the widowed Fatima, sixty-eight years of age and called Hajji by everyone because she has completed the hajj to Mecca, one of the duties incumbent on all Muslims during their lifetime. She married at seventeen and lived with her husband for four years before he died. For a woman of her generation there was never any possibility that she could remarry, and so she has remained a widow all her adult life. Hajji has two children, a son and a daughter, but in Arab tradition only the son stays in the family home after marriage, while the daughter goes off to live with her new husband. So Hajji's son, Hassan, fifty, and his wife, Samira, forty-seven, live with her in the building, and the couple's two unmarried grown-up sons, Khalil and Waleed, have their own apartments there in preparation for their marriages. Hassan and Samira's two eldest daughters, Heba and Omayma, are married and so have left home to be with their new families, though they spend a large part of their time visiting their parents and helping in the house. That leaves only Suad, aged seventeen, the one daughter still at home.

Although that is the core of the family, it extends much further. Hajji's own father married twice, so we have a vast network of aunts, uncles and cousins, and half-aunts, half-uncles and half-cousins, who come to visit and drink coffee with us in Hajji's apartment. They are all related in complex patterns that I cannot even begin to unravel but that the rest of my family understands intimately. Unlike me, they are helped by a lifelong familiarity with their extensive family tree and by the Arabic language, which has adapted to accommodate these relationships in more sophisticated ways than English. Aunts, uncles and cousins have titles which denote the blood relationship to each parent's side of the family. For example, the word "ami" tells any Arab child that one of his father's sisters is being referred to, while "hali" reveals that one of his mother's sisters is being identified. The English equivalent for both words, "aunt," is far less helpful.

And then beyond the extended family there is the bigger family structure, known as the "hamula," or clan. There are four main hamulas in Tamra—the Abu Hayja, the Abu Romi, the Diab and the Hijazi—with each controlling a portion of the town, its quarter. My own family, as its name suggests, belongs to the Abu Hayja hamula, which dominates the southern side of Tamra. The hamula system means that everyone in our neighbourhood is related to us, even if it is in some very distant fashion. The importance of the hamula cannot be overstated: it is the ultimate body to which members of traditional Arab society owe their loyalty. In the West the hamula, or tribal system, is seen as backward and a block to progress, but I soon realised that this is a gross simplification. In Middle Eastern countries the tribe still fulfills a positive role (one usurped in the West by the welfare state), ensuring that its members have access to land, housing, jobs, loans and a pool of potential marriage partners. The hamula is the best protector of its members' rights, and it provides an impartial forum for arbitrating disputes. It is revealing that in Israel, where a strong welfare state has developed, at least for Jewish citizens, the hamula still plays an invaluable role in many Arab citizens' lives. Because the state continues to behave as though the Arab citizens are not really its responsibility, many choose to rely on the traditional tribal structure for support.

The hamula serves other functions. It is a crucial point of social reference, a guarantor, if you like, of an individual's good family name. For example, I soon noticed that when two Arabs met for the first time, they would spend several minutes trying to establish a significant mutual acquaintance. Evidently it was important for them to identify each other's place in relation to the various hamulas. Sometimes there would be a series of "Do you know so and so?" questions until both parties could relax at the discovery of a common bond; things could be tense if it took them some time to reach that point. Now, when people are introduced to me, they ask similar questions of me and are reassured by my link to the good name of the Abu Hayja hamula and my immediate family.

For me, as for the rest of my family, the centre of gravity in our lives is to be found in a single figure: Hajji. Her ground-floor apartment is where we often congregate for food, and I like to sit with her on a stool outside her front door first thing in the morning while she makes us strong black Arabic coffee over a stove. The ritual of coffee-making is taken very seriously in all Palestinian households, and Hajji is an expert practitioner. Over a gas flame she dissolves a home-made mixture of coffee and cardamom powder with water and sugar in a small open pot. Just before the liquid boils over she pulls it away from the heat, stirs it until it settles and then heats it again, repeating this process up to half a dozen times. Finally the pot is left standing for five minutes, with a saucer over the top, as the sludge sinks to the bottom. When the coffee is ready, it is poured into tiny cups.

In the time I have been in Tamra, Hajji and I have forged a very deep bond, despite communication difficulties. Speaking in a mixture of broken English, Hebrew and Arabic, we laugh about our common ailments and our love of flowers and nature. Hajji is an authority on traditional Arab remedies, and when I damaged my knee, she suggested wrapping cabbage leaves around it to draw out the fluid.

Widowed at twenty-one, Hajji has known severe economic hardship and raised her family in extreme poverty. She tells stories from her youth of going out into the fields to catch hedgehogs and, desperate for protein, stripping the animals of their prickly skin and roasting them on a spit. Hajji's skills in making the most of the little she has are phenomenal. She knits beautiful children's clothes without a pattern to follow; it's all there in her head. She also has a profound understanding of nature, which I marvel at whenever I watch her in the garden. She has large hands with delicate fingers that plant seeds at high speed and deftly pick out herbs. She selects the Arab mint, sorrel and chamomile plants for our tea, picks off the parts she doesn't want, and lays the rest out to dry in large round wooden sieves. Later she breaks them up into small pieces for storage in jars. There is a calm, rhythmic quality to her work that I find reassuring and meditative.

But she is getting weaker with age, and nowadays she has trouble visiting the rest of the family, who live on the first and second floors of the building. So family occasions are invariably held in her flat. The family jokes that the only time Hajji leaves her apartment is when someone in the extended family has a child, gets married or dies. It's more or less true. Recently, though, she has started going to an old people's centre, where she does embroidery and knitting. She is collected in the morning and arrives home early in the afternoon. But she generally prefers to be at home, and I don't like it when she is away too long. I never really knew either of my two sets of grandparents, and even though she is little more than ten years older than I, Hajji, I think, has become my surrogate grandmother.

Hajji and her daughter-in-law, Samira, together form the backbone of what in the West would surely have become a small business. Downstairs, next to Hajji's apartment, is a garden and a covered area where they produce, manufacture and store the huge quantities of food the family needs. We are a restaurant, plant nursery, canning and pickling plant and bakery all in one. Every week there seems to be a different task, each one defined by the particular growing season. It might be pickling cucumbers, cauliflowers and carrots for use during the rest of the year; or going to collect zatar (a herb akin to thyme and oregano) in the wild, then bringing it back to dry it, mix it with sesame seeds and grind it; or buying staples like rice, flour and bulgur wheat for storage in big containers. There are always piles of boxes, sacks and barrels waiting to be labelled and put away.

A special occasion is the olive harvest in late October, when we all disappear to the edge of town, to a small patch of ground where the family has an olive grove. There for three or four days we crowd among the trees, climbing ladders to pick off handfuls of the green and black fruit and throw them onto tarpaulins below. At the end of the day the tarpaulins are gathered up and the olives are bagged into sacks. Some we later pickle in glass bottles, while the rest goes to the press in town. After the harvest in my first year in Tamra, the family gave me the first bottle of oil as a gift.

Much of our diet, however, grows next to us in the small garden. That is the traditional way in Arab communities, although it is a way of life slowly dying because of both the arrival of out-of-town supermarkets and the extensive confiscation of Arab communities' agricultural land by the Jewish state. Some Arab areas have lost all their farming lands, but Tamra has managed to hold on to some. The ever-increasing territorial confinement of the town, however, means that few families can spare what little land they have left to grow subsistence crops for their own use. Instead they have tended to construct homes for other family members, building ever more tightly next to each other.

In my family's garden a huge number of herbs, some of which I do not know by any English name, grow amid the more common vegetables, such as cabbages, peppers, courgettes, cucumbers and beans. We have our own orange and lemon trees, figs, pomegranates and vines. The leaves of the vines, like other vegetables, are cooked after being stuffed with a mixture of rice and meat. But first the leaves must be stripped from their stalks, an art that both Hajji and Samira mastered decades ago but that I cannot perform without tearing the leaves, despite many attempts.

Many of the dishes we eat here are uncommon to Western eyes, even though they are just as delicious and healthful as the cuisines of Mediterranean countries such as Italy and Spain. We serve up a huge array of stuffed vegetables, not just the more familiar vine leaves and peppers but also artichokes, cabbage leaves, courgettes, aubergines and small marrows known as kari'a. Other traditional dishes are okra in a rich tomato sauce (bamiye) or with beans (lubia); a dry lentil and onion stew (majedera); a tasty paste of green leaves known as mloukiye; and a seasonal thorny weed called akoub that is found in Galilean fields and has to be carefully prepared before eating. These dishes are made in large pots for lunch, the main meal, and are then kept hot with a thick blanket wrapped around them so that family and visitors can eat at any time during the rest of the day.

Given the size of Arab families and the need to have something on the stove ready for guests, Hajji and Samira also make lots of healthy snack food. There are always large quantities of freshly made hummous available, far better than anything you can buy in a shop; a creamy sesame paste called tahina mixed with parsley; a puree of broad beans, tahina and garlic known as fool; a mash of aubergine and tahina called mutabal; and a tart home-made yoghurt known as labaneh. All of these are served up with the local pitta bread, which we bake ourselves in a special oven. The equivalent of pizza here is something known as manakiesh, a bread topped with melted salty cheese or zatar. Hajji squats on the floor, as Africans do when preparing food, to roll out the dough. For special occasions the family will also make finger food: pastry parcels (ftir) stuffed with cheese, spinach or zatar, or mini-pizzas topped with meat and pine nuts (sfiha). The most prized dish of all is tabouli, a salad of minutely chopped parsley, bulgur wheat, tomato and spring onion, soaked in olive oil and lemon.

My apartment in Tamra was never meant as a temporary base, nor as a social experiment. It is as much my home as Tel Aviv was when I first arrived in Israel six years ago, or as London was before that. This is where, aged fifty-six, I am choosing to root myself for the foreseeable future. I have filled my apartment with all the most precious things I have collected over a lifetime: mementoes of my childhood in Britain, of my many travels to South Africa, where much of my family still lives, and of my more recent life in the Middle East. I have original paintings by South African and Palestinian artists, Bedouin carpets on the floor, stacks of CDs of music from around the world, and a wide range of books on subjects that especially interest me, from psychology and politics to biographies. My father instilled in me a deep appreciation of Jewish culture and ethics, and many of my favourite books reflect that. Like me, my home is an eclectic mix.

From my balcony the main view is of Tamra, its grey homes pressing upon their neighbours, offering no privacy at all. Electricity and telephone cables are slung haphazardly across the streets, attached chaotically to metal pylons or wooden poles, many of which are planted in the centre of roads, creating a major traffic hazard. The roads themselves drop precipitously in a network of lanes that it appears no one ever planned, their surfaces only half made or scarred by potholes. Every street is lined with rubble or rubbish, and piles of dust swirl in the wind. Children with no parks or even gardens to play in squat in the streets, making games with stones, discarded bottles or sticks and dodging the passing traffic. In the winter, which is when I arrived, showers instantly overwhelm the drains, sending torrents of water washing down the streets, a miserable stain of brown and grey.

But the story inside people's homes is very different. Amid all this public squalor, everyone maintains his or her private space in meticulous order. Homes are cleaned daily, and the surfaces are so spotless that you could eat off them. Even the poorest families invest their energies in making their homes bright and attractive, bringing as much colour into their domestic lives as is possible within Tamra's dour surroundings.

Despite the oppressive atmosphere, there are many compensations to living in Tamra, including the warmth and friendliness of the people and the town's location. Here in the Galilee the air is clean and the light pure. From my lofty position both on a hillside and on the building's top floor, I overlook my neighbours to see far to the north, to the high hills of the Upper Galilee and almost to Lebanon. The rocky slopes embracing Tamra change colour through the day, settling into wonderful hues of orange and purple at sunset. In the late afternoon the shadows of the tall cypress trees lengthen rapidly, like nature's timepieces. I love to look out at the clear sky at night, as the stars slowly emerge and a luminous moon rises over the horizon. Out on the nearby hills an amazing variety of wildflowers are to be found in the spring, including breathtaking displays of baby cyclamen and anemones. In the summer the air is filled with the perfume of the blossoms of jasmine, hibiscus, orange and oleander, all of these plants somehow managing to root themselves in spite of the concrete. Fig and pomegranate trees are everywhere, affording another of the great joys of living here: being able to pluck the heavy fruit directly from the trees as one walks in the street.

Moving into an Arab community in Israel, however, means changing one's definition of privacy. There is no sense of the anonymity that is a major component of life in Tel Aviv, New York or London. Hajji's door is never closed, unless she is out. And it would never occur to anyone in the family to knock before entering her home or to ask before opening her fridge. That doesn't go just for Hajji, it applies to everyone here. (Apart, I should add, from me. A special allowance is made in my case, and the family knocks before entering my apartment.) I find this lack of barriers both a reward and a drawback. In my first few weeks I was invited to an art exhibition in Haifa by a well-known Palestinian artist, Salam Diab. We arrived back home late to find, unusually, that the lights were still on. I went inside to say hello, only to discover Hassan and his two sons, Khalil and Waleed, sitting in a row on the sofa watching the television and nervously awaiting my return. When I saw their worried faces, I looked at Hassan, more than five years my junior, and announced, "I'm back!" We both started laughing. Nowadays I always make sure that they can reach me on my mobile phone, because I know they worry about my safety. At first this seemed like an intrusion, but now I have come to see the advantages. Being absorbed into the family means that I enjoy its protection and its concern for my welfare.

Not all the loss of privacy is cultural, however. Someone I met in my first week in Tamra equated living here with being in a goldfish bowl. I already knew what she meant. On my first morning in my new apartment I opened the blinds of my bedroom window, at the back of the house, to find that I was staring directly across at my neighbours' house a few metres away—and at my neighbours, who were looking out from their own window. On all sides of the house, apart from my balcony at the front, neighbours' homes are pressing up against mine. If I have the blinds up, there is almost nowhere in the apartment where I can be free from prying eyes. Ghetto living is more than just a feeling of confinement; it is a sense of suffocation too. During my first weeks the sense of being watched followed me into the streets. Walking around Tamra, I felt like a specimen in a zoo, as if every article of clothing I wore and every movement I made were being observed from a thousand different angles. When I went to the shops, everyone stared at me. Everyone. People would stop dead in their tracks, and on a few occasions there were nearly traffic accidents—the drivers couldn't quite believe what they were seeing. What, their eyes were asking, was a blond woman doing here alone? There was never any enmity in their looks, only surprise or bewilderment.

I cannot claim to be the only non-Arab woman ever to have lived here. There are a few others, though you'll find them concealed by the hijab, the Islamic headscarf. These women have found love with local men who studied or worked abroad and returned home with them. There are even former Jews in the town, women who maybe met their husband-to-be at university or through work. But they have all converted—as they must do by law in Israel, where there is no civil marriage—and live here as Muslims. Many of these newcomers struggle with culture shock and the lack of amenities. A young doctor recently left Tamra with his new Romanian wife to live in the more cosmopolitan city of Haifa, perhaps the one place in Israel where Jews and Arabs can live in some sort of mutual accommodation, if not quite equality.

But for a woman to be living here without an Arab husband is unheard of. And for her to be a self-declared Jew is off the register. As I negotiated the town's streets during the first few weeks, learning Tamra's chaotic geography, I would see groups of people sitting outside their homes drinking coffee and chatting. The women's heads would move closer together as I went past. They never pointed—Arabs are far too polite for that—but it was clear I was the topic of conversation. After a few days, the odd person worked up the courage to stop me in the street and strike up a conversation. These people always addressed me in Hebrew, a language Arabs in Israel must learn at school. This made me uncomfortable, especially after an early warning from one of my occasional neighbours, Dr. Said Zidane, the head of the Palestinian Independent Commission in Ramallah, in the Palestinian West Bank. His mother lives next to me, and on a visit to see her he advised me not to speak Hebrew, as it might arouse the suspicion that I was working for the government or the security service, the Shin Bet, which is known to run spies in Arab communities. He suggested that I exploit my lack of fluent Hebrew and speak English instead.

Always I would be asked where I had lived before moving to Tamra, and the questioners would be amazed by my reply. "Why would you want to live here after living in Tel Aviv?" they would ask. Why not? I would say. "But it's obvious: Tel Aviv has cinemas, theatres, coffeehouses, proper shops, tree-lined streets, libraries, community centres, a transport system . . ." The list was always long. Their incomprehension at my choice revealed the difference between my life and theirs. Although I choose to live in Tamra, as a Jew I am always free to cross back over the ethnic divide. I think nothing of an hour's train ride from Haifa to Tel Aviv. But for them a trip to Tel Aviv involves crossing a boundary, one that is real as well as psychological. To be an Israeli Arab visiting a Jewish community is to be instantly a target, an alien identifiable through the giveaways of language, culture and often appearance. They must enter a space where they are not welcome and may be treated as intruders. The danger, ever-present in their minds, is of encountering hostility or even violence. They know from surveys published in local newspapers that a majority of Israeli Jews want them expelled from the country. They also hear about frequent attacks on Arabs by Jewish youths and racist policemen. Many of my Arab friends have told me how uncomfortable they feel about going to Jewish areas. In my house, Khalil, who is a film-maker, travels to Tel Aviv only when he has to, on business or to buy new equipment, and he leaves as soon as his work is done.

Unlike the cold, impersonal atmosphere of Tel Aviv, Muslim communities like Tamra take pride in their hospitality to friends and strangers alike. But when you are living in—as opposed to visiting—an Arab community, the hospitality comes as a double-edged sword. One March morning I told Hassan I was going to the chemist, a couple of hundred metres down the hill. I was gone for an hour and a half: on the way, at least fifteen people stopped me to chat or to invite me in for coffee. On my return, Hassan asked with concern where I had been. When I told him, he laughed and suggested I start wearing the veil. "At least that way you can go about your business without attracting so much attention," he joked.

It's true that trying to get things done always seems to take longer in Arab society, and although being welcomed into people's homes is a wonderful thing, it can be inconvenient, time-consuming and stifling. The fear of insulting a neighbour or a friend by refusing an invitation for coffee or a meal can make a quick trip to the shops a dismaying prospect. Invitations to people's homes follow a vague formula, which in essence involves being offered a cold drink, possibly accompanied by nuts, fruit or biscuits. There may be tea later, or a meal, depending on the time of day and the closeness of the relationship. The signal that the host needs to get on with something else—or is tired of your company—usually comes when he or she produces a pot of coffee.

Conversations in people's homes are wide-ranging, particularly with older Tamrans, who have experienced enough earth-shattering events to fill anyone's lifetime. One old man told me in detail about the different train routes that one could take from the Galilee all over the Middle East before the creation of Israel, when the borders existed as no more than lines on maps produced by the area's British and French rulers. Here in the Galilee, he told me, we were at the very heart of the Middle East, with all the region's biggest cities—Beirut (Lebanon), Damascus (Syria), Amman (Jordan) and Jerusalem (Palestine)—a two-hour trip or less away. Today only Jerusalem is easily accessible; Beirut and Damascus are in enemy states, and Amman lies across a heavily guarded international border. I felt frustrated at being barred from visiting most of these places, but for Arab citizens the borders represent something tragic. Many people in Tamra, like other Palestinians, have loved ones still living in refugee camps in Lebanon and Syria, more than five decades after they were forced to flee during the war that founded the Jewish state. Israel refuses to let the refugees return, and neither Israel nor Lebanon nor Syria wants its population crossing over the borders. So a meeting between separated relatives—even brothers and sisters, and in a few cases husbands and wives—remains all but impossible.

Few Israeli Arabs in the Galilee, apart from an educated elite, know much of the world outside their immediate region. Many venture no further than Haifa, less than twenty-five kilometres away. Few can afford to travel to Europe for a holiday, and most of the Arab states are off limits. People can at least go by bus to Jordan and Egypt, which have signed peace treaties with Israel, but even then the reception is not always warm. Egyptians in particular have difficulty with the idea that someone can be an Israeli and an Arab at the same time. The assumption—shared, to be honest, by most Westerners—is that if you are Israeli, you must be Jewish. "I get fed up hearing the Egyptian taxi drivers telling me that I speak good Arabic for a Jew," Khalil once remarked to me.

Many conversations in Tamra concern the town's history. It has often occurred to me that Tamra looks much like a refugee camp. Like other Israelis, I have seen plenty of television images of the bleak camps of Gaza and the West Bank, the background to Palestinian children throwing stones at Israeli tanks. Those camps, some no more than an hour's drive from Tamra and other Palestinian towns and villages, are inhabited by more than three and a half million Palestinians who are not Israeli citizens but live under Israeli military occupation. When I arrived in Tamra, what shocked me was that, as Shaher observed, the town looked much the same as Gaza and the West Bank; only the tanks and the soldiers were missing. But Tamra's inhabitants, unlike those of the occupied territories, are not at war with Israel. They are citizens of a democratic state.

During a conversation one morning over coffee with Hajji, I learned that my observation about the town's appearance was far nearer the truth than I could have imagined. Much of Tamra in fact used to be a refugee camp. It was like a dark, ugly secret that no one would dwell on for too long. But photographs from 1948, the year in which the Jewish state was declared, prompting a war with the indigenous Palestinian population, show not only a scattering of Tamra's stone houses but also a sea of Red Cross tents housing refugees from the fighting.

In 1947 Tamra had a population of no more than two thousand people, but a year later that figure had risen to three thousand. Today, according to Amin Sahli, a civil engineer and the local town planner, a third of Tamrans are classified as internal refugees, people who are refused permission ever to return to their original homes. In the callous, Orwellian language of Israeli bureaucracy, they and another quarter of a million Israeli Arabs are known as "present absentees": present in Israel in 1948, but absent from their homes when the authorities registered all property in the new Jewish state. Everything these refugees owned, from their land and homes to their possessions and bank accounts, was confiscated and is now owned by the state. They and their descendants lost everything they had in 1948. The members of my own family are refugees too, having fled from neighbouring villages in the Galilee.

More than four hundred Palestinian villages were destroyed by the Israeli army during and after the war of 1948, to prevent the refugees from returning. A special government department was even created to plan the destruction. So why did Tamra and another hundred or so Palestinian villages remain relatively untouched by the fighting? Amin told me that the town survived for two reasons: first, it was located off the main routes used by the advancing Israeli army, and therefore its defeat was not considered a military necessity; and second, Tamra was a small community that had a history of, to phrase it generously, "cooperating" with the pre-state Jewish authorities as well as with local Jewish businesses. It was, in other words, a useful pool of cheap labour in the area. Soon the farmers of Tamra were turning their skills to the advantage of Jewish farming cooperatives like the kibbutzim or were being "reskilled" to work at building cheap modern estates of homes for the Jewish immigrants who flooded into the new state of Israel. Tamrans lost their traditional skills of building in stone and wood and learned to construct only in the bland, grey, concrete garb of modern Tamra.

According to Hajji, the first refugees in Tamra were sheltered in the homes of the existing inhabitants. But soon the town was being overwhelmed: hundreds of Palestinians arrived from the destroyed villages of Damun, Ein Hod, Balad al-Sheikh, Haditha and Mi'ar. The warm welcome turned much colder. Most of the new arrivals fell under the responsibility of the Red Cross, who housed them in tents, but after a few years the international community passed responsibility for the internal refugees' fate back to Israel. It was some fifteen years before the last tents were gone, recalls Hajji, as many people were reluctant to give up the hope that one day they would be able to return to their original homes.

Stripped of all their possessions, the refugee families had to work and save money to buy land from the original inhabitants of Tamra, so that they could turn their fabric homes into concrete ones. That fact alone goes a long way to explaining the unplanned, chaotic geography of Tamra and other Israeli Arab communities. The roads, originally designed for the horse and cart, were simply diverted around the maze of "concrete tents."

During the subsequent decades, Israel has rezoned most of Tamra's outlying lands as green areas, doing yet more damage to the town's already unnatural development. Hemmed in on all sides by land that it cannot use, the rapidly growing population has been unable to expand territorially. Instead it has had to grow much denser. Today's twenty-five thousand inhabitants live in a town that in reality barely has room for a quarter of that number. This is apparent in even the tiniest aspects of Tamra's infrastructure. Consider the toilets, for example. Nothing has been spent on improving the sewerage system since the days, more than a half-century ago, when the few dozen houses here each had a basic hole in the ground. Now all families own a flushing toilet, but these all feed into an overstretched network of ancient pipes that catered to a different reality. In my first few days, the family tactfully explained to me why there was a bucket by the toilet. If I continued to flush toilet paper down the bowl, they warned me, I would block the pipes in no time.

Overcrowding isn't restricted to the humans of Tamra. Everywhere there are animals—not cats or dogs, but those more familiar from the farmyard. In the early evening it is common to see teenage boys riding horses bareback down the streets at high speed, jostling for space with the cars. When not being ridden, these horses are to be found tethered in families' tiny backyards or under their houses, where there are also pens of sheep and goats and chicken sheds. In some parts of Tamra, particularly in the Abu Romi quarter, every home seems to be operating as a cramped small farm. Sheep and goats are often penned up in the space where one would expect to find the family car. I found this quite baffling until Hajji explained the reason. Before 1948 most of Tamra's families either farmed commercially or owned land to subsist on, but in the intervening years Israel either confiscated or rezoned their fields. Families lost their crops, but they were at least able to hold on to their animals by bringing them to their homes. Samira's daughter Omayma, who lives with her husband's family in the middle of town on the main street, has a vast collection of animals. Until recently they included an impressive flock of geese, but the geese's numbers were slowly whittled down by a pack of wild dogs.

Another striking feature of Tamra is the apparent absence of shops. None of the Israeli high street names are here, nor are the international chains. It is not for lack of local interest: Tamrans will drive long distances, to Haifa and elsewhere, to shop at the larger clothes stores, and they are as keen to eat an American burger as any Jew. Presumably, however, these chains are too nervous to set up shop in an Arab town. (McDonald's Israel claims to have a branch in Tamra, but in truth it is to be found well outside the town, on the opposite side of the dual carriageway, where it services the passing traffic.) The town's shops are all local businesses, though their presence is largely concealed. Apart from a couple of dozen clothes, fruit-and-veg and electrical goods stores on the main street, it is impossible for a visitor to know where Tamrans do their shopping. The hairdressers, doctors and dentists, furniture shops, pharmacies and ice cream parlours are invariably in anonymous houses, hidden behind the same grey concrete and shutters as residential properties. The local inhabitants, of course, know precisely where to find them, but for quite some time the lack of clues made shopping a nightmare for me.

Such difficulties were exacerbated by the problem of orientating myself. Because of the unplanned streets and the lack of regulations on construction, the local council has never attempted to name roads or number houses. So if I asked directions, the reply would always involve telling me to turn right or left at a building that obviously served as a landmark for the local population but that to me looked indistinguishable from the rest of the concrete. After a year I started to recognise at least a few of these landmarks. One felafel shop might be used as a signpost rather than its neighbour simply because it had been around for decades and the community felt its long-term usefulness had been established.

In the early days I would think, "I will never find my way around this place; I will never understand how to get from A to B." I started walking every day to learn the complex patchwork of alleys and side streets. I was immediately struck by the huge number of roads that were incomplete, unsurfaced or scarred by endless potholes. Streets would come to an abrupt end or peter out. I had embarrassing moments when, having started to rely on a shortcut, using what I thought was a footpath or an empty piece of ground, I would find one day that it was now blocked by concrete walls. A family, someone would explain, was squeezing yet another house into one of the last remaining spaces open to them. Because it was me, no one ever showed offence at the fact that I had been tramping through his yard.

The sense of community in Tamra is reinforced by its festivals. Anyone who has been to the Middle East quickly learns that public space is treated differently in Arab countries. On their first night, foreign visitors usually wake in the early hours of the morning, startled by the noisy wailing of the local imam over the mosque's loudspeakers, calling the faithful to prayer. For the first week or so these calls to prayer, five times a day, disturbed me too, but they soon became part of the background of life, as reassuring as the sound of church bells echoing through an English village.

One of the things I soon noticed about Muslim festivals is how much they resemble those celebrated by religious Jews, including the Orthodox members of my own Jewish family. When Dr. Asad Ghanem, a political science lecturer at Haifa University and one of the country's outstanding Israeli Arab intellectuals, took me to Nazareth for a Muslim engagement party, he asked me on the way back, "So, how was it at your first Arab party?" He laughed when I told him, "It's just like being at an engagement party in North London. I feel like I'm living with my first cousins." Israel, and more recently the West, spends a lot of time warning us about the dangers of "the Arab mind," instilling in us a fear of Arab culture and of Islam by accentuating their differences from us and by removing the wider context. Even though intellectually I knew that Jews and Arabs were both Semitic races with their roots in the Middle East, I was still unprepared for the extent to which the traditions in Islam and Judaism and the two cultures are so closely related.

Take, for example, death. The rituals of the two faiths closely mirror each other. The most important thing is that the dead person must be buried on the same day, before sundown, or, failing that, as soon as possible. So when Samira's sister died early one morning, she was in the ground by 1 P.M. As in Orthodox Judaism, the family and close friends went to the home and gathered around the body to pray while it was washed and the orifices were stuffed with cotton. After the body had been buried, the family sat in the house for a three-day mourning period, during which guests were welcomed to share in the sorrow (in Judaism this period lasts seven days). The purpose in both religions is the same: to expunge the grief from the mourners' souls in a communal setting and thereby allow them to move on. In both faiths the family continues to mark its grief for a longer period by abstaining from celebrations and parties and not playing music. During the three days of mourning the family's house is open from early morning to late evening, with the men and women sitting apart. Another tradition the religions share is that neighbours bring food to the dead person's family during the grieving period. That is what happened when my mother died in London.

In Tamra we laid out a large meal of meat, rice and pine nuts for the mourners. On the second day I took coffee and milk to the women for breakfast.

The most joyous and lavish occasion is a wedding, which can last from three days to a week. If it is the marriage of the eldest son or an only son, the celebration is always huge. The basic schedule is three days: one for the bride's party, one for the groom's, and the third for the wedding itself. On each occasion the party starts at sunset and goes on till the early hours, with a guest list of a few hundred family members and friends. Often the road on which the family lives will be shut down to accommodate the party as it spills into the street. Music is played very loudly, with wild, throbbing, hypnotic beats that reverberate around the town. During the summer months, there is rarely an evening when you cannot hear the thumping boom of wedding songs somewhere in Tamra. The noise is like an extended invitation, ensuring that everyone can join in—at a distance—even if they have not been officially invited.

On the bride's day the women come together to eat, dance and talk. I found it fascinating to see so many women, their heads covered by hijabs, dancing together. You might expect their dancing to be modest, but there is something very sensuous and provocative about the way Arab women dance, slowly gyrating their hips and swaying as they twist their arms and hands in the air. The messages are very conflicting. At my first Arab wedding I felt overwhelmed by the noise, the rhythmic dancing and the huge number of bodies packed together. Later in the evening a group from the groom's side was allowed to join the party. Arriving in a long chain, these people danced into the centre of the celebrations, with the other dancers standing to the side and clapping their hands rhythmically. As the noise grew louder, the clapping turned ever more excited, until people were opening their arms wide and snapping them shut together, like huge crocodile jaws. Finally a pot of henna was brought, and the bride's fingers were decorated with her own and the groom's initials entwined. Her palms and the back of her hands were painted with beautiful patterns to make her more attractive for the wedding.

The second party, for the groom, follows a similar sequence of eating and dancing. At the end of the night the groom is prepared for the wedding day with a ceremonial shaving. Carrying a tray bearing a bowl, shaving cream and a razor, his mother and sisters dance towards him. Just as with the henna, the tray is decorated with flowers. Then, as they sing, the closest male relatives put him on a chair raised up on a table and begin to shave him with a great flourish of excitement. Soon foam is flying in all directions, with the raucous men smearing it over one another's faces. Everyone is having so much fun that they are often reluctant to finish the job. But once the groom is smooth, he is held aloft on the shoulders of a strong male relative, who dances underneath him as he moves his arms rhythmically about. The symbolic significance of this moment of transition into manhood is immense; close relatives often burst into uncontrollable tears.

On the final day, the groom's family must collect the bride from her parents' home and bring her to her new family. As in Judaism, there is no equivalent of the church ceremony familiar in the West. Before they set off, the groom's family invites everyone for a great feast of meat and rice followed by sweet pastries. Then the groom's closest friends wash him, while the women dance, holding his wedding clothes. He is dressed, and the family is then ready to fetch the bride. At one of the family weddings I attended, we formed a long convoy of cars and took a circuitous route through Tamra so that we could toot our horns across the town, letting everyone know we were coming. The lead car was decorated with a beautiful display of flowers and ribbons. The bride's family welcomed us with drinks and plates of delicate snacks while the bride stood by in her white dress. As the moment neared for her to leave, small goatskin drums were banged and the women ululated a traditional song, which to my ears sounded sad and tragic but which actually wishes her health and happiness in the future. It is an emotional moment for the bride, who often cries. She dances on her own, holding in each hand a lighted long white candle, surrounded by a circle of relatives. When she is finished, she steps on the candles to extinguish them and leaves.

The highlight of the year for me is Ramadan, the spiritual month of fasting that commemorates the first revelation of the Muslim holy book, the Koran, to the Prophet Mohammed by God. No food or drink may be consumed from the moment the sun rises till the moment it sets. Muslims are expected to reflect on their behaviour at this time of year, during which they should not lie, cheat or fight. Special TV programmes concentrate on the spiritual aspect of Ramadan, showing live footage from Mecca and talks by religious leaders. It is a very physically demanding time: we have to rise at 4 A.M. for breakfast and then endure the heat of the day without any sustenance. Some Middle Eastern countries effectively grind to a halt during Ramadan, and offices and shops close during the day. But in Israel no allowances are made for non-Jewish religious festivals, so people have to carry on with their normal work.

During Ramadan, the imams call out a special prayer on the mosques' loudspeakers just before sunset. This is the signal to the community that they can start eating again. I like to think that at the precise moment the imam begins his prayer, the streets of every Muslim community in the world are like ours: deserted and profoundly quiet, in a way unimaginable at any other time. Nothing moves or makes a noise. Even the birds seem to know they should not stir. Inside the houses, families start with a watery soup to accustom their stomachs to food again, then tuck into a table filled with their favourite foods. By the end of Ramadan people have lost weight and look tired; it asks a lot of them.

Unlike Judaism, which has many festivals, Islam has only two major feasts: the three-day Eid al-Fitr, which marks the end of Ramadan, and the four-day Eid al-Adha. There is a huge celebration in Tamra at both times of year, as improvised stalls are set up along the edge of the main road in the centre of town, selling children's toys and sweets. Teenage boys show off their horse-riding skills while younger children are pulled along more sedately in a horse-drawn carriage painted in vivid colours. Tamra has no parks or public spaces where these festivities could be held more safely, so the stallholders, children, horses and cars simply jostle for priority.

Both of these eids entail endless visiting of relatives, especially for the younger children, who are dressed in smart new clothes for the occasion. They receive money as a gift from each relative they visit. Unfortunately, the boys invariably choose to spend their windfalls on toy guns—convincing replicas of the weapons they see being used by Palestinian gunmen and Israeli soldiers on the television.

Homes are stuffed with sweets, chocolates, dried fruits and special shortbread biscuits filled with date paste. Extended families congregate in large circles, eating and drinking tea or coffee while they chat. But the main celebration at each of these festivals is the barbecue, when huge quantities of meat are consumed. The Eid al-Adha (Feast of the Sacrifice) is, as its name suggests, a celebration of meat consumption. The feast commemorates the familiar Biblical story in which Ibrahim (Abraham in Christianity and Avraham in Judaism) is asked by God to sacrifice his son Ishmael as a sign of devotion. Ibrahim proves his faith, but God substitutes a sheep for his son at the last moment. For Muslims this story is quite literally reenacted, with blood running in the streets as each family slaughters a sheep, cutting its throat for the barbecue. I found it a shock to see an ancient story I had learned as a schoolchild coming to life before my eyes. Once the sheep has been butchered, the meat is cut into three equal parts: one portion for the immediate family, one for the extended family, and one for the poor. We then eat barbecued meat for four days.

At other times of the year, leisure time in most families revolves around a single object: the nargilleh, or what we in the West refer to as the hookah or water pipe. The popularity of the nargilleh in Tamra doubtless partly reflects the fact that there is no equivalent of the pub here. Although alcohol—mostly beer and whisky—is sold in a few grocery shops, people rarely drink outside the privacy of their home. But puffing on a nargilleh for an hour or so can be just as intoxicating as a few beers. The nargilleh plays a central role in my family's life; there is rarely an evening when I don't see Waleed or Khalil cleaning or carefully preparing the pipe before loading it with apple-flavoured tobacco. They own several nargillehs, large and small, each decorated in different colours. The family forms a circle of chairs around the pipe outside Hajji's house and begins smoking. Although I occasionally puff on the nargilleh, the other women in the house do not. It is generally considered unbecoming for a woman to smoke in public.

In the West, the most identifiable and controversial thing about Islam—after Osama bin Laden and al-Qaeda—has become the hijab, the headscarf, which is widely seen as part of a system of oppression of women. The arguments against the hijab rarely touch on its significance in the lives of modern Muslims. I once asked seventeen-year-old Suad which tradition meant the most to her, and was surprised when she replied, "The wearing of the hijab." Her head is uncovered and she is a very modern teenager, so I asked her why. "Because it makes you proud of your femininity." I asked what she meant. "When you are covered by the hijab, it is the opposite of being repressed—you feel free and proud to be a woman. It gives you your dignity." Part of the problem in the debate in the West is that it focuses exclusively on the hijab, without seeing that the headscarf is only one—if the most visible—of the dress codes that apply to all Muslims, both men and women. The concept of personal and family dignity is deeply important to the society, and clothing is one of the overt ways in which a person demonstrates that he or she deserves respect.

Showing a lot of one's body to people outside the family suggests quite the opposite. How that rule is interpreted can appear very arbitrary and eccentric to outsiders. For example, I quickly found that whatever the heat, the men in Tamra would not dream of wearing open-toed sandals or shorts outside the immediate environment of the home. A code applied to them too: if they wanted to be accorded respect and earn it for their family, they had to dress in respectable ways. In the case of women, this policy of covering up can seem oppressive to Western eyes, which have become used to the idea that women *should* show as much flesh as possible. Since living in Tamra, I find myself appalled every time I return to Europe or America to see the virtually pornographic images of women, and even children, crowding high street billboards. As they go unnoticed by everyone else, I can only assume that living in Arab society has fundamentally changed my perception.

This did not happen overnight. I arrived in Tamra with suitcases full of thin, almost see-through linen garments that I had relied on to cope with the Tel Aviv heat. I knew I had to be much more careful about the way I dressed in Tamra but was unsure exactly where the boundaries lay. Certainly I was not about to wear the hijab, but that did not mean that I was going to refuse to accept any limitations. So during my first summer I would dress each morning and go down to Hajji's flat for a clothing inspection. She would extend her finger and turn it round to show that she wanted to see me from every angle. She would look at me in the light and out of the light, and then if she couldn't see anything, she would give me the thumbs-up. T-shirts that showed my shoulders were out, as were skirts higher than the knee and tops that had plunging necklines. Some of my thinnest tops, I realised, I would have to wear with something underneath. Now this self-discipline has become automatic and unthinking. I long ago threw away all the tops that revealed too much. Visitors to Tamra are shown great tolerance when they break these unwritten rules, but living here, I decided it was important for me to earn people's respect by showing them similar respect.

Nowadays I find it shocking to return to Tel Aviv in the summer and see women, including older women, wearing crop-tops that expose their tummies or blouses revealing their bras. It seems vulgar in the extreme. I regard the Arab women around me as much more dignified; they even seem to move in a more upright, graceful manner. I now find the idea of being covered liberating in much the same way as Suad does: it frees me from confrontations with men, the kind of situation I had experienced all my life without fully realising it. If my body is properly covered, men have to address what I am saying rather than my body. It was only after covering myself that I started realising that most of my life I had been used to men having conversations with my body rather than with me.

Also, covering up gives me a sense of independence and self-containment that still surprises me. Like other Westerners, I had always assumed that Muslim women were oppressed, but I now know that's far too simplistic. Although in places the hijab is misused to limit women's possibilities, that is not by definition true. I have met plenty of professional Palestinian women, in Tamra and elsewhere, who wear the hijab but are strong-willed, assertive and creative. They expect men's respect and they are shown it.

Not that women's lives here are without problems. I find it difficult to accept the social limitations on young unmarried women, including the fact that they can never venture out alone in the evenings. Teenage girls are definitely *not* allowed to date, or in many cases even openly to have a boyfriend. When I asked Suad how she coped, she admitted it was hard. She felt torn between two cultures: the Western way of life she sees on television and in many Jewish areas, where girls do what they please, and her own Arab traditions, of which she is proud and which she wants to obey. My own daughter did not hesitate as a teenager in London to tell me she was going to the pub or the cinema with a boyfriend, but girls here simply are not allowed to do that. For a long time I wondered how anyone found a marriage partner, with all these restrictions. But in reality many girls have secret boyfriends whom they "date" over the phone. The arrival of mobile phones has quietly revolutionised the dating game in Muslim communities. Even so, I still marvel how a girl ever finds a husband. In many cases she has few opportunities to meet men outside events like weddings, and so her choice of partners is pretty much limited to the men inside her hamula. But slowly, with more education about the problems caused by marrying a first cousin and the genetic legacy for the offspring, such marriages are being discouraged. The situation is far from static.

Although as Westerners we are encouraged to believe we have a right to sit in judgement of other cultures, what I heard from women in Tamra alerted me to the weaknesses in our own culture—flaws we are little prepared to acknowledge. For example, one evening a group of about a dozen local women visited me in my home so that we could learn more about each other. They were keen to know both why I had left my children behind in Britain after my divorce and how I managed living alone in Tamra. In Arab society, a woman would never separate herself from her family, even her grown-up children. Because I had left

Britain, they assumed I had abandoned Tanya and Daniel; they were astonished that I could turn my back on my children, even though they are in their late twenties and early thirties. I had to explain that in Britain, grown-up children leave home, often moving long distances from their parents. Many mothers are lucky if their children visit more than a couple of times a year. The women were appalled, and pointed out the huge advantages of having families that remain together for life. When I see how we all gather in Hajji's apartment, how she is never alone unless she wants to be, I can see their point. I have concluded that there are many benefits to having your family around you as you grow older.

The central place of the hamula in organising not only the lives of Tamra's individual families but also the political life of the whole community became clear to me during the first municipal elections after my arrival. It was an uncomfortable lesson, revealing a side to Tamra that dismayed me. As one Israeli Arab academic, Marwan Dwairy, has observed, "In politics we still have parties dressed up as families and families dressed up as parties." Israeli intellectuals often cite the aggressive and tribal nature of political campaigning in Arab areas as proof of the primitive character of Arab societies and their inability to cope with modern democratic principles. Apart from glossing over the tribal nature of Jewish politics inside Israel, that argument misses a larger point. The continuing feudal nature of Arab politics in Israel is neither accidental nor predetermined by the "Arab mind"; it results from the failure of Israeli Jewish society to allow the country's Arab minority to join the national political consensus. Arab politicians are considered hostile to the state unless they join a Zionist party, and Arab parties have been excluded from every government coalition in Israel's history. These coalitions are a hotchpotch of diverse, often antagonistic and extremist political parties, but the bottom line is that they must be

Jewish. When Arabs are excluded from the Knesset table, it is not surprising that they fight for whatever municipal scraps they can get. Sensing that their voice is irrelevant to the process of their governance, they end up seeking solace in the kind of posturing and feudal politics familiar from the days of their grandfathers.

I experienced this in a very direct way during Tamra's local elections. I was quickly sucked into the town's hamula-based politics. The fervour and excitement surrounding the elections was something I had never witnessed anywhere else, and it contrasted strongly with the calm, slightly stultifying atmosphere of a British municipal election. In the final week of campaigning there were fireworks and street parties every night, with loud music and mountains of food on offer. The tribal divisions within the community were far more visible than usual, not least because the two candidates for mayor were the heads of the two largest hamulas. The campaign, it was clear, was less about competing political platforms than about rivalry between the family leaderships. On one side was Adel Abu Hayja, standing for the Communist Party, and on the other was Moussa Abu Romi, the incumbent mayor, representing the Islamic Movement. The victor would be in charge of the town's limited municipal budget for the next five years and so, in the great tradition of patronage systems, would be able to reward his followers. The stakes were therefore extraordinarily high, as each of the two biggest hamulas fought to secure the floating votes of the two smaller hamulas with promises. In the run-up to the election, young men from one hamula even occasionally pulled guns or knives on those from another.

By election day the temperature in Tamra had rocketed. The whole town was alive with activity, with party buses roaming the town looking to transport supporters to the polling booth. Since I lived inside the Abu Hayja hamula, my support for Adel Abu Hayja's candidacy was taken for granted. There was never any question whom I was expected to vote for: I would vote for the family.

It was widely known in Tamra that I was making history: this was the first time that an openly Jewish woman had voted in a municipal election in an Arab area. When I arrived at the school on the hill above my home where I was due to vote, I found complete pandemonium. Everyone was pushing and shoving and shouting. People who thought they had been waiting in line too long started hitting those in front of them and trying to push past to get to the room where the polling booth was located. Standing in their way was an old wooden door holding back at least 150 people, who were pushing one another up against it. One policeman was inside, desperately trying to keep the door closed as the crowd pressed forward, and another was doing his best, without success, to keep order. Finally a huge man lost control and started hitting the women in front of him before lunging for the door. Using all his might, he managed to push it open and get inside. The door closed behind him.

Hassan, the head of my family, who had come with me, was outside in the street but could see that I was getting crushed. He is a big man, and he forced his way through the crowd to reach me so that he could hold me tightly around my shoulders, using his arms to protect me. I could sense how much he feared for my safety, because it is rare for Arab men and women, even husband and wife, to touch in public. But it was the only way to keep me on my feet. When a brief gap appeared in the crowd, he pushed me forward and I was propelled through the door. The door slammed shut, but with all the hammering on it I feared it would come down. I found myself in a tiny room with a small window, and I remember thinking with a little relief that if I could not get out through the door, at least I could climb through the window.

I gave my ballot card to the Jewish official who was overseeing polling at the station. I also had to give him my ID card, and when he saw that I was a Jew and living in Tamra, he gave me a strange look, as though there had been an administrative mistake he could not quite figure out how to correct.* But after a pause he pointed me towards the booth. Behind the curtain were two piles of official voting slips, with the names of Moussa Abu Romi and Adel Abu Hayja. Just before polling day, a rumour had been circulating that supporters of the incumbent mayor, Abu Romi, were planning to sabotage Abu Hayja's chances by printing his voting slips in an ink that would disappear over time, so that when it came to the count all his votes would be blank. My family had persuaded me that I must take another slip supplied by Abu Hayja's party, and I had hidden it in my purse. Standing in the booth, I hurriedly took it out and slipped it into the ballot box. The family's absolute belief in the truth of the story of the fading ink had led me to believe it myself. I had been so drawn in by the fervour of the elections, by the supreme importance attached to the outcome, that I could willingly abandon the normal rules of democratic participation.

When I reached the exit door, I wondered how I would ever get out alive. The policeman opened it and I was confronted by a wall of agitated faces. And then the people in the crowd appeared to come to their senses. Most of them I had never met before, but it seemed that they knew who I was. In Arab communities, the idea of a local newspaper almost seems redundant: by some kind of osmosis, everyone knows everyone else's news, good and bad. So, as if I were Moses facing the Red Sea, the waves parted. For the first time that day, there was total silence.

*Until recently, all Israeli ID cards divulged the ethnic group of the holder. New ID cards often have a row of stars in the place where nationality is identified (see Glossary on citizenship, page 277). It is widely believed that the cardholder's ethnic group is revealed by the ID number.

As I walked past, people reached out to shake my hand. But as soon as I reached safety, the scrum resumed.

Apparently there was no truth to the tale of the fading ink, as Abu Hayja was comfortably elected as mayor. Not all of Abu Romi's supporters accepted the result; some took to the streets with firearms, and there were several days of fierce confrontations, including a gun battle that resulted in one man's being taken to hospital, seriously wounded. My family warned me not to go out in the streets. The violence ended only after the imam called out passages from the Koran over the mosque's loudspeaker, to calm everyone down.

Word of my presence in Tamra quickly spread further afield, to Haifa and beyond, assisted by an interview I gave to the country's most famous Hebrew newspaper, *Ha'aretz,* in September 2003. A short time afterwards I received a phone call from Michael Mansfeld, a senior partner in a firm of architects in Haifa. He said he had been impressed by my critical comments about Israel's not having invested in any new housing schemes for the Arab minority in the state's fifty-seven years, although the population had grown sevenfold. He told me his firm had been appointed by the Interior Ministry to draw up the master plans for Tamra's development till 2020, and he wanted to explain what the government had in store. He said I'd be impressed by what I would see. I was sceptical but keen to see the plans, about which no one in Tamra seemed to have been consulted. I invited the newly elected mayor, Adel Abu Hayja, and Amin Sahli, the town planner, to come to my home to see Mansfeld's presentation. But before the meeting I talked to Mansfeld privately. I told him about the severe land problems facing Tamra and explained that I didn't see a future for Israel unless Jews and Arabs were able to become equal partners. When he agreed, I challenged him: "Why do so many Israeli Jews agree with me in private but refuse to speak out?" He replied that if he spoke publicly, things could be made difficult for him and his business, and he said that his family was his first priority. His words reminded me that it is not only the Arabs who live in fear of their own state, but Jews of conscience too. It was a depressing realisation. Mansfeld, whose father won Israel's most prestigious award, the Israel Prize,* is part of what might be termed the establishment Israeli left. If he does not feel he can stand up and be counted, who can? And without more people who are prepared to speak out and expose the crisis at the heart of the Jewish state, what kind of country will we leave to our children?

The presentation which was supposed to impress us boiled down to the fact that Tamra's inhabitants would have to accept that there was a shortage of land in Israel. In Mansfeld's words, "From now on we must all build upwards." Afterwards I took a copy of the plans to Professor Hubert Law-Yone, a Burmese academic who came to Israel after marrying a Jewish woman and who is an expert on town planning, based at the Technion in Haifa. He did a few quick calculations and concluded that the plan was bad news for Tamra: based on the assumption that the population would grow to forty-two thousand by 2020, it required very high-density living—eighty-eight people per acre. He suggested that the Interior Ministry brief probably had a hidden agenda, one familiar to the Arab population: the maximum number of Arabs on the minimum amount of land. Its reverse is, of course, the minimum number of Jews on the maximum amount of land. That is why the Jewish communities around Tamra—farming cooperatives and small luxury hilltop settlements like Mitzpe Aviv—have been allotted land that once belonged to Tamra. That's also why Tamra's Jewish neighbours have impressive villas with big gardens, often including swim-

*Since 1953 it has been awarded each year to an Israeli citizen who has demonstrated excellence or broken new ground in a particular field.

ming pools, and communal parks and playing areas for the children. The plan for Tamra, in contrast, envisages ever more crowding in a community already stripped of all public space. In Professor Law-Yone's words, "There is plenty of land in Israel. Building upwards is just code for cramming more Arabs in."

Speaking to Amin Sahli later, I sensed that that Tamra could do almost nothing to change its bleak future. The government bodies and the planning committees that set the guidelines for these master plans are always Jewish-dominated and often have no Arab members at all. Arab citizens have no voice in their own future, let alone the state's. Amin was deeply depressed. He had just returned from a meeting of the Knesset's economics committee, which, at the instigation of an Arab Knesset member, Issam Makhoul, had discussed the land and housing crisis in Tamra. Amin had compiled figures which showed that the town had little more than a thousand acres for building, all of which was developed. The rest of its six thousand acres were zoned either for farming or as green areas, which could not be developed. Because the Interior Ministry refused to release any new land for development, he told the committee, young Arab couples had no choice but to build their homes illegally, often on their own land which was zoned for agriculture. Their parents could not build upwards to provide them with an apartment, as Mansfeld had suggested, because they had already reached the building-regulation limit of four storeys for their homes. One hundred and fifty buildings in Tamra were under demolition orders, threatening hundreds of young couples and their children with homelessness and destitution.

I found that I could say nothing to reassure Amin as he spoke in a tone of absolute despair about Tamra's future. He had exhausted all the official channels, commuting to Jerusalem regularly to try to persuade Jewish officials and politicians of Tamra's crisis, only to be met by a lack of interest or condescension. It seemed to me the height of irony, given our history, that the Jewish state has so little concern about the ghetto living it has forced on its Arab citizens. Amin said he felt humiliated and powerless every time a young couple came to him seeking help with their housing problems. All he could do was to turn them away empty-handed. It was not as though they had other choices available to them. Israel makes it virtually impossible for Arabs to live in Jewish communities, and other Arab communities are in the same dire straits. Couples would simply be moving from a ghetto they know to one they do not, to a place where they could not even rely on the support of their hamula.

"You know, Susan," Amin said, "even dying is a problem if you are an Arab in Israel. In Tamra we have run out of land to bury our dead."

I asked him how he felt about living here. With his head in his hands, he told me he was thinking about a way to leave Israel with his wife and three young children. If he did, he would be joining his three siblings, all of whom are doctors, in exile: his two brothers are in the United States and his sister is in France. "It feels to me like a subtle way of ethnically cleansing me off my land," he said. Today equal numbers of Jews and Arabs are living in the Galilee, he pointed out, but it is obvious from looking at the region's development plans that one ethnic group is benefiting at the expense of the other. "These plans are about making life impossible for us, the Arabs, to remain here. Israel destroys the structure of our family life, making us weak and fragmented. If it continues like this, anyone who can leave will do so. I want to stay here, to raise my children in their homeland, but I have to be realistic. How can I stay when all the messages my state sends me are that I am not welcome?"

2

DEATH OF A LOVE AFFAIR

Inside the information pack from the Jewish Agency office in London was a badge and an accompanying letter: "Wear this as you walk off the plane to begin your new life as an Israeli citizen," the instructions stated. So on 10 October 1999, as I made my way down the flight of steps onto the tarmac of Tel Aviv's Ben-Gurion International Airport, I had a badge pinned to my chest bearing the slogan "I've come home."

The thought that I and the hundreds of other new immigrants arriving each week on El Al flights from all over the world were reclaiming a right that had lain dormant for two thousand years did not strike me as strange. For the thing that brought me late in life to Israel, with only a couple of suitcases of belongings, was a dream I had secretly harboured since childhood. The object of my desire was to make aliya, the Hebrew word for "ascent"—the idea that in returning to Israel, a Jew is fulfilling a divinely ordained mission. At the age of fifty, I was leaving behind my home in Wimbledon, South London, two grown-up children, Daniel and Tanya, a recently failed marriage and my work as an AIDS/HIV counsellor. Other than these attachments, not much stood in my way: Israeli law entitles me and every other Jew in the world to instant citizenship if we choose to live in Israel. There

are no visa applications, points systems or lengthy residency procedures. As a Jew, I had a right to Israeli citizenship by virtue of
my ethnicity alone. The Jewish Agency in London had been able
to process my application for Israeli citizenship in just a week,
and it made sure the immigration process was as painless as possible. My flight ticket was paid for, and accommodation was provided while I found my feet in the Promised Land. The only
hesitation on my part was a reluctance, when confronted by an official issuing my Israeli identity card, to adopt a Hebrew name.
My friends suggested I become either Shashana or Vered, the
names of two flowers, but at the last minute I decided to stick
with Susan.

I am not sure I can identify the exact moment I became a
committed Zionist, but I do know that a single childhood incident changed the direction of my life and my understanding
of what it was to be a Jew. I was eleven years old and on an out-
ing with some girls from my boarding school to nearby High
Wycombe, one of the many commuter towns that ring London.
Browsing through the shelves of a small bookshop in one of the
back streets, away from the other girls, I stumbled across the
most horrifying picture book. As I leafed through its pages, I
found photo after photo of emaciated corpses piled high in pits,
of men ripping gold fillings from teeth, of mountains of hair and
shoes. At such a young age I was not aware that these were pictures of the Holocaust, an event that was still fearsomely present
in the imaginations of Jews around the world fifteen years after
the end of the Second World War. But the awfulness of the images transfixed me.

I learned the story behind these photographs from my parents shortly afterwards, and so began my compulsive interest in
the Holocaust and Jewish history. The following year, 1961, after
I had moved to a new boarding school in Buckinghamshire, the
trial of the Gestapo leader Adolf Eichmann began in Jerusalem.

I read the newspapers every day, appalled by the accounts of the "final solution," Hitler's attempt to exterminate the Jewish people. I also recall spending weekends poring over copies of the *Jewish Chronicle* in my parents' home, reading in the personal columns the notices from individuals and families still searching for relatives in Europe from whom they had been separated for as long as two decades. These heart-rending messages were an uncomfortable reminder that the legacy of loss and destruction wrought by the concentration camps was continuing. My exposure to the Holocaust, and my new understanding that millions of Jews had died at the hands of the Nazis, launched me on an ever wider quest for knowledge, not only of what had happened to its victims but also of what had led to such barbarity.

My own family, I was soon aware, had only narrowly escaped—by a quirk of destiny—the tragedy that had consumed so many others. My father's parents, before they met, were refugees from the pogroms in Lithuania in the 1880s, fleeing separately to Odessa, where they hoped they might catch a ship to Hamburg and a new future in Germany. But when they arrived at the port, they and many other refugees found the ship full and were forced to travel on the only other vessel, bound for Cape Town in South Africa. As we now know, their fates and their children's were transformed by that missed boat: instead of finding themselves caught up in the rise of European fascism, they watched the horrific events unfold from the safe distance of Cape Town. My father, however, was in Europe at the outbreak of war. He had left South Africa in the late 1920s, a penniless but brilliant medical student travelling steerage class on a boat bound for Ireland. He enrolled at Trinity College, Dublin, where he was mentored by Chaim Herzog, the chief rabbi of Ireland and the father of Israel's first president, also named Chaim, who helped him become a passionate Zionist. By the time Nazism was on the rise in Germany, my father was a leading surgeon in London, where he met my mother, a nurse. They spent the war tending to the injured at the Tilbury docks in Essex, one of the most heavily bombed places in Britain.

If my family had survived the war unscathed, the plight of the many who had not touched me deeply. As with many others, my perception of the tragedy that had befallen my people was shaped by the story of the *Exodus,* as told by the novelist Leon Uris. I read of the ship that left Europe in July 1947, its decks choked with Holocaust survivors in search of sanctuary in what was then Palestine; of the refugees who tried to jump ship and reach the shores of the Promised Land; of the decision of the British to send the 4,500 refugees to internment camps in Cyprus, because they had agreed to limits on Jewish immigration to avoid further antagonising the local Palestinian population and neighbouring Arab countries; and of the horrifying eventual return of the ship and its Jewish refugees to Germany. I was outraged by the thought that British soldiers, ruling Palestine under a mandate from the League of Nations, could have acted with such callousness. My alienation from my country, Britain, began at that point.

The middle classes exercised a subtle, sophisticated discrimination against Jews in postwar Britain, which was apparent enough to make me increasingly aware of my difference. There were the comments about my "funny name" (my maiden name is Levy). I heard tales that disturbed me about the clubs that excluded Jews as policy. Among my parents' friends there were worried conversations about quotas on Jewish children, which might prevent their offspring from being admitted to a good school. And my mother, who was born a Protestant but converted to Judaism after marrying my father, told how everyone in her family apart from her mother disowned her for choosing to marry a Jew.

During my childhood, at the rural boarding schools where I

spent most of my time, I felt as if I were wearing a yellow star, as if my Jewishness were a visible stain to the teachers and other pupils. These were demonstratively Christian schools, with chapel services and morning prayers. I was aware of my vulnerability, too: out of hundreds of children in the senior school I attended, only four others were Jewish. I swung between contradictory emotions. On the one hand I feared appearing different, and on the other I wanted to own that difference proudly. Although I did not have the courage to refuse to attend morning prayers, I resolutely kept my mouth closed during the hymns. It was a very isolating experience: I felt outside the consensus, subtly but constantly reminded of my difference. This is, I think, a common experience for Diaspora Jews, but one little appreciated by Israeli Jews who were born and raised in a state where they make up the majority.

My growing distance from British society was reflected in an ever greater attachment, if only emotionally, to Israel. I was raised on stirring stories of the great and glorious Jewish state. For non-Jews it is perhaps difficult to appreciate what an enormous impact the creation of the state of Israel had on us. It reinvented our self-image, anchoring our pride in a piece of territory that had been our shared homeland two thousand years before. It satisfied our sense of historic justice and showed that we could forge our own place among the modern nation-states. But more than that, many Jews, myself included, were excited by the triumphs of our army, particularly those of 1948 and 1967, when Israel took on its Arab neighbours and won substantial territory from them. Here we were, a persecuted, isolated people, freeing ourselves from the ghettos of Europe and rising like a phoenix from the ashes of the gas chambers to become warriors. No longer a helpless minority always at risk of persecution, we were a proud people reclaiming our homeland, willing and able to fight to defend it on the battlefield. Young Jews could imagine a future not just as either merchants or intellectuals but rather as brave and courageous soldiers. We could call ourselves sabra, identifying with the prickly Middle Eastern cactus that flourishes in even the most hostile terrain.

I married Michael Nathan, a successful lawyer, in 1970, at the age of twenty-one. My early marriage, frowned on by my parents, brought me into the embrace of a much more religious family than my own. Michael's mother and father were traditional and Orthodox, in sharp contrast to my parents' secular, liberal background, and our differences in upbringing, culture and outlook would eventually push Michael and me apart. During the twenty-six years of our marriage, however, we only visited Israel together once, when we went to see Michael's brother in Jerusalem. Michael never shared my attachment to the Jewish state, and on the seven other occasions when I visited, I was always alone. Our two children forged their own relationships with Israel, touring the country as part of youth groups or working on kibbutzim. But although this was officially my state, I always left Israel as a tourist, an outsider, with a feeling that its inner substance had not been fully revealed to me.

So when I arrived to claim Israeli citizenship in 1999, my head was still full of romantic notions of Zionism and the Jewish state. The Jews had reclaimed an empty, barren land—"a land without people for a people without land." We had made the desert bloom; we had filled an uninhabited piece of the Middle East with kibbutzim, the collective farms that were the pioneering backbone of the state. At that stage, the thought that the country was full of strangers, people whom I and my countrymen lived alongside but entirely apart from, did not enter my mind. The one million Arabs who share the state with Jews—Palestinians who remained on their land after the 1948 war that founded Israel, and so by accident rather than design became Israeli citizens—were invisible to me, as they are to almost all

Israeli Jews. Their culture, their society and their story were a mystery.

The excitement of being in Israel did not quickly dissipate. My first months were filled with thrilling moments of feeling, for the first time in my life, that I belonged to the majority. I did not need to explain my family name, nor did I have to hide my pride in my Jewishness. I could have walked down the street with a Star of David emblazoned on my lapel if I wanted to; no one would have batted an eyelid. There was even a strange sense of liberation in calling a plumber and opening the door to a man wearing a kippa, the small cloth disc worn by religious Jewish men as a head covering. It made me think, *I really am in the land of the Jews.*

The stories that had inspired me as a child now came dramatically to life. Soon after my arrival I was hanging laundry outside the kitchen window of my Tel Aviv flat when I noticed an old woman waving down to me from a neighbouring apartment block, a dilapidated building erected in the early 1950s. Noticing a new face in the area, she called out that her name was Leah and asked who I was and where I was from. I told her, then asked whether she had been born in Israel. No, she replied, she had been born in Poland. During the Second World War she had been separated from her parents, who were later killed in a concentration camp. She went into hiding in the woods, staying with several Russian families until envoys from the Jewish Agency tracked her down and put her on a ship to Palestine. That ship was the *Exodus*. She recounted the story of the trip in the packed boat that I had read about in my teenage years, and explained how they were turned back to Germany. She told me of the horrific overcrowding on the ship, of the bodies stuffed together, but also of the excitement as they neared the Promised Land. Here in Leah I had found a living, breathing piece of history, a woman who made flesh all the reasons that I felt attached and committed to Israel.

Most Jews are all too ready to tell you how much Israel means to them as a sanctuary. How safe they feel, knowing that there is a country they can flee to if anti-Semitism raises its ugly head again. How reassuring it is to have a country that will protect them, having inherited the legacy of centuries of persecution and the horrors of the Holocaust. What they are much less ready to admit is that Israel is not just a safe haven and a homeland; it also embodies the value of naked Jewish power. What I felt when I arrived in Israel—as I suspect many other Jews do—was that through my new state I was defying a world that had persecuted my people. Being in the majority, and not needing to explain myself, was a condition I was unfamiliar with. The sense of being in charge, of putting the boot on the other foot, was more than a little intoxicating.

I did not come to Israel the easy way, though as a middle-class Londoner I could have strolled into any flat in Tel Aviv. I chose instead a path that I believed followed in the footsteps of the pioneering Jewish immigrants to Palestine. I arranged with the Jewish Agency in London to spend my first six months in an immigrant absorption centre in Rana'ana, close to Tel Aviv. I knew what I was letting myself in for: an apartment shared with strangers newly arrived from all over the world, separated by different languages, cultures and traditions. All we would have in common was the knowledge that we were Jews and that we wanted to become Israelis.

These first months presented a culture shock that tested the resources of many of the inmates. I arrived with my British culture, but the absorption centre was also home to people from many other cultures, including Americans, Dutch, Russians, Swiss, French and South Americans. All of us had to adjust both to these other cultures and to the new Israeli culture. We also struggled with the abruptness of Israelis, which many took for rudeness. The Rana'ana centre has perhaps the most privileged intake of

Jewish immigrants anywhere in Israel, with most coming from developed countries. It beats by a considerable margin the caravan transit camps reserved for Ethiopian Jews, the Jewish group most discriminated against inside Israel. Many of the one million Russian Jews who arrived in Israel during the 1990s, following the collapse of the Soviet Union, also stayed in far less salubrious surroundings.

Nonetheless, the absorption centre was a tough and uncomfortable introduction to Israel, and I remember that it left several people close to a nervous breakdown and ready to fly back home. I still have a cutting from a local newspaper, *Ha Sharon*, headlined "Immigrants Complain of Poor Conditions." A letter written by some of the French and American inmates to the absorption centre's management is quoted: "The apartments are old and full of mould and fungus. The kitchens are broken, the showers don't work properly, the walls are peeling and we have no air-conditioners." And it is true that in many ways Rana'ana was as much a prison as a melting pot. Having spent my childhood from the age of seven on, however, in the harsh, disciplinarian atmosphere of British boarding schools, I found that coping with these material hardships only slightly marred the wonderful experience of being absorbed into a new country and culture and meeting so many like-minded Jews.

But in these early months I started to experience darker moments. It was a big disappointment that the only family I had in Israel, religious cousins living in the southern city of Ashdod, who originally approved of my decision to make aliya, kept their distance from the moment I arrived. They did not even meet me at the airport. For a while their attitude baffled me, but eventually I came to understand how my migration challenged their sense of their own Israeliness. They belong to the right-wing religious camp and still hold on to a vision of Israelis as pioneering frontiersmen, settlers implanting themselves in hostile terrain. I think they were convinced that with my "European softness," I would not be able to stay the course. And when I confounded them by almost immediately securing a well-paid position in Tel Aviv teaching English to business professionals, my easy assimilation served only to antagonise them further.

My job involved travelling from one office to the next, which meant that I quickly learned my way around Tel Aviv. I also met and got to know a range of Israelis with different political views and insights into the "Israeli experience." I heard from some of them about their own problems as immigrants being absorbed into Israeli society, about their concerns for their children serving in the army and about the country's economy.

Four months after my arrival, I suffered a devastating blow when I was diagnosed with a rare form of eye cancer. I had to begin a crash course in negotiating my way single-handedly around Israel's health care system, and eventually I found myself in Jerusalem's Hadassah Hospital, awaiting an operation. Hadassah occupies a striking position, set in a pine forest overlooking the old stone houses of Ein Kerem, a Palestinian village that was cleansed of its population in the 1948 war and is now a wealthy suburb of Jerusalem to which many rich Jews aspire to move. The hospital has state-of-the-art medical equipment and is staffed by a mix of Israeli Jews and Arabs, and it was there that I got my first sense that the country I had so longed to be a citizen of might not be quite what I imagined. I was lying in a ward surrounded by beds filled not just with other Jews but with people from many of the diverse and confusing ethnic and religious components of the Holy Land: Jews, Christians, Muslims and Druses. This was before the intifada of September 2000, but still it was surprising to see Israelis and Palestinians sharing the same ward. Even more confusingly, many of the Palestinians were Israeli citizens, members of a group I discovered were commonly referred to as the "Israeli Arabs." The Jewish state was clearly a lot less ethnically pure than I had been led to believe.

Another experience on the ward started me questioning what was really going on inside Israel. One day a young Orthodox woman arrived, clutching her month-old baby, who had just undergone surgery on an eye. That evening her husband came to visit. He was wearing a knitted kippa, long sidelocks, a pistol on one hip and a rifle slung casually over his shoulder. This is the uniform of the nationalist religious right in Israel, better known abroad as "the settlers." The thought that a heavily armed civilian could wander freely around a hospital where women and children were ill appalled me. I engaged him in conversation as he was leaving. In a strong American accent he told me, "I've just requisitioned an Arab home in East Jerusalem. I never leave home without a weapon." I argued that he would be better off living in the Jewish quarter in the Old City. No, he retorted. "All of East Jerusalem belongs to the Jews."

His words left a nasty taste in the mouth. Why was he stealing a home from Arabs in the Palestinian part of the city, the section captured by Israel in the 1967 war, when there were vast tracts of the country he could choose to live in? And why did I appear to be the only person on the ward who thought it strange for a visitor to a hospital to arrive wearing a gun? I left the hospital confused by the signals Israel was sending me. Here was a state that prided itself on having one of the best medical systems in the world. And access to health care seemed not to discriminate overtly on the grounds of race or creed. But it was also clear that some Israelis had an unhealthy admiration for violence and an appetite for what did not belong to them. Israel did not appear to place many controls on their behaviour.

My strong humanist values derive from an understanding of both my family's history and my people's. My father raised me on stories about my great-grandfather Zussman Hershovitz, who lived in one of the Jewish ghetto communities, the shtetls, in Lithuania. I was taught as a small child the consequences of being Jewish for men like my great-grandfather—how it was not possible for him to go to school as a boy, how he ended up as a peddler moving from place to place to avoid the pogroms. In addition, my father, Samuel Levy, a respected Harley Street doctor, instilled in me a deep appreciation of Jewish ethics, culture and history. I cannot claim he was a good father. Much of my childhood was spent living in terror of his rages and under the shadow of his disappointment. But outside the immediate family circle he was never less than a fiercely loyal and dedicated healer. Although he was very successful, he believed he had wider social responsibilities than simply accumulating money from the wealthy clients who visited his London practice. He continued to dedicate much of his time to a practice he started when he was younger, in a deprived part of Essex. After he retired, in 1973, he returned to the country of his birth, South Africa, to be a medical health officer and practise in a clinic for blacks only in Groote Schuur, Cape Town.

So even though I was soon earning good money as an English teacher in Tel Aviv, I could not simply accept the privileges that came with being a successful new Israeli. A few months after I recovered from the eye operation, I was approached by a student organisation called Mahapach, which had heard of my experience in community work and raising money for AIDS charities in London. They asked if I could write a funding application in support of their work for disadvantaged communities inside Israel, particularly the indigenous Arab population and the community of Jews of Middle Eastern descent, known in Israel as the Mizrahim. Much of Mahapach's work involves encouraging students to go into deprived communities to teach youngsters core subjects like Hebrew, Arabic, English and maths outside the often limiting arena of the formal classroom.

I sat down and read about these communities and their problems. I knew about the difficulties of the Mizrahim, who, because of their Arab culture—they originally came from Morocco, Iraq, Syria and Egypt—have long been treated as inferior Jews by the European elite, the Ashkenazi Jews, who run Israel. But questions quickly began to surface in my mind about the indigenous Arab communities. Where did these Arabs I was reading about live? Why had they been so invisible, except briefly when I was in hospital, during my first two years in Israel? In those days I had little time for anything except my work. I would usually be up at 5 A.M., start work at 6 (before my clients' offices opened) and finish at 8 or 9 P.M. Still, I was not satisfied with simply regurgitating the dry statistics I found in newspaper articles, which suggested that Israeli Arabs were discriminated against. They were as faceless and unconnected to my life as bacteria living at the bottom of the ocean. I wanted to meet these Arabs for myself. When the chance arose to visit an Arab town as part of the research, I leapt at it. The destination was Tamra, in the western Galilee.

Within minutes of driving into Tamra I felt that I had entered another Israel, one I had never seen before. It was almost impossible to believe that I could turn off a main highway close to the luxurious rural Jewish communities of the Galilee and find myself somewhere that was so strikingly different from any Jewish area I had ever visited, and not just culturally. It was immediately obvious that Tamra suffered from chronic overcrowding. The difference in municipal resources and investment was starkly evident too. And a pall of despair hung over the town, a sense of hopelessness in the face of so much official neglect. It was the first time I had been to an Arab area (apart from visits as a tourist to the Old City of Jerusalem), and I was profoundly shaken by it. A disturbing thought occurred to me, one that refused to shift even after I had driven back to Tel Aviv. Tamra looked far too familiar. I thought, *Where have I seen this before?* I recognised the pattern of discrimination from my experience of apartheid South Africa, which I had visited regularly during my childhood. I could detect the same smell of oppression in Tamra that I had found in the black townships.

These initial impressions were reinforced by a meeting at the home of Dr. Asad Ghanem, who lives in the neighbouring village of Sha'ab. One of the few prominent Arab academics in Israel, Dr. Ghanem impressed me with his direct and unemotional explanations of the discrimination exercised in all spheres of Israeli life against the Arab population, from employment and education to land allocations and municipal budgets. But he found it difficult to remain detached about one topic he brought to my attention, an issue that would later become the theme of many conversations with my new Arab neighbours and friends. In Arab communities across Israel, tens of thousands of homes are judged illegal by the state and are under threat of demolition. In Tamra, Dr. Ghanem told me, 150 homes were facing destruction. Intermittently the police would target an Arab community, bring in bulldozers at the crack of dawn and tear down the illegal homes. Razing these buildings, some of them up to four floors high, might mean that dozens of extended families, comprising hundreds of people, were made homeless at a stroke.

I knew from my research that illegal building was widespread in Arab communities. This was regarded by the Israeli authorities as the action of law-breakers, people who were squatting on state land or who did not want to pay for a building licence. But as Dr. Ghanem pointed out, no one chooses to invest his life savings and his dreams in a home that might be razed at any moment. Arab families have been forced to build illegally because in most cases the state refuses to issue them with building permits. And then he delivered the knockout blow: he told me that his own beautiful home was illegal and threatened with demolition.

There can be little doubt that the land on which Dr. Ghanem's home stands has belonged to his family for generations. From the salon, visitors can see the old stone foundations of his grandparents' house. A few years before, he had decided, with the arrival of his children, that he and his wife, Ahlam, could no longer live in his parents' apartment; they would build a home on the only land the family had left, even though the planning authorities refused him a building permit. Effectively branded criminals by the state, like tens of thousands of other Arab families, he and Ahlam had been paying heavy fines ever since—as much as £15,000 sterling at a time—to ward off demolition. Their lives have become a routine of paying the state to prevent the destruction of everything they hold dear.

The question that echoed in my mind as I heard Dr. Ghanem's story was, where were he and his family supposed to live? What was the future envisaged for them by the state? I knew well that endless housing developments were springing up all over Israel, and illegally in the occupied territories, for Jewish families. But where was the next generation of Arab citizens to live? Dr. Ghanem and Ahlam are pillars not only of their own community in Sha'ab but of the whole Arab community inside Israel. Nonetheless, the state is forcing them to live with a terrible threat hanging over their heads. They are raising their children in an environment of continual insecurity. Every day when they leave home, they do not know whether they will return to find a pile of rubble. They have been made to live in a unstable world, which I have no doubt is deeply damaging to them and their children.

My meeting with Dr. Ghanem ended uncomfortably. In a matter-of-fact tone he asked me whether I had made aliya, whether I had claimed my right as a Jew to come to live in a country from which the overwhelming majority of his people had been expelled little more than half a century earlier. These Palestinians still live in refugee camps across the Middle East and are refused the opportunity to return to their former homes in Israel. It was the first time I hesitated to answer this question. I understood that my privileges as a Jewish immigrant had come at the expense of his people. Sitting in his home, I finally faced reality. The intoxicating power trip had come to an abrupt halt.

As is my way, I could not continue to live in ignorance. So I began the long and difficult task of becoming informed. I read and absorbed anything I could find on the position of the Israeli Arabs, questioning the official narrative. My left-wing friends in Tel Aviv, mainly academics and people working in nonprofit organisations, whom I had met through a fellow inmate of the absorption centre, were quick to reassure me they had Arab friends. I asked, who exactly were these friends? Where did they live? What did they talk about together? The reply was always more or less the same. They were on good terms with the owner of an Arab restaurant where the felafel was excellent. Or they got their car fixed in a garage in an Arab village where the prices were low. What did they talk to these "friends" about? When did they meet outside these formal relationships? What intimacies did they exchange? The Tel Aviv crowd looked at me aghast, as if I were crazy. They did not have *those* sorts of relationships with Arabs.

In fact, it was clear they had no Arab friends at all. I was mortified. The revelation that I had stumbled across the same kind of master-servant relationship that existed in South Africa was something I was little prepared for. For a week I was racked by pains in my stomach and head. It was as if I were purging myself of all the lies I had been raised on.

When I was stronger, I returned to Tamra. Ahlam Ghanem invited me to spend the night with her family. We ate dinner together, and then she and I sat on the terrace in the warm evening air and talked. We exchanged confidences and intimacies that people rarely share until they have known each other for a long time. I remember thinking as we sat close together that here were an Arab and a Jew getting to know each other at a very deep and personal level, and that this was the way it was supposed to be. Cut off briefly from a society that always privileges Jews, we could feel like equals. I went back to Tel Aviv firm in my resolution that something in my life would have to change. Israel, as it was presently constituted, required me to choose a side. Would I carry on with my life in Tel Aviv, turning a blind eye like everyone else to the suffering of the Arab population, or would I do something to highlight the reality and work towards changing it?

As it happened, my mind was effectively made up for me. I started to see much more clearly the paternalistic and colonialist attitudes of my left-wing friends. Being around them became unbearably suffocating. When Asad invited me in the winter of 2001 to teach English to Arab professionals at his Ibn Khaldun Association in Tamra, I had little hesitation in agreeing to take up the position. The Abu Hayjas, whom I knew through my work for Mahapach, offered to rent me the empty top-floor flat in their home, on the hillside overlooking the town's central mosque.

I knew that breaking away from the Jewish collective would be traumatic, but I could not know how profoundly I would alienate those I thought I was close to. Almost overnight I lost my Jewish friends. Individualism is highly prized in many societies, but not in Israel, where the instinct of the herd prevails. Doubtless the reasons can be found in Jewish history, in the centuries of persecution culminating in the Holocaust. There is an attitude of "you're either with us or against us." No one should step outside the consensus, or question it, because this is seen as weakening the group. But human beings are immeasurably more important to me than labels or institutions. By choosing to live as a Jew in a town of Muslims, I hoped I could show that the fear that divides us is unrealistic. It is based on ignorance, an ignorance that the state of Israel tries to encourage among its Jewish citizens to keep them apart from their Arab neighbours. I know Jews who have lived on a left-wing kibbutz near Tamra yet have never ventured into the largest Arab community in their area.

I have pondered long and hard why I was able to break away from the Jewish collective when other Israelis and Jews feel so bound to it, prisoners of a belief that they must stand with their state and their people, right or wrong. At the core of modern Jewish identity is the idea of victimhood, shaped by our history of persecution and the singular outrage of the Holocaust. The sense among Jews in Israel and the Diaspora that they are uniquely victims, both as individuals and as an ethnic group, cannot be overstated. Victimhood has become something akin to a cult among Jews, even among the most successful in Europe and America. It is developed as part of the ideology of Zionism, creating an Alice-through-the-looking-glass world for most Jews: they sincerely and incontrovertibly believe that Israel, a nation with one of the strongest armies in the world, backed by the only nuclear arsenal in the Middle East, is in imminent danger of annihilation, either from its Arab neighbours or from the remnants of the Palestinian people living in the occupied territories. They can safely ignore the improbability of this scenario, however, as long as suicide bombers wreak intermittent devastation on crowded buses in Tel Aviv and Jerusalem.

No one can say I do not understand the suffering inflicted on families by these attacks. One day I was waiting at Ben-Gurion Airport for a flight to the U.K. when a good friend called, her voice barely audible, to tell me that her son, a serving soldier, had been badly injured by a suicide bomber. I had introduced this young man to my daughter, Tanya, the previous summer, and the two had formed a deep bond. Since then he has undergone more than thirty-five operations to try to repair the damage done to his body. His father has suffered eight heart attacks. All their expectations about their life were destroyed in an instant. That suicide bombing has torn apart the lives of my friends as easily as a piece of paper can be ripped.

But while I know that these attacks can be terribly destructive of Israelis' lives and their sense of security, they can easily become an excuse not to confront the reality of what is taking place, the wider picture. They can simply reinforce in a very negative fashion this sense of Jewish victimhood. I understand this well. Like most Jews, I was brought up to see myself as a victim too: in a collective sense, as a Jew raised in the shadow of the Holocaust, and in an individual sense, as a Jew growing up in a postwar Britain tinged with anti-Semitism.

I was born in January 1949 into the grey, tired world of Britain under rationing. My family in Grays, Essex, appeared to me even at a very young age to be unlike those around me: there were no grandparents, brothers, sisters, aunts or uncles. My father's family were thousands of miles away, in South Africa, and my mother's immediate family were all dead, victims of the First World War, tuberculosis and bad luck. There was only me and my parents. But my isolation did not end there. My parents, preoccupied with the heavy duties of running a successful medical practice, abandoned me to the care of the cleaning lady. I was forbidden to play with the local "rough" children, who arrived with the building of a council estate near our home, and instead consoled myself with games with our golden retriever, Laddie, and my rubber doll, Pandora, in the back garden.

My only recollection of true early friendship is with a black servant called Inyoni, who looked after me, effectively as a substitute mother, when I was two years old, when my father briefly returned to South Africa. The experiment did not last long; after spending six months just outside Cape Town, we headed back to Britain. But Inyoni is a vivid feature in all my memories of that period in South Africa, much more so than my grandparents, whom I can barely recall. In that half-year I formed a deep attachment to him. He taught me to strap Pandora to my back and carry her the way the local black women carried their babies. (Back in Essex I would see other little girls in the street holding their dolls in their arms and tell them off, showing them how to do it properly.) I also spent hours squatting with Inyoni on the floor in his quarters at the back of the house as he prepared the vegetables. At other times we would play tea-party games on the lawn with Pandora. After my family left South Africa in 1952, I felt the loss of Inyoni deeply.

I was a sickly child, suffering repeated bouts of severe sinusitis, which served only to provoke anger and resentment in my father, whose interventions with drugs and operations failed to improve my condition. In total contrast to the way he treated his patients, he had no sympathy for my suffering and would simply tell me to get a grip on myself. I suppose to a highly respected doctor my recurrent illnesses must have seemed like a reproof: in the very heart of his family was a sick child he was powerless to heal. This failure was compounded, in his eyes, by my lack of success at school by any of the yardsticks he held dear. The many days I missed from school and his overbearing demands took their toll on my academic performance. I was constantly being dragged to teacher-parent meetings to discuss my poor results. Eventually, at the age of seven, I was packed off to the first of my boarding schools, cut off from contact with my parents apart from one weekend out of every three. Even when I returned home, my father was usually too busy with patients to spend time with me.

Before I left for boarding school, during the long periods when I was sick, my father would lock me in my room with what he considered educational material. He would give me a *National Geographic* to read, or throw me a pile of postcards he had been sent from around the world and demand that I find the country or city they had been posted from in an atlas. Sometimes he would want me to draw the outline of the country too. I was beaten if I could not answer his questions when he returned. By the age of six I was an expert at finding foreign places.

There were compensations for this harsh regime, trapped in the small world of my bedroom, deprived of companions. The biggest was the *National Geographic*, which opened up another, far more exciting world to me. In my head I had incredible adventures in places most British children had never heard of. Remote South American hill tribes became my friends, as did the Pygmies of the Congo. They never seemed any stranger to me—maybe less strange—than the children at school. My favourite place was the Himalayas, somewhere that looked awe-inspiring and magnificent; I thought that if only I could climb to the very top, I would be able to see the whole world. I felt a huge desire to go to these places and experience them for myself.

One of the features in the *National Geographic* that fascinated me most was about India. I was attracted to the pictures of that country, as I was to those of Africa, because of the bright colours, the beauty of the landscapes, the different way of life and the great variety of groups living on one subcontinent. What fascinated me most about India was the caste system, in particular the group classified as the lowest caste, the untouchables. I would study the pictures that accompanied the article and then read the copy that explained that the untouchables were supposed to be the ugliest, dirtiest, stupidest Indians and had to live on the outskirts of the towns. I would trace my fingers first around the faces of the untouchables and then around those of the highest caste, the Brahmans, flicking backwards and forwards between the pictures. But however long I looked at them, I could not see where the difference lay. Why were the untouchables supposed to be uglier? I could not understand how you could designate one group as dirtier or less worthy than another.

Although I have always rejected this fear of the Other and the racism that it inevitably fuels, I have learned from experience that it is a deeply rooted need in the human psyche. At the slightest provocation we will put distance between ourselves and those we cannot or do not want to understand.

At an early stage of the AIDS crisis I trained to be a therapist at Great Ormond Street Hospital in London. In the late 1980s, when, without the slightest shred of scientific evidence, there were stories all over the British media warning that AIDS was highly contagious, I was working at the London Lighthouse Project with infected women and children and with the partners of infected people. At the project we tried to challenge people's prejudices by bringing AIDS into the community; we even established a commercial restaurant, where the staff had AIDS or were HIV-infected, so people could see that they were not going to catch the disease simply by eating there. Nonetheless, some evenings I would attend social functions with my husband, Michael, and wait for the moment when another guest would ask what I did. My reply—that I was an HIV/AIDS counsellor—always elicited the same response: overwhelmed with revulsion, the other person would take a step back. There was a double disgust: the fear that I might be carrying that terrible disease, and also the incomprehension that a nice, presentable middle-class woman would be doing a "dirty" job like mine. It was as though people thought they were shaking the hand of a Brahman, only to discover that they had been tricked into making contact with an untouchable.

Moving to Tamra seemed to cause equivalent offence to my former Jewish friends. While Israeli Jews looked at the Palestinian uprising and responded by choosing to disengage, either by building a wall to separate themselves from the occupied population their army rules over or, inside Israel, by boycotting Arab areas and refusing to buy felafel or get their cars fixed in Arab garages, I elected to put myself right in the middle of the problem—to join the untouchables. The response of my friends, like that of the well-heeled party crowd in London, was to withdraw in revulsion. Now that I am outside the Jewish collective, outside the herd, I must be treated like the enemy, as if I have committed a crime of treason or incitement.

Although the decision to leave Tel Aviv and cross the ethnic divide seemed the natural reaction to my new understanding of what was happening inside Israel, it was never easy. On some days I felt tearful and isolated. I cried not out of fear but out of a terrible sense of how much my country was failing not just its Arab citizens but also its Jewish ones, and how catastrophically fragmented it was growing. It soon dawned on me that I had to be 100 per cent committed to my new course. My Jewish friends chose to dismiss my decision as a silly passing episode, and even some of my new friends in Tamra appeared to doubt whether I could withstand the pressures. Hassan's son Khalil said to me in the first few days, "After three months you'll go back. You won't be able to stand it here, without cinemas at the end of the road or elegant restaurants."

Neither side could understand why anyone would choose a primitive life over a sophisticated one. There was a double error in this thinking. First, I never saw Tamra as more primitive than Tel Aviv. Life was simpler, certainly, but my view has always been that life's greatest pleasures are simple. Second, it ignored the fact that some values are more important than being comfortable, such as developing a consciousness about the rights and wrongs of the society one lives in and an awareness of what each of us can contribute to improving it. In this sense the sophistication of the West increasingly appears to me to be a ve-

neer, concealing the fact that most of us have lost our understanding of where our communities are heading. We are encouraged to believe in the sanctity of the safe little bubbles we
inhabit, to the point where we can imagine no other life, no
other possibilities.

My rejection by my Jewish friends was matched by suspicion
about my motives and my seriousness expressed early on by a
few people in Tamra. An Israeli newspaper took pleasure in
quoting a former Arab Knesset member and resident of Tamra,
Mohammed Kaanan, when he was asked about me: "I want to
believe she is an innocent woman working in the interests of the
inhabitants here, but if a suspicion arises that she is working for
an organisation that is against the Arab population, that may
harm her. We won't stand for it." I was saddened by Kaanan's
comments but understood where such distrust springs from. For
the first two decades after the state of Israel was born, the Arab
minority lived under harsh military rule, and today their lives
are still controlled by a special department of Shin Bet, which
runs a large network of informers inside Arab communities. In
the circumstances, good intentions from Jews are treated with
caution.

Far more disorientating was the initial reaction of a Tamran
woman who would later become one of my closest friends. I met
Zeinab, an English teacher at the local high school, on my first
trip to Tamra, when I was doing research for Mahapach. In her
home she greeted me warmly and invited me to sit with her and
have coffee while we discussed discrimination in education. She
told me about the smaller budgets for Arab schools, the bigger
class sizes, the shorter learning days, the shoddy temporary
buildings in which Arab children learn and which usually became permanent classrooms, the severe restrictions on what may
be taught (restrictions that do not apply to Jewish children), and
the rigid control exercised over the appointment of Arab teach-

ers and principals by the security services, which weed out anyone with a known interest in politics or Palestinian history. She
added that Jewish schoolchildren receive benefits not afforded
Arab pupils, such as double the school allowance if their parents
serve in the army. I learned that by law all classrooms must be
built with air conditioners, a requirement strictly enforced in the
construction of Jewish schools but usually ignored in Arab ones.
And she explained that in most cases heating equipment, com-
puters and books have to be bought by Arab parents, because
Arab schools lack the funds to pay for them. Then, after calmly
informing me of this discrimination, her eyes turned glittery
with suppressed anger and she asked, "Why all of a sudden are
you so interested in the Arabs? Is it because of 9/11?" It had not
occurred to me that there was a connection between my being
here in Tamra and what had occurred in the United States. But
her accusing tone suggested otherwise; it was as though she were
saying, "We have been here all these years with the same problems and you Jews have always neglected us. Why the interest
now?" As our meeting came to a close, she showed me to the
door and said, "You are always welcome in an Arab home." I had
rarely felt less welcome in my life. Although I felt confused by
her barely contained rage, I was also impressed by her and
wanted to know her better.

On my subsequent visits to the Galilee, I always called on
Zeinab, and she was one of the first people I informed of my
planned relocation to Tamra. As the day of the move neared, I
rang her from Tel Aviv. She answered, saying she had been cleaning the house and thinking about me. I asked her what she was
thinking. "I was wondering whether I will be able to trust you,"
she replied.

It was at this moment I started to understand the roots of
Zeinab's anger. I realised that she had always been let down by
Jews, even those left-wingers who claimed to be on her side, and

she had no reason to think I would be any different. The few co-existence groups in Israel operate mainly in the Galilee, often bringing together Jewish and Arab women, but they are almost always run by Jews, and the debate is always controlled and circumscribed by the group's Jewish members. Politics is usually off limits, which in effect means any discussion that touches on the power relationship between Jews and Arabs is off limits. These groups almost universally failed to survive the outbreak of the second Palestinian intifada in September 2000, precisely because the central concerns of their Arab members had never been addressed. The Jewish participants were not prepared to make any sacrifices to promote equality, believing that if they did so, they would undermine the thing they hold most dear, the eternal validity of a Jewish state. Allowing their Arab neighbours an independent voice was seen as threatening the Jewishness of Israel. I felt that Zeinab had set me a test, convinced I would betray her like all the other well-intentioned Jews she had known. I began to persuade her otherwise by the very fact of moving to Tamra; she was soon at my door with a bowl of beautiful cacti.

In those early days in Tamra I also came to understand that my image as a Jew was problematic. Months before my move, in the spring of 2002, Israel had launched a massive invasion of the West Bank, known as Operation Defensive Shield, in which the army reoccupied the towns that had passed to the control of the Palestinian Authority under the 1993 Oslo Accords. All summer and winter, families in Tamra sat each night watching disturbing images on Israeli television and the Arab satellite channels of Israeli soldiers ransacking Palestinian homes in Ramallah, Nablus and Jenin, or of tanks ploughing down the streets, crushing anything in their way, from cars to electricity pylons. For people in Tamra, as in other Israeli Arab communities, these were even more dispiriting times than usual. Many had held out the hope that with the arrival of a Palestinian state next door, maybe they would finally come to be accepted as equal citizens of the Jewish state rather than as a potential fifth column. Now they saw that hope unravelling before their eyes.

Several disturbing incidents at this time brought home to me the fact that I had little control over how my image as a Jew was being shaped and distorted by my country, my government and my army. One came when I joined Suad, then fifteen, for a walk on the far side of Tamra. We reached a spot where a group of a dozen or so children aged between seven and eleven were playing outside the neighbourhood homes. It is a point of honour for most Arab families that they and their children are immaculately dressed, but these children were wearing ragged clothes. When they saw us, they rushed out shouting to Suad, "Is she a Jew, is she a Jew?" and "Jews are dirty, they kill people." Looking upset, Suad refused to translate straight away and called out to them, "Stop it!" She wanted to run, but I told her to stay calm. As we walked away, the children picked up stones from the roadside and threw them in our direction, though not strongly enough to hit us. It was a symbolic demonstration. Shaken, I thought afterwards that I understood their message: "We hate Jews, so stay away. They only ever bring trouble with them."

On another occasion, when I was out with Samira, we took a shortcut through a school playground in front of a group of transfixed ten-year-olds. A few came running up behind me, shouting, "Yehudiya, Yehudiya!" and throwing handfuls of leaves that I could feel caressing my back.

When I reflected on these incidents, I understood that what most Arab children learn about Jews comes from the media, and what they see is violence, oppression and abuse. The image of the strong, aggressive Israel that had so enthralled me in my early Zionist days I now saw in a very different light. These children, lacking the sophistication to discriminate between the media image of the Jew as an ever-present, menacing soldier and the reality of many kinds of Jews living in different circumstances all around the world, related to me in the only way they knew. They saw the children of Jenin or Ramallah throwing stones at the Jewish soldiers, and now they were mimicking them.

This problem was illuminated for me on another occasion, when I visited the home of Asad Ghanem. As he introduced me to his two young children, they asked, "Is your friend who doesn't speak like us a Jew?" Asad answered, "Yes, but she's a good Jew." I had been reclassified in a way that shocked me: I was not a human being, not an Israeli and not even a Jew, but a "good Jew." I came to realise that for most Arab children living in Israel, the first lesson—something they learn from watching what happens in Jenin, Nablus, Hebron or Gaza—is that Jews are bad. They have to be taught that not all Jews kill and destroy. This is something the older children understand: they have learned it as part of their survival training for later life, when they will have to venture into a society which will mostly treat them as an enemy. When they are old enough to leave the safety of Tamra, they must know when to conceal their Arabness and keep their mouths shut.

When I think of those children throwing stones at me, I get angry not with them but with all those Jews who tell me that the Palestinians living inside Israel are unaffected by the occupation, that it has nothing to do with them. They forget or choose to ignore the fact that although Palestinian citizens of Israel are separated from Palestinians in the West Bank and Gaza by the reality that one has citizenship and the other does not,* the

---

*Citizenship offers protections to Israeli Arabs not afforded to Palestinians of the West Bank and Gaza. The rights and duties incumbent on Israeli citizens, Jews and Arabs, are set out in Israeli law, whereas Palestinians living under occupation are judged according to a complex

bonds of their shared nationality—the fact that they are all Palestinians—are far stronger. Many Palestinian citizens, whether living in Tamra, Nazareth or Haifa, have family living under occupation in refugee camps in the West Bank and Gaza or in extreme poverty in Lebanon and Syria. When they see a child being shot in Jenin or Nablus, it could be a cousin or a nephew. Even progressive Jews appear deeply blocked in understanding this. When I explained the complex identity problems faced by Israeli Arabs to a left-wing friend from Tel Aviv who belongs to Rabbis for Human Rights, an organisation which vehemently opposes the occupation, he told me simply, "But they live in the state of Israel. The occupation doesn't touch them."

How wrong he is was proved one evening while I was still smarting from the stone-throwing incident. I was sitting in my home with a group of twelve Arab friends watching a video of Mohammed Bakri's controversial documentary film *Jenin Jenin*, originally banned in Israel. It is a powerful record of the traumatic effects on Jenin's inhabitants of Israel's violent invasion of the West Bank city in the spring of 2002. It was a disturbing moment at many levels. Sitting there as the only Jew, I was aware that I had to choose where I stood in this battle between two peoples, and that I had to be committed to the cause of justice and humanity. I watched the film through my Arab friends' eyes, learning exactly how they see us Jews as occupiers and oppres-

---

mix of local laws that applied before the occupation, Israeli laws, Israeli military decisions and international humanitarian law. Israeli military judges have wide discretion in applying these laws, often in apparently arbitrary fashion. Nonetheless, Israeli Arabs still face considerable discrimination, mainly because Israel lacks a constitution codifying basic rights, such as equality, freedom of speech and religious freedom, and because important national group rights, which determine resource allocations, are only recognised for Jewish citizens.

sors. It made me question very deeply how I had been able to identify with a country that could send its child soldiers to behave in this fashion.

The film prompted me to recall a conversation I had had on one of my increasingly rare and strained visits to my religious cousins, Jeffrey and Doreen, in Ashdod shortly after Operation Defensive Shield. Their granddaughter's husband, a medic in the reserves, had been sent to the Jenin area, and Doreen was apoplectic at the media's suggestions that there had been a massacre there. "Good Jewish boys who serve in the Israel Defence Forces, like our Ofer, don't harm people," she asserted confidently. And then, as if providing the proof, she told me that Ofer had even been asked by his commanders to give medical assistance to a Palestinian woman who was having a heart attack during the invasion. This level of naïvety and self-satisfaction I found profoundly unsettling. I told her, "The reality is that no one can know what their children get up to in a war. Soldiers carry secrets they will never divulge to their families."

Although I am sure some soldiers attempt to hold on to their humanist values while in uniform, I am also convinced that the inherent immorality of enforcing an occupation makes good intentions almost futile. Worse than this, there is plenty of evidence that many soldiers lose their judgement entirely under the pressure of the barbaric tasks they are ordered to carry out. One need only consider the reports in the Hebrew media of high suicide rates in the army, of the number of soldiers who are receiving psychological help and counselling or who are discharged from duty, to know the truth of this. But on this matter Israelis are in denial.

Later, after visiting Jenin, I was convinced that something terrible had happened there and that atrocities had been carried out by the Israeli army. When I watched the film, before I had been there, I was unprepared for the horrifying details of what had taken place and the terrible destruction wrought on the inhabitants' lives as well as on the centre of Jenin camp.* Watching the survivors, broken-hearted amid the rubble of their homes, hopeless and understanding that their voices would never be properly heard, I felt their rage. It dismayed me to realise that I too was seeing the Israeli army, full of those "good Jewish boys," as a terrorist army, and that for the first time I was beginning to understand the emotions that can drive a suicide bomber to action. I could see how unfair it sounds to a Palestinian to hear a suicide bomber being labelled a terrorist when we refuse to do the same if an Israeli soldier bulldozes a house with a family inside.

As I attempted to cope with these images on the screen, I was also confronted by the unexpected reactions of my Arab friends watching alongside me. Afterwards we talked about the film, and though I felt near to tears, they were smiling as they spoke about the horrifying events. I vividly remember Heba, from my family, talking about one particularly unpleasant scene, when an old man tells of being shot in the leg at close range by a soldier, and all the while she maintained a fixed smile. I thought, *Is this a mask—is this the only way she can contain her emotions, suppress the pain? And if it is, is the mask reserved for me, the Jew here, or is it one*

---

*Jenin exists as both a separate town and a refugee camp, living side by side, the dividing line between them unclear except to the inhabitants. Both the town and camp consist of concrete homes but the camp's residents are refugees (as registered with the UN) from the 1948 and 1967 wars when they were driven from their lands inside what is today Israel. Residents of Jenin town, on the other hand, are mainly from families that lived in the town before the waves of refugees swelled the community's numbers. Interestingly, the Israeli army appears to note the difference: it famously leveled the centre of Jenin camp but barely touched Jenin town during the incursions of Operation Defensive Shield in spring 2002. Most West Bank cities, such as Nablus, Tulkaram, and Ramallah, have significant refugee camps next to them.

they maintain with each other too? The answer came when the group got up to leave. Zeinab turned to me at the door and said, with the same fixed smile and glittering angry eyes I had seen before, "Sweet dreams." It was as if I had been hit in the stomach. I desperately wanted to say, "But that's not me—don't hold me responsible, I'm with you." But anything I said would have been inadequate. Maybe that night was the ultimate test for me in Zeinab's eyes. Maybe she thought I would go running home to Tel Aviv the next day. But I didn't; I stayed. And afterwards our friendship deepened and strengthened.

Listening to and coming to understand the Palestinian narrative was an important part of unlearning my lifelong Zionist training, which had dismissed the Palestinians' history and culture as irrelevant or nonexistent. One of the most poignant episodes occurred when I was reading the autobiography of the Jerusalem doctor Mufid Abdul Hadi, which had been given to me by his nephew, Dr. Mahdi Abdul Hadi, the director of the Palestinian Academic Society for the Study of International Affairs (PASSIA), based in Jerusalem. A moving passage concerning his escape from Palestine in 1948, after the Israeli state was declared, concludes with a scene on a boat, *al-Malik Fuad,* which heads for Sweden packed with Palestinian refugees being taken away, most of them forever, from their homeland and their families: "When *al-Malik Fuad* lifted its anchor and began its westward-bound journey, it met another ship going in the opposite direction. Its gunwale was occupied by hundreds of singing and rejoicing people, who were greeting 'The Promised Land' for the first time. The happy people greeted our ship by waving the Jewish state's flag."

Here was the flip side of the *Exodus* story that had inspired my love affair with Israel. In all my time as a teenager learning my people's history, I had never been encouraged to think in those terms—that our people's rejoicing came at the cost of another's bereavement. The Zionist story I had learned was that this country was "a land without people." But here was one of those supposedly nonexistent Palestinians telling me his story of loss and betrayal. I thought how much we could change history if we could raise Jewish children with that simple understanding.

The obstacles to doing it are huge. The apparent inability of Jews in Israel and the Diaspora to address the true roots of the Middle East conflict and accept their role in the Palestinians' suffering is given an alibi by their fears, which are in turn stoked by stories in the media of the ever-present threat of anti-Semitism, a Jew-hatred in both Europe and the Arab world that, we are warned, has troubling echoes of the period before the Second World War. A disproportionate part of the media coverage of anti-Semitism concentrates on tarring critics of Israel with this unpleasant label. Anyone who has disturbing things to say about what Israel is doing to the Palestinians is, on this interpretation, an anti-Semite. I have little doubt that the motivation of Israel's defenders in many cases is to silence the critics, whether their criticisms are justified or not.

My own critique of Israel—that it is a state that promotes a profoundly racist view of Arabs and enforces a system of land apartheid between the two populations—risks being treated in the same manner. So how does one reach other Jews and avoid the charge of anti-Semitism? Given the sensitivities of Jews after their history of persecution, I think it helps if we distinguish between making a comparison and drawing a parallel. What do I mean? A comparison is essentially a tool for making quantitative judgements: my suffering is greater or lesser than yours, or the same. Jews have a tendency to demand exclusive rights to certain comparisons, such as that nothing can be worse than the Holocaust, because it involved the attempt to kill a whole people on an unprecedented scale. Anyone who challenges that exclusive right, for example by suggesting that Israel is trying to ethnically cleanse the Palestinians from their homeland, is therefore dismissed as an anti-Semite. The debate immediately gets side-tracked into the question of whether the argument is anti-Semitic rather than whether it is justified.

Drawing a parallel works slightly differently. It refuses, rightly, to make lazy comparisons. Israel is neither Nazi Germany nor apartheid South Africa. It is unique. Instead, a parallel suggests that people can find themselves in similar circumstances, or that one set of events can echo another. Even more important, the emotions people feel in these circumstances may share some of the same quality. That common quality is what allows us to see their suffering as relevant and deserving of recognition, without dragging us into a debate about whose suffering is greater.

I will give an example from my first few weeks in Tamra. I had been visiting families and hearing stories of what had happened to them in the war of 1948, when 750,000 Palestinians were either deported or terrorised from their homes by the Israeli army and sent to refugee camps across the Middle East. This event is commemorated by Palestinians as the Nakba (the Catastrophe), the loss of their homeland to the Jewish state and the dissolution of the Palestinian people as a nation. About 150,000 Palestinians managed to avoid this fate, remaining within the borders of the new state of Israel and becoming Israeli citizens. Nonetheless, many of them had experiences similar to the refugees'. All the members of my family in Tamra, for example, were internally displaced in the 1948 war. They lost their homes and most of their possessions when they were forced to flee from villages in the Galilee.

The family of Hassan's wife, Samira, were expelled from a small coastal village near Haifa called Ein Hod. She once tried to visit her parents' home there, which still stands but for decades has been occupied by Jews. When she knocked on the door to ask whether she could look inside, the Jewish owners angrily told her to go away. She has not dared to go back. When I talk to Samira, I see the pain she feels at being uprooted, at living only a short distance from her family's home but having no access to it or right to reclaim it. In fact, she does not even have the right to a history: the state refuses to remember her story, commemorate it or teach it to new generations. Her past is denied her, which damages her sense of who she is. It is a feeling we Jews should know only too well. After all, Jews have campaigned for the right to reclaim their properties in Europe, seek restitution, win recognition of the wrongs done to them and build museums. In this battle they have been increasingly successful. Why is Samira's pain not equally worthy of acknowledgement?

This lesson was reinforced by Rasha, a bright eighteen-year-old girl to whom I taught English, who is hoping to go to Haifa University to study psychotherapy. During a tutorial I asked her how she felt about life in Tamra, and she replied that she always felt afraid. This was clearly a sensitive topic, and I proceeded carefully. I asked her what she knew of her family history. Did she know where her parents were born? She said they were born in Tamra. And what about your grandparents? I asked. She said she knew they weren't from Tamra. "They came from a village," she added, revealing only with hesitancy that they were among the hundreds of thousands of refugees forced out of some four hundred villages by Israeli soldiers in the 1948 war. I asked if her parents ever talked about this with her at home. "No, because they are afraid too," she said. "I ask them questions, but they don't like to talk about it."

Rasha, it struck me, was living in fear of connecting with her past and her roots. Her eyes filled with tears. I thought, this is the story of this country. How can we educate our Jewish children about the Holocaust, the centuries of discrimination against Jews, and yet here sitting next to me is a Palestinian child who has been forced by the Jewish state to cut herself off emotionally and psychologically from both her personal story and her people's narrative, who is truly afraid to learn about her past? I asked her how she felt about not knowing the truth and not being able to talk about it in her home. She replied, "I don't feel like I have a future."

Other families told me of the massacres that took place in their villages and of the tactics used by soldiers to frighten them from their homes. These are not fanciful stories; they are supported by the research of respected Israeli Jewish historians who have spent years trawling through Israel's state and military archives. I heard one such disturbing account from Adel Manna, a history professor at Hebrew University and a fellow of the Van Leer Institute in Jerusalem, Israel's leading centre for intellectual thought. Dr. Manna was born in late 1947, a few months before the creation of the state of Israel, in the Galilean village of Majd al-Krum, a few kilometres from Tamra. In November 1948, he told me, the advancing Israeli forces reached Majd al-Krum, causing the irregular Arab militia that was supposed to protect the village to flee. The local leaders surrendered to the Israeli army, promising to hand over all weapons in return for a pledge not to bulldoze their homes or kill the villagers, as had happened in other places. The next day both sides kept their part of the agreement.

However, a week later, Dr. Manna explained, another unit of Israeli soldiers arrived at the village and gave the inhabitants twenty-four hours to hand over their weapons. The unit returned the following day to the central courtyard, but the village leaders said that they had already surrendered their arms. Unpersuaded, the Israeli commander warned them that if no guns were produced within half an hour, he would begin executing the inhabitants. The mukhtar, the village head, repeated that he knew of no more weapons, and said that if someone was hiding a gun, he would be too afraid to admit it. "But after half an hour the army took three men and shot them in front of the villagers," said Dr. Manna. The commander told the mukhtar that in half an hour three more villagers would die, and that is what happened.

Later that day, continued Dr. Manna, three more people, a woman and two men, were shot dead as they returned to Majd al-Krum from the nearby village of Sha'ab (the home of my friend Asad), taking the death toll to nine. They did not know of the soldiers' presence there, and according to Dr. Manna they were killed in cold blood as they entered the village. "The massacre was only stopped by accident," he said. "An Arab man married to a Jewish woman who was serving in the Israeli army came to visit relatives in Majd al-Krum. He was working for the intelligence services and knew that the village had already surrendered a week earlier. He persuaded the commander to stop the killings."

The horror did not end for the villagers, however. Many fled northwards after the massacre and hid in the surrounding hills and among the trees. By the time they found the courage to return, the new Israeli government had adopted a policy of expelling as many Palestinians remaining in the Galilee as possible. The army came to Majd al-Krum twice more and deported a total of 535 villagers—mostly young people and couples, including Dr. Manna's family—to the West Bank, which by then was under Jordanian control. Dr. Manna's family became refugees in Nablus, while others ended up in Jenin.

Determined that the family should not remain refugees, Dr. Manna's father began plotting a route back to the village. They crossed over to the east bank of the Jordan River, then moved up into Syria and finally went to Lebanon's Ein Helweh refugee camp, where they lived for the next two years. When Dr. Manna's mother fell pregnant with their second child, her husband de-

cided the dangerous return to Majd al-Krum must be under-
taken quickly. "He told my mother he would not allow a child of
his to be born in a refugee camp," said Dr. Manna. Along with
fourteen other refugee families, they secretly took a boat from
Lebanon to Acre in Israel and walked through the night to Majd
al-Krum. Eventually the family managed to get Israeli citizenship,
claiming they had been missed in the registration drives during
all the chaos following the war. "My uncle was too frightened to
make the journey, and his family are still living as refugees in Ein
Helweh," Dr. Manna explained.

Most families have stories like these, if not as expertly re-
searched as Dr. Manna's. I remember one family telling me how
the men were away working in the fields when the Israeli army
arrived at their village. The soldiers burst into the homes and
started to undress, so the terrified women ran away. When the
men returned later in the day, they were shot. In the middle of
the night, hours after hearing this story, I awoke in a panic. I sat
bolt upright in bed, covered in sweat even though it was a cold
winter night. I had been dreaming that I was running through
the streets of Tamra in my nightgown while tanks and soldiers
chased me and my neighbours from our homes. I remember the
oppressive feeling that there was nowhere to flee to. It was then
that I realised I was experiencing the life of the Arab community
as they live it. I became consumed by Rasha's fear. I began to
have a sense of what it means to lose your home, to have your
land confiscated, to live in a state which does not truly accept
your right to be there, to have no sense of where you really belong. And that reminded me of the perennial suffering of the
Jewish people: the discovery that the place where you thought
you belonged rejects you.

Soon after that night I went to see Roman Polanski's film *The
Pianist*, which documents the experience of Jews under Nazi rule
in Warsaw. I watched the scenes of Polish Jews being herded

from their homes into the ghetto and later being transported in cattle cars to the gas chambers. As I looked at the pictures of their belongings littering the empty streets of the ghetto, I could not help but see a parallel with what had happened to hundreds of thousands of Palestinians only three years after the Holocaust.

3

SECOND-CLASS CITIZENS

Soon after my move to Tamra, Samira's sister Nawal, who was in her early fifties, was diagnosed with an advanced brain tumour, which her doctors said was inoperable. However, a surgeon in Frankfurt was willing to perform the operation, and the people of the town rallied round to raise the money needed to send her to Germany. A few days before her journey, the family called Rambam Hospital in Haifa, where Nawal was staying, to sort out arrangements for the flight. She would be transferred by ambulance to the airport, then carried by stretcher onto the plane. When Abed, the husband of Samira's eldest daughter, Heba, called the Magen David ambulance service, the man on the other end of the line asked for the patient's name. His suspicions aroused by Abed's reply, he asked, "Is she a Jew or an Arab?" Abed wanted to know what difference it made. The man from Magen David said, "If she is a Jew, they can carry her straight onto the plane, but if she is an Arab she will have to undergo security checks first." Nawal, close to death, would have to be questioned and searched by Israel's security services.

In the end Nawal was spared the indignity and humiliation of the airport security procedures reserved for Arabs. A Jewish friend of the family was able to use his personal connections to persuade Ami Ayalon, a former director of the Shin Bet secret services, who has grown a little left-wing in his old age, to intervene. The airport security staff agreed to drop the normal checks. Nonetheless, I was appalled that this terminally ill woman could so readily be stripped of her dignity simply because she was an Arab. It reminded me of an incident during a holiday in Durban, in the apartheid days of South Africa, when I was a teenager. I had opened the local newspaper to discover that a black man stabbed in a street fight had been rejected by the crew of a passing ambulance because it was reserved for whites only. The man bled to death while he waited for the ambulance for blacks to arrive. The blinkered and callous racism at the heart of the apartheid system seemed to have a disturbing echo in the airport procedures of Israel.

There cannot be an Arab citizen of Israel who has travelled abroad who does not have his or her own personal horror story of dealing with the security procedures at Ben-Gurion Airport, just outside Tel Aviv. An Arab's status as a citizen inside the Jewish state is immediately made clear the moment he enters the airport and produces his passport for inspection by one of the young Jewish officials who are charged with assessing the security threat posed by each passenger. The main criterion used by the security personnel is not whether the traveller is an Israeli or a non-Israeli but a Jew or a non-Jew. Jewish passengers are almost always allowed to pass without further checks. Foreigners are asked questions about their activities, including whether they have had any dealings with Arabs, including Arab citizens, and their bags are X-rayed and possibly inspected. Arab citizens are assumed by definition to pose a security danger and are treated accordingly. They are subjected to lengthy questioning about their activities, their acquaintances and their reasons for travelling. If they pass these checks, their bags will be X-rayed and then intimately searched, and finally they may undergo a body search.

Where I stood in this hierarchy of security classifications after my move to Tamra was apparent whenever I passed through Ben-Gurion. The moment the airport officials realised I was living in an Arab area, the respectful initial interview would switch into a full-blown interrogation in which I was left in no doubt that I was considered a suspect. I would be asked endless questions about why I lived among Arabs, then a series of absurd enquiries about which Arabs I knew in Tamra, whether an Arab had brought me to the airport, what conversations I had had with Arabs, whether I spoke Arabic, and whether I knew any Arabs in the country I was travelling to. The first few times this happened, I quickly tired of the interview and suggested that if the security staff suspected I was a terrorist, they should skip the questions and simply get on with X-raying my bags. "Oh, don't worry, madam, we will be getting to that," they would say. "But you don't understand the way we work. We must ask you these questions first."

This humiliating treatment is not reserved for Arabs known to have been involved in subversive activities. It is not even reserved for those who fit a general security profile—male, young, not married, politically active—which suggests to the authorities that they ought to be treated with caution. All Arabs, whether Israeli citizens, Palestinians in the occupied territories or Arabs from abroad, are assumed to be a danger, without exception. Thus, hardly an eyebrow was raised when the Israeli media reported that one of the most respected Arab journalists in the country, Lutfi Mashour, the editor of the *Sinara* newspaper, was forced to abandon his trip as part of an official press delegation accompanying the Israeli president, Moshe Katsav, to France in February 2004. Mashour, the only Arab in the thirty-five-person party, was singled out for extra searches; when he refused, he was told he would not be allowed to board the flight. A few months later another senior Arab journalist, Ali Waked, who works for the website of the biggest-circulation Hebrew newspaper, *Yedioth*

Ahronoth, was prevented from boarding a flight after he had been invited to join the foreign minister, Silvan Shalom, on a state visit to Egypt. On neither occasion did the Jewish journalists and officials in the delegations protest against the treatment of their Arab colleagues.

The damage that such wanton discrimination does to the identification of Israel's Palestinian citizens with their state was illuminated for me during a conversation with Dr. Manna at the Van Leer Institute. He told me, "I often ask the security people at the airport, 'What does an Arab have to do *not* to be a suspect?' I try to imagine what the profile of a suspect is. If I am in my fifties, a professor at Hebrew University, travelling with my wife and daughter, and they need to check us this thoroughly, what are they doing with everyone else? How can an Arab avoid being a suspect in this country? The officials never have an answer when confronted with this question. They tell me, 'We do this to everyone.' And I clarify for them, 'You mean everyone who is not a Jew.' Then they tell me to complain to their line manager. But the problem is with the system, not with the individuals in it. Often I find myself getting intentionally provocative. I say, 'Do you sleep well at night?' and they ask why. 'Don't you see that you are implementing a racist, discriminatory policy against Arabs?' I tell them. 'No, sir,' they reply. 'We are only doing our jobs.' And then I say, 'Well, you know, the Nazis said they were only doing their jobs.' That always outrages them. 'Are you comparing what we are doing with what the Nazis did?' 'Not exactly,' I say, 'but I want to make you uncomfortable, to get you to think a little about what you are doing. You know that if I was born to a Jewish woman you would not be doing this to me. You are doing it to me because I am an Arab.' The reply is always the same: 'Well, sir, those are the orders.' But anyone can say they are following a policy; the problem is that the policy is a racist one."

The blindness of Israeli society to the extent of this state-sanctioned racism, and the damage it does both to the Jewish officials who implement it and the Arab victims who have to endure it, cannot be overestimated. I innocently asked Dr. Manna what effect, if any, his being Palestinian had on his nonprofessional life. Little did I realise the Pandora's box I was opening. Momentarily he looked thrown by the question—I don't think anyone had ever asked him before—and then slowly he recalled one example of racism at the hands of officialdom, followed by a second, and a third, and a fourth. The catalogue of the abuse and humiliation he had endured came to an end only because we ran out of time for our meeting. He told me that one incident was at the front of his mind: the next week he was due in court to contest a heavy fine issued by a policeman because Dr. Manna supposedly had a worn tyre and faulty brakes on his car. He said that at first the policeman had been courteous when he stopped him for a spot check, but that he had soon grown suspicious, possibly because of Dr. Manna's accent when speaking Hebrew, or because of some written material in Arabic he had on the back seat of the car. "The policeman asked to see my driving licence. As soon as he saw my name, he dropped the 'sir' and I became simply 'Adel.' " Although the car had only recently passed its annual test, and despite Dr. Manna's protests, the policeman gave him a fine and told him to get the tyre and brakes fixed immediately.

Dr. Manna took the car to a nearby Arab garage in East Jerusalem and asked the mechanic to check it. He could find nothing wrong with it. Dr. Manna asked him to check again, especially the tyres and the brakes. Again the man gave the car the all-clear. "I asked him to give me a certificate that my car had passed the test. He wanted to know why, because it was another ten months before the current certificate ran out. So I told him the story. When he heard what had happened, he shouted at me, 'Are you crazy? You want me, an Arab, to give you a certificate against the police? They will come and close the garage tomorrow! Where do you think you are living?' He was very angry, cursing me and telling me to get lost. I asked him what I could do. He said, 'Go to a Jewish garage. Are you a simpleton? They are the landlords of this country. Get out of here now.' I followed his advice. When the Jewish garage also found that the car was fine, I told the owner the same story and asked for a certificate. He said, 'No problem.' I asked him, 'Aren't you afraid of the police?' 'Of course not,' he replied."

Dr. Manna has his own airport horror stories, one of which will suffice. Two years ago his son Shadi went on holiday with his American Jewish girlfriend to the Greek island of Kos with the Israeli charter company Israir. When it was time for their return flight, they took the shuttle bus from the hotel with the fifty other Israelis on their package tour. Shadi was near the front of the queue for the initial security check at the airport, but when the official saw the name on his passport, he asked him to stand aside while he dealt with the other passengers. Shadi asked why. "Because you will take more time, and I have lots of other passengers to do. I will come to you afterwards," he was told. Shadi's girlfriend, who was next in line, said she was with him. The official was surprised. "But aren't you Jewish?" he asked. "Yes," she replied, "but I am his girlfriend." She was told to stand aside too.

After the other passengers had been cleared, Shadi was told he and his girlfriend would not be able to catch the flight. He asked why not. "Because it will take us at least two hours to check your luggage, and the plane can't wait for you," the official said. Shadi tried arguing that he and his girlfriend had been in a group and that it was the official's fault for pulling them out of the line. The man said no discussion was to be had; they would have to wait for the next flight. When would that be? "Maybe tomorrow, maybe next week," Shadi was told.

"My son rang me and his girlfriend rang her parents in Chicago," said Dr. Manna. "Then I got a call from her parents, very upset and asking whether our son had been in jail. Of course he had not, I said. 'Then why won't they let him on the plane?' they asked. 'This is Israel, not Chicago,' I told them." Dr. Manna called his other son, a lawyer, who rang the airport and threatened legal action against the security official. The man started to sound nervous and said he would no longer speak to any of them. He told Shadi there would be another flight in eight hours, and he could catch it if he signed a waiver declaring that it was his fault he missed the earlier flight because he arrived at the airport late. "My son refused, and was told he would not be allowed on the next flight. In the end a law professor friend told me the form was of no legal significance and that Shadi should sign it, adding the words 'under the circumstances.' " Later, after a precedent-setting legal battle, Dr. Manna won damages from the Israeli government, Israir and the national carrier, El Al, which is responsible for security at airports.

If this is what one of the most influential and well-connected Arab men in Israel suffers, what is the situation of most other Arab citizens, who are not friends of a battery of law professors? "Even for me it's exhausting, humiliating and depressing," Dr. Manna said. "You can't go fighting the system in court every other day, for yourself, your son, your wife or your daughter. I don't have the energy or the time to do it. You just have to accept that this is your life. You fight sometimes, but in most cases you have to let it go."

Many leading figures in Israeli life admit that there is rampant discrimination against the country's Arab citizens, but they usually excuse it as an unattractive trait shared by most democratic countries where a distinctive minority population is to be found. For example, Amnon Rubinstein, a law professor and one of the founding members of the left-wing Meretz Party, has often observed in his newspaper columns that black citizens of Britain and America face the same discrimination as Arabs in Israel. But

while racist attitudes undoubtedly pervade even the highest echelons of officialdom in Western countries, Rubinstein's comparison is pure sophistry. In Europe and America, such racism exists
only insofar as officials break the rules of state institutions and
the country's legal codes; in Israel, such racism is not only state-
sanctioned but actually encouraged by the institutions themselves—as is demonstrated by the security procedures at the
airport. The only recourse an Arab citizen has is a lengthy, ex-
pensive and often futile fight through the courts.

Some of the problem stems from the fact that Israel's legislators have refused to draft a constitution, partly because such a
document would lack international legitimacy unless it enshrined principles of equality that would strengthen the Arab
minority's hand in legally challenging acts of discrimination by
state bodies. Instead, Israel has constructed a legal system that
carefully veils its discrimination. Although the Law of Return
openly states that it offers special privileges to Jews only, other
laws make the same distinction without being so explicit, often
by stating simply that the benefit applies to anyone who qualifies
under the Law of Return—that is, Jews. Other laws and government decisions apply only to those eligible for military service,
again a code for Jews.

After my move to Tamra, I quickly discovered for myself how
the state had cultivated an atmosphere in which neglect and
abuse of Arab citizens' rights were the norm. I also learned how
wearying the struggle for equal recognition and treatment is,
and how much it damages both one's sense of belonging to the
state and one's sense of self-worth. On crossing the ethnic divide, I noticed almost immediately that I had been redesignated
by the state bureaucracy as a nonperson. For example, I rang the
state-owned airline, El Al, to check how many points I had accu-
mulated on my frequent flyer card. The woman who answered
asked for my personal details, including my address. I told her

that I had moved from Tel Aviv and was now living in Tamra. "Tamra?" she asked after a few moments. "I can't find it on the computer." I told her it was an Arab town close to Acre in the Galilee. "Are you sure you don't live in Timrat?" she asked. The inhabitants of Timrat, a small rural community built on land that the state confiscated long ago from the expelled Arab villagers of Malul, near Nazareth, are exclusively Jewish. It was clear that Arab communities were not listed on El Al's system, because Arabs were not expected to have frequent flyer cards. "I live in Tamra," I repeated. "But you must live in Timrat," the woman insisted. "That's what I have on the computer." I have subsequently learned that few Israeli computer systems include Arab communities, because for most Jews they simply don't exist.

On another occasion I stayed in the Sharon Hotel in Herziliya, by the coast a little north of Tel Aviv. On arrival I handed over my ID so the staff could prepare my bill before my departure. As I was about to leave two days later, I noticed on the bill that I had been registered as "Susan Nathan, from Tamara, Kfar Sava." I called the manager over and pointed out that this was not my address. "But you live there," he insisted. I asked him to look again at the address on my ID card and tell me what it said. "Tamra," he said sheepishly. When I asked why he had invented a fictitious address, he said he had been unable to find Tamra on the computer system. He began checking again. "Don't bother," I said. "I'm sure it's not on there."

The fact that I had become a nonperson insofar as I was a resident of Tamra had many other troubling aspects. For example, the public utility companies clearly had little interest in servicing customers living in Arab areas. It is a scandal rarely mentioned inside Israel, or outside, that employment in the country's huge public sector is reserved almost exclusively for Jews. Nachman Tal, a former deputy head of Shin Bet, found that only six of the thirteen thousand employees of the Israeli Electricity Corporation are Arabs. A similar number of Arabs are believed to be among the ten thousand people who work for Bezeq, the national telecoms company.

When I was living in Tel Aviv and I changed apartments, I could visit or phone any of several Bezeq offices, and the next day an engineer would come to install a telephone line. In Tamra there is no Bezeq office; one must travel to Acre or Haifa. After warnings from local families about the lack of telephone services in Tamra, I rang Bezeq, three weeks before I moved, to book a time for an engineer to install a new line in my apartment. He never showed up. When I rang the company to protest, I was told, "Well, you've got a cell phone, haven't you?" I badgered the Bezeq office every day, telling them how urgently I needed a phone line, but nothing ever happened. In the end I managed to get the number for the company's northern head office and tracked down the direct line of the chief engineer. I told him I would go to the media and explain that Bezeq was discriminating against me for living in an Arab community if the line was not installed immediately. The next day he showed up at my home himself.

Interestingly, the Bezeq office had blamed their inability to install a line on recent storms, which, they said, had brought down many phone lines in the Galilee. I could not remember any such storms, and I received a very different explanation from the chief engineer: "We don't like coming to Arab areas because when they see a Bezeq van, they all come out of their houses saying that they have a problem that needs fixing and that they've been calling for months." From what I had seen, that seemed a more than plausible scenario. Friends in Tamra told me that they believed the Jewish staff of the public utility companies were afraid to come to Arab areas because they feared they would be attacked. When I eventually managed to get a man from Tevel, the cable TV company, to connect up my television, he was so nervous he couldn't remember what he was supposed to do. In the end Khalil had to take over and do the work for him. Some friends in the nearby Arab city of Nazareth found they could not get IKEA to deliver a bedroom suite they had ordered from the store in Netanya. No one from the company would tell them what was causing the hold-up. However, a few weeks later the Israeli media revealed that another IKEA customer, the mayor's son in the Arab village of Kalansua, had been refused delivery of his furniture too. He was told it was company policy not to deliver to areas considered "dangerous."

I couldn't help thinking that such fears were preposterous. But if Jewish employees really were afraid to work in Arab areas, wasn't the obvious—not to say the fairest—solution to employ Arabs, so that they could do the jobs their Jewish colleagues were too frightened to touch? In one of those paradoxes that underpin life in Israel, many Jews have been boycotting Arab communities—refusing to eat in their restaurants or get cars fixed in their garages—since shortly after the start of the intifada, in October 2000, when the Israeli police shot dead thirteen unarmed Arab demonstrators across the Galilee. At the time I was living in Tel Aviv, and these killings barely penetrated my consciousness. Like other Jews, all I heard from the Israeli media was that there had been what they termed "Arab riots" in the north; the deaths were presented as the price that had to be paid for the defence of our state.

In fact, something rather different had taken place. The country's Arab citizens had staged official demonstrations and protests inside their communities against the killing of Palestinians in the occupied territories at the start of the intifada. In particular, their anger had been inflamed by television images of twelve-year-old Mohammed Durra being killed in a hail of bullets from an Israeli military position in Gaza as he shivered in terror, sheltering behind his father. The police in the Galilee either chose on their own initiative or were ordered (we are unlikely ever to know for sure) to strike pre-emptively to break up these protests. They stormed into towns and villages without riot gear but armed with rubber-coated steel bullets. Arab youths, outraged that their communities were under fire and that other young men had been killed and injured, retaliated by throwing stones. When the police ran out of rubber bullets, as several policemen later testified during an official inquiry, they simply switched to live ammunition. A team of police snipers was also deployed in two towns, Nazareth and Umm al-Fahm, where several protesters were killed.

Those thirteen deaths, and the severe injuries inflicted on hundreds more, have scarred the imagination of Israel's Palestinian citizens ever since, reminding them both that they have little reason to identify with their state and that the country's security officials do not recognise them as citizens with rights comparable to those of Jews.

Several people in Tamra observed to me that a massacre of the country's Arab citizens has occurred once a generation, as if to remind Arabs that they should not forget the insecure nature of their citizenship. In 1956, when the Arab minority was living under martial law, forty-nine men, women and children were shot dead in cold blood by Israeli soldiers after the army placed a curfew on the village of Kafr Qasem at short notice. Villagers who were working out in their fields and thus unaware of the curfew were killed at a roadblock as they returned home in the evening. The commander who gave the order, Colonel Isachar Shadmi, was put on trial and fined one piaster—the lowest sum possible—by the judges.

In the second massacre, twenty years later, the police stormed the village of Sakhnin, close to Tamra, to prevent a demonstration against a wave of confiscations that were stripping the community of its last land reserves. Six unarmed Arabs were killed.

"Now it is the turn of our generation to learn that Israel does not tolerate dissent when it comes from non-Jews," said Wahid, one young man in Tamra. He and many others told me that after the thirteen deaths, the police had stormed Arab communities in the Galilee, randomly rounding up men and boys, some as young as ten, and jailing them. Tamra was relatively quiet during the protests, but Wahid and his two brothers were arrested and spent several days in jail. "We were lucky," he said. "Our father had connections with the local police commander and was able to get us released. But hundreds of other youngsters were detained for months by the police."

An official judicial inquiry into the police shooting spree in the Galilee did not hold any of the police officers to account for the killings. But it did conclude that the police force held a common prejudice, shared across the ranks, that the country's Arab citizens were "the enemy" and needed to be treated as such. During my conversation with Dr. Manna, I told him that it seemed to me this attitude had polluted every area of life in the country. For example, I had read that month in *Ha'aretz* about an official fraud that had been perpetrated in Arab areas for the past year by the Israeli Broadcasting Authority, the national body that regulates the television industry. The IBA had set up illegal checkpoints at which officials menacingly demanded money from Arab motorists to cover TV licence fee debts, often sums invented on the spot. More than $5 million was taken in this fashion. Off-duty policemen hired to man the roadblocks were authorised to confiscate the driving licences or ID papers of drivers who couldn't or wouldn't pay. I said to Dr. Manna that I could hardly believe such an illegal practice by an official body had continued for so long without any actions being taken. If Jews had been targeted in this way by the IBA, the story would have been front-page news the next day.

"Actually, I was caught in one of those roadblocks myself," he said. Why didn't human rights and legal groups not challenge the action earlier? "There are so many cases of discrimination, you have to prioritise. There are Arab villages without water or schools or electricity. Are you going to try to help those people or drivers being harassed for money in the street? The system is designed to exhaust not just the Arab public but the nonprofit organisations and the public institutions designed to protect them. They are overwhelmed by the discrimination and harassment."

Dr. Manna's description of the problem is not exaggerated. My impression is that this panoply of discriminatory measures by official bodies is designed with one end in mind: to keep the Arab population ghettoised, afraid to leave the narrow confines of its towns and villages. An Arab citizen can avoid most dealings with the authorities—and therefore avoid getting into trouble— if he stays penned up in his community. The moment he steps outside, into Jewish public space, he faces physical, bureaucratic and legal challenges. From the state's point of view, as long as an Arab citizen is cooped up in his village, scared to leave, he is invisible, weak and silent. No wonder an exceptional, irrepressible man like Dr. Manna, who spends much of his time moving between cities and countries, has such a difficult time with Israeli state officials.

I raise these examples of discrimination because they give a flavour of the different meaning of citizenship as it is experienced by Arabs and Jews inside Israel. Overt and state-sanctioned racism at the airport, from the police and by the public utility companies erodes the identification of Arab citizens with their state and their identity as Israelis. They are made nationless. How profoundly dislocating and damaging this experience is was revealed to me during a series of discussions with Arab friends and students about two topics that touch their lives most directly: education and employment.

My early conversations with Zeinab had opened my eyes to injustices in the Israeli education system, but as our friendship grew deeper and I talked with other teachers, I started to learn a great deal more about how the country's Arab schools operated. Israel has developed two separate school systems, one for its Jewish population and another for its Arab minority. The official justification is that the separate tracks allow the Arab population to preserve its culture, language and heritage. In practice, this is nonsense. Having separate Arab schools has simply allowed Israel to maintain a weaker, underfunded Arab system to ensure that lower educational standards prevail, to permit Jewish officials to interfere in the curriculum to remove any trace of Palestinian history or culture, and to intimidate Arab teachers and principals into silence on key issues concerning their schools.

The biggest crisis in the Arab school system is not a financial one, though that is severe, but results from the state's continual undermining of the status of education among the Arab population. A former principal in Tamra, who has taught for more than twenty-five years, explained to me the damage being done: "I remember from my youth that teaching was always held in the highest regard—it was revered as a profession. This is the traditional Arab view of education. In the Arabic language we have a word, ustaz, meaning 'teacher,' which we use to address anyone who deserves to be emulated. But the problem in the Israeli educational system is that no Arab child respects or wants to emulate his teacher, because he knows that the Israeli security services vet all appointments in his school and control all promotions. Teachers themselves lose heart. They understand that their progress depends not on their skills in the classroom or their dedication to educating young minds but on whether they are seen to be 'reliable' by the Shin Bet. In fact, the better you do as a teacher in an Arab school, the more tainted you become in the eyes of the other teachers and the pupils. The system of surveillance and interference corrodes the values of education."

I heard similar claims from other teachers, including Zeinab, and could not help wondering whether they simply reflected the mildly paranoid, if natural, suspicions of a minority group. But in 2004 I learned from a very reliable source—Israel's most serious newspaper, *Ha'aretz*—that everything I had been told was true. In the spring a former senior Shin Bet official, Reuven Paz, admitted to the paper a long history of interference in the education system by the security services: "The Shin Bet not only determined and intervened in the appointment of principals and teachers, but even decided who the custodians and janitors that clean the bathrooms in the Arab schools would be." And later, in the autumn, *Ha'aretz* reported that the director-general of the Education Ministry, Ronit Tirosh, admitted that the Shin Bet was still approving every appointment to Arab schools and that it had no intention of discontinuing such practices. "Due to the sensitivity of educational positions, all [Arab] teachers undergo security, personal and criminal background investigations before being assigned to a position," she said.

According to the newspaper, the vetting process is overseen by an official in the Ministry of Education, Alex Rosman. The reason for such intensive surveillance of the Arab education system is clear: to prevent any discussion of Palestinian history or culture in classrooms. Teachers are effectively banned from teaching about the Nakba or about their people's connection to Palestinians in the West Bank and Gaza and in refugee camps across the Middle East. If they break this rule, they are certain to be dismissed. As a result, pupils grow up with little or no knowledge of their heritage and their people's history, apart from confused and confusing titbits picked up from older family members, as I found in conversations with pupils and adults in Tamra.

One woman, Manal, had spent three years training to be a teacher before abandoning her studies in the final year. "I slowly realised I had no faith in the values taught in Arab schools. I started to look back on my own years at school and see them as empty years, years that were stolen from me. I think now of how I trusted my parents and teachers and feel like I was lied to," she explained. The system as crafted by the Shin Bet, I realised, was designed to strip Palestinian citizens from a young age of their political awareness, to make them a malleable, identity-less mass that could be better manipulated and exploited by the state.

Another teacher recalled her own experience of the Shin Bet's involvement in her school in Sakhnin: "Parents and children know that teachers have to be approved by the Shin Bet; it is an open secret. But they also know—and this is much less spoken about—that the Shin Bet recruit spies among the pupils, usually via parents who are themselves in the pay of the Shin Bet. I will give you an example. A colleague of mine was teaching a class of sixteen-year-old boys who would not settle down. Instead of concentrating on the lesson, they kept asking him about the Palestine Liberation Organisation. This was before the Oslo agreements were signed. Maybe some of the boys had been having an argument about the subject in the playground before the class. Other teachers would simply have shut down the discussion, but he was a good teacher, committed to the values of his profession, so he gave them a brief history of the PLO. I knew this teacher, and he was not politically active by any stretch of the imagination. He simply told them what the PLO is and what it stands for according to its charter. The next day he was summoned to the local police station to 'discuss' what had happened in class the day before. A few days later he lost his job. Now, who knew about that lesson? Only the boys in the class. So one of them must have given the information to the police. What kind of effect on the learning environment do you think that has?"

How teachers and children are supposed to develop an atmosphere of trust and respect under these circumstances defeats me. But according to the former principal in Tamra, just as damaging as the Shin Bet's intrusive surveillance of schools are the efforts of Israeli politicians to erode the status of Arab teachers and education by demanding that they promote Zionism and Jewish culture in the classroom. "Imagine it: we are the remnants of the Palestinian people who lost almost all of our homeland in 1948, whose relatives were forced to flee into refugee camps, who have had our lands and homes confiscated by the state," he told me. "Today we are sort of semi-citizens, not even included in the description of our country as a Jewish state. And how does the Ministry of Education want us to respond? It issues directives telling us to raise the Star of David flag above our schools, when the children know the Palestinian flag is banned, to sing the national anthem, even though its verses speak of the Jewish people returning to their homeland, and to teach a curriculum which highlights the great victories of Zionism in founding a Jewish state and extols the virtues of Jewish culture. What do you think it feels like being a teacher when that is your job description? And what do you think the pupils make of the teachers who force-feed them this stuff every day? We are totally discredited in their eyes—and our own."

Talking to my teenage students in Tamra, I got a sense of how the school system was eroding their self-image, their relationship with the state and their future prospects. One day Suad showed me an English textbook that is used in Jewish and Arab schools. It was full of picture stories about Jewish kids with names like Gideon, Avner, Daphna and Anat wanting to be astronauts, actors and firemen. The book contained a single story of Arab life: two boys named Mahmoud and Yousef asking their uncle, Sheikh Salem, about how to become a good camel driver. It was bad enough that images of Arabs were almost entirely absent from the curriculum, but that offence was then compounded by their brief appearance as an outdated and racist stereotype. Apart from a few tens of thousands of Bedouins in the country's southern Negev Desert, Israel's Arab children have no more contact with camels than Jewish children do. I am still waiting to see my first camel in the verdant hills of the Galilee. And given Israel's determined policy of stripping all Arab communities of their farmlands, the idea that any of these children could aspire to be camel herders—let alone would want to—was almost comical.

But more harmful than the racist representations of Arab life in textbooks is the paucity of the wider curriculum. Despite claims that the separate educational system is designed to protect Arab culture and heritage, the Ministry of Education has ensured that these are the main elements excised from school courses. Almost all great Palestinian and Arab literature is off limits to Arab pupils. The spotlight was briefly turned on this issue in 2000, when the former education minister, Yossi Sarid, from the left-wing Meretz Party, provoked a huge row by trying to include the most famous Palestinian poet, Mahmoud Darwish, on the country's literature courses for Jews. Although it is now technically possible for Jewish pupils to study Darwish, his writing is still banned from Arab schools. The curriculum used in Arab education is one agreed to in 1981 by a committee whose sole Jewish member vetoed any works he thought might "create an ill spirit," which apparently meant literature that might connect Arab pupils to their heritage and culture.

"Studying Darwish for me is only a dream," said Butheina, one of my female students. "In school I have much lower expectations than that. I would just like to be allowed to read a modern love poem in Arabic. Instead, all we can read are what are called the jahiliya poets, who lived hundreds of years ago and write in a language we can barely understand." The experience of Butheina and her classmates was the equivalent of British students being forced to read only Chaucer. "I know the classics are important, but they offer us a very limited understanding of our past, and it puts off the great majority of students. It makes our culture seem fossilised and irrelevant." I feared that was probably the intention.

All my pupils told me about the lack of resources at their schools. Many studied in crowded temporary buildings that had long ago become permanent. They rarely had access to a computer, and the schools did not have the funds or teachers to offer the kind of after-school learning programmes that are common for Jewish children. One girl told me that when she took home her tattered Arabic textbook, her mother said she had used the same book twenty years earlier. "Jews hardly ever learn Arabic, and so they don't bother updating the Arabic language textbooks," she said. In contrast to the colourful illustrated Hebrew language textbooks, the pages of Arabic textbooks were a forbidding mass of endless text.

Comparative visits I made to schools in Tamra and in the deprived Jewish town of Kiryat Shemona as part of my work as a supervisor for Mahapach left me in no doubt about the rank discrimination in the funding of Arab education. Rather than accepting my view, consider the school funding figures for 2001, published by the Central Bureau of Statistics in 2004. Each Arab student in Israel received resources (after teachers' salaries had been excluded) of £105 a year, less than a quarter of the £485 spent on Jewish pupils in secular state schools. The state discriminated yet further in allocations to Jewish religious schools, where each pupil was getting resources woth £1,340, or twelve times as much as an Arab pupil. This has been achieved by a duplicitous system of double funding that allows religious Jewish schools to apply for money from both the Education Ministry and the Religious Affairs Ministry. (Almost no funds are available for the funding of non-Jewish religious schools.) As a result, many Jewish parents, including secular ones, choose to send their children to extremist religious schools so they can benefit from the higher budgets. The dangers of this should have been apparent to the succession of education ministers who allowed the practice to continue. The religious schools take a less than enlightened approach to subjects such as modern science and issues like women's rights. A serious question mark hangs over why Israel should want to encourage this brand of Jewish fundamentalism among the most impressionable members of its society.

The level of discrimination against Arab students is so great that in places where Jewish and Arab communities live close together, there are increasing reports of Arab parents trying to get their children registered for Jewish schools. In Haifa, for example, the Arab Parents' Forum announced that the standards at the local Arab junior school were so dismal they wanted to register their children at Jewish schools for the 2004 academic year. Their efforts were blocked by the Education Ministry's regional chief, Aharon Zavida, who said such a transfer was impossible because Arab pupils were in "a separate registration area."

The best hope for most Arab parents, if they can afford it, is to send their children to one of the few private mixed Jewish and Arab schools. The Ministry of Education has tolerated a handful of these, categorising them as special-interest schools, though it has been taking a much harder line of late. A government-appointed committee, the Dovrat Commission, recommended in early 2004 that no more special-interest schools be allowed, arguing that they are "elitist." The opening of a bilingual school in the Arab town of Kafr Kara, the first mixed school in an Arab community, was blocked in June 2004, again by Mr. Zavida.

Two other bilingual schools have been operating for a few years, one in Jerusalem and the other close to Tamra, in the Jewish community of Misgav. Asad Ghanem decided that he was going to send his young daughter, Lina, to the Misgav junior school, which teaches classes in Hebrew and Arabic. I asked him what advantages he saw in her meeting Jews at such a young age. Might she not get a misleading picture of Israeli life? Her equal treatment with the Jewish pupils at the school would not prepare her for the racism and discrimination she would face in later life. "I know from the activities at the Misgav school that the Arab pupils there are much more open and have much more confidence than children in Arab schools," Asad said. "At least the teachers and the principal are appointed by a nonprofit organisation that recruits them for their professional competence, and not by state officials working for the Shin Bet. As for the ideological effect of the school on her, I hope it will lead her to understand that our reality here is full of contradictions, that we must cope with a Jewish reality and a Palestinian reality. It's not that I am against sending her to an Arab school, it's just that I think she will be better prepared for the challenges she will face in later life if she masters these contradictions and the issues surrounding her complex identity from a young age. When you live inside Israel, I don't think you can really open your eyes to what it means to be Palestinian until you meet Jews. In this school, where she will get the chance to meet the Other, she will learn who she is and where she belongs. For me, I didn't mix properly with Jews until I went to university, and that is too late."

I still wondered whether his daughter, aware of her Palestinian identity, culture and heritage from her private schooling, might not then find her move to university a damaging experience. Israeli universities, far from being the beacons of academic freedom celebrated in the international media, are part of the same system of racist control. Despite pressure from the Arab community, the state has refused for more than five decades to create a single university teaching in Arabic. Fewer than one per cent of the country's university lecturers are Arabs, and many of the Jewish lecturers and researchers are "sponsored" by national security bodies that require them to teach in military and police colleges as well. There are also severe restrictions on the forms of political protest open to Arabs, particularly at Haifa University, which has the largest Arab student body. If an Arab student even waves a Palestinian flag at a demonstration, he or she might be arrested.

The entry requirements of Israeli universities are also skewed to favour Jewish over Arab applicants. For example, the matriculation exam on which the universities base their decision awards extra points to the best students of Hebrew but not to students of Arabic. The psychometric tests are also weighted in favour of Jewish students, because of their bias towards Western cultural norms. When the system was briefly reformed in 2003, in an attempt to help students from "weaker" sections of society, the biggest beneficiaries were Arab candidates rather than Jewish candidates from deprived communities. When the Israeli Committee of University Heads realised that the number of successful Arab candidates had risen significantly in the first year of implementation, it immediately abolished the new system and reintroduced the old tests. The committee's reason, in its own phrasing, was that "the admission of one population [Arabs] comes at the expense of the other [Jews]." The Arab student body is about 8 per cent of the total, even though Arabs make up 24 per cent of that age group.

Asad had no doubts about the advantages for his daughter of attending a mixed school: "If you are telling me that the outcome of this choice is that my daughter will go to university with higher expectations, that she will be more mobilised and angered by the discrimination she encounters there and that she will resist it more strongly, then that is one goal. I teach all my students [at Haifa University] that they have the right and the ability to achieve anything they want, so that when they go out into the wider world and find that they are denied their basic rights, they will be readier to fight for equality and to effect change. I see that as a positive thing."

I knew from my own teaching in Tamra that in general the Arab children who got to university had to study far harder, were far brighter and were far more committed than Jewish children. The reason so many adults in Tamra speak a language in addition to Arabic and Hebrew, such as English, German, Russian, Italian, or more obscure languages like Bulgarian, Romanian and Moldovan, is that their families have been forced to spend their life savings to send their children abroad to study, often in cheap East European states, because their own country makes it so difficult for them to acquire higher education.

These difficulties were highlighted when seventeen-year-old Samiha, one of my cleverest students, applied for a place at university. She had worked tirelessly for her exams in the hope of winning a place at medical school, and she achieved outstanding marks in her matriculation exam. However, when she started searching for courses, she discovered that either she did not qualify because she had not served in the army or she would have to wait another three years before she could begin, because the entry age for many courses is adjusted to enable Jewish youngsters to finish their army service first (three years for men, two years for women). She decided instead to apply for a place on one of the best law courses in the country, at the Netanya Academic Institute. When she told the admissions staff of her high mark in the matriculation exam, they said they still had many places to fill and she should send in her form immediately. She and her family were sure that acceptance was a formality. But a few weeks later she received a letter saying she had been rejected, without even the offer of an interview. When the family called, the college refused to give a reason.

I was appalled that this talented young woman was being cast aside so casually. In other countries the outstanding children of disadvantaged communities are given every assistance to advance themselves; in Israel it looked to me as if obstacles were being thrust in her way to break her spirit. My fear that Samiha would scale down her ambitions and that her family would resign themselves to this rejection were soon confirmed: she started applying to poorly regarded colleges for courses in physiotherapy.

While living in Tamra, I have been trying to help reverse some of the damage done to such pupils by the Israeli education system, through both my work as a supervisor for Mahapach and my involvement with the only Arab music conservatoire in Israel, Beit al-Musica (Music House). Mahapach, founded by Jewish and Arab university students in 1997 as a way to bridge the vast educational gaps in Israel by helping disadvantaged children, has built seven "learning communities" in Jewish and Arab towns. The students work privately with young pupils once a week to help build their confidence. Mahapach widens the meaning of education to include the environment in which pupils learn, acknowledging that economic and cultural factors play a role in students' ability to develop and prosper. In each town, children are encouraged to take a more active part in their communities by improving their educational achievements, honing leadership skills and promoting community projects that relate to educational, environmental and housing issues. Children from the different ethnic communities are also given the chance to step across the barriers designed to separate them and meet the Other. The need for this kind of programme is particularly strong in Arab communities, because their inhabitants lack even the most tenuous bond to the state. Denied the chance to serve their country— neither they nor their state want them fighting in the army—and deprived of an Israeli identity, Arab youngsters are not able to establish a connection to Israel at the national level. But by volunteering, whether by helping old people, establishing groups to empower women or campaigning for improved services, they can contribute to a better life for themselves and their town. It is a long, hard battle to develop that connection, but given time, Mahapach can help them to create their own meaning of citizenship.

A good example is a Mahapach project currently being developed by a group of sixteen-year-old students in Tamra to give names to the town's streets and numbers to the houses. Most of the Arab towns and villages in Israel do not have official street names, largely because the state has taken all formal planning controls from the minority. Instead, Tamra, like other Arab communities, has developed in a higgledy-piggledy fashion, like a refugee camp. Overcrowding and the consequent illegal building by families, often in the form of extensions, mean that numbering systems break down. The only way people from the outside world can send mail to us in Tamra is through a post office box. The priority the children have given to assigning names to their streets and numbers to their homes reflects their recognition that this is vital to their sense of belonging. "Here we are on the map," they are saying. "This is our town, this is where we live." For them, it means they can be identified, and just as important, they cannot be ignored.

Through Mahapach I am also attempting to encourage a pride among the youngsters in their culture and history. In Tamra we have been organising after-school classes where students can discuss the aspects of their past that are withheld from them in school, and we have created an atmosphere in which they feel confident to speak their own language, Arabic. Although Arabic is an official state language, many children and adults are reluctant to use their mother tongue outside the confines of Tamra, because they are afraid of being overheard by Israeli Jews. They fear the aggressive reactions that using their language may provoke.

The state, as might be expected, is trying to undermine the

work of Mahapach, an organisation with few resources on which to draw. For example, the thirty or so student workers developing projects in Mahapach's seven learning communities should each be entitled to a government scholarship. These funds are one of the main sources of revenue supporting the organisation's work. But despite its legal obligations and in a clear example of racist policy-making, the Ministry of Education is honouring the scholarships of only the Jewish students who participate; Arab students cannot receive a scholarship unless they agree to work in a Jewish community. Faced with this outrageous condition, Mahapach has two stark choices: the unacceptable one of pulling most of the students out of Arab areas and concentrating on the Jewish communities, or footing the bill for its Arab students. The large burden of this extra cost is threatening the long-term survival of the organisation. It could challenge the government policy in court, but the directors are afraid that if it does so, it may lose the scholarships of the Jewish students too. To an extent this divisive government policy, intended to empower Jewish students while disenfranchising Arab students, is working.

Another important way of countering the damaging effects of Arab education is by encouraging a greater awareness in local children of their rich Arab and Palestinian heritages. Few opportunities to do this exist, especially after decades in which Israel has sought to strip both its Palestinian citizens and the Palestinians of the occupied territories of much of their cultural heritage—mainly as a way to deprive them of a sense of their shared identity.

This destruction of Palestinian culture has been well described by Omar Barghouti, a writer who is also the choreographer of the award-winning El-Fanoun folk dance troupe in Ramallah, which has been hounded by the Israeli authorities over much of the past twenty years. Some of its leaders have even been arrested. Barghouti observes that bemused visitors often ask why the dancers are so committed to their art when tanks and soldiers are wrecking buildings and lives all around. "I never asked myself that question," he told me. "Do we have to stop creating dance, music, art and literature to join the battle of 're-construction'? Is reconstruction only applicable to devastated buildings, roads, water pipes and electricity poles? How about shattered dreams and shaken identities—don't they need reconstruction as well?"

Barghouti believes that the need to reassert and reinvigorate a Palestinian identity derives from a collective sense among these people of the failure to prevent the destruction of the Palestinian nation in 1948. Palestinians in the occupied territories have come to realise that only through establishing a strong sense of who they are can they hope to withstand the ever greater erosion of their rights at the hands of Israel. "Our very humanity has been restricted, hampered, battered by the relentless dehumanising efforts of our tormentors," Barghouti explains. "As a reaction, the process of decolonising our minds assumes crucial precedence. Restoring our humanity, our dreams, our hopes and our will to resist and to be free therefore becomes even more important than mending our infrastructure. Thus, we dance."

This is an eloquent statement of the need for all Palestinians to connect to their past and their future. It is a process well under way in the West Bank and Gaza but only in its infancy inside Israel, where Palestinian citizens have been severed from their culture and history for nearly six decades. One institution that is beginning to repair that damage is Beit al-Musica, based in the Arab town of Shefaram, near Tamra, and run by the inspirational figure of Amer Nakleh. A distinguished oud player, Amer has worked tirelessly since the 1990s to bring his love of traditional Palestinian music first to the youth of Shefaram and now to the whole Arab community in Israel. Beit al-Musica teaches a vast array of classical Arab instruments unfamiliar in the West, such as the oud, the Middle East's lute; the derbeki, a goatskin drum in the shape of an hourglass; and the qanun, an Arab zither played on the lap of the musician.

Confronted by the unstintingly high standards of musicianship at Beit al-Musica, the Israeli Ministry of Education finally agreed to recognise it as the country's first Arab music conservatoire in 2004. This achievement will have impressive cultural benefits for the Arab population. As well as classical Arabic music, Beit al-Musica promotes a rich tradition of modern songs and poetry set to music, a knowledge of which is essential for Palestinians to revitalise their culture. Many of these songs deal with the community's longing for the land that has been lost to them and with their sense that they are now strangers in their own country.

It is to be hoped that with official recognition of Beit al-Musica, its activities can expand. Already its programme ranges from introducing children of kindergarten age to musical games to training some of the finest professional musicians in the country. It had plans to organise a major concert with leading black South African jazz musicians to forge ties between the two country's musicians, but, in a sign of how short South Africa's memory is, that country's authorities have repeatedly denied funding.

I have been raising money for Beit al-Musica by launching a programme for local and international donors to sponsor gifted children who have little hope of developing their talent without financial help. Jewish children, of course, can rely on many scholarships and grants paid for by the Israeli government or Jewish organisations overseas. Little of this money is available to Arab children. As a first step, I have sponsored a ten-year-old boy named Fadi, who is an exceptional oud player but whose musical career was in jeopardy after his mother fell ill with cancer and his father lost his job.

Another inspirational figure in the Arab community is Saed Abu Shakra, a talented artist and the founder of the Umm al-Fahm art gallery. Umm al-Fahm is a deprived part of Israel in an area known as the Triangle, in the centre of the country next to the West Bank, and it is not an obvious place to find one of the nation's most important exhibition spaces. The gallery's success can be attributed to Saed's vision, his single-mindedness and his refusal to be intimidated. His own art, however, reveals his fraught relationship with the state. I remember him once taking me round the school run by his wife, Siham, and finding myself stunned as he showed me a small walled-off square of tarmac, measuring a mere twenty-five metres square, that served as both the staff car park and a playground for eight hundred pupils. I found the idea that eight hundred children could even squeeze into this space, let alone play there, almost inconceivable.

Saed, a former police officer who worked with Arab juvenile delinquents, is putting his art gallery to very worthwhile communal use, as a place not only where the community's imaginative horizons are extended but where mentally and physically disabled children and those from deprived families can express themselves through art and drama workshops. The proportion of children suffering disabilities is far higher in the Arab minority than in the Jewish population, largely because of the traditional practice of first cousins marrying each other. Nonetheless, the state makes almost no investment in special-needs schools for Arabs, though of course they exist for Jews. Saed has been doing his best to fill the gap.

The discrimination that destroys most Arab children's hopes of ever realising their full potential, or of understanding who they are and where they belong, follows them throughout their lives. Just as they are made fully aware that they are second-class citizens in the classroom, they understand that their parents are second-class citizens both in and out of the workplace. When periods of high unemployment arrive, Arab citizens are always the first to lose their jobs, and even the highly educated often find themselves forced to work in construction, quarrying or factories because little work is available in what is effectively the Jewish economy of Israel. By the "Jewish economy," I mean the significant areas of the economy that are off limits to Arab citizens, usually on the pretext that the work is security-related. These include not only the vast array of military industries, such as the Rafael Armaments Authority, the nuclear reactor at Dimona and the country's secret nuclear weapons factory, but the prisons, the Israeli Aircrafts Industry, the national carrier, El Al, and the country's airports. Also falling under the security rubric are the giant government corporations, such as the telecoms firm Bezeq, the Mekorot water company, the Electricity Corporation, the state textile industry and even the Bank of Israel.

In addition, Arab citizens are excluded from most of the vast civil service, the country's biggest employer, except for the health, religious affairs and education ministries, where they are needed to provide services to Arab communities. Areas such as engineering, surveying and architecture are also difficult for Arabs to enter, because the work is regarded as security-related—possibly because these professions are intimately involved in planning the infrastructure of the illegal Jewish settlements in the occupied West Bank and Gaza and the roads that connect them to Israel proper. State employers therefore make it abundantly clear that they regard Arab citizens as "the enemy" in precisely the same way as the airport security staff and the police force do.

Before 1948, most Palestinian families outside the cities relied for their living chiefly on agriculture. Today that course is no longer available to them: the state has confiscated most of their lands and passed them to Jewish farming communities such as the kibbutzim and moshavim, which receive big subsidies on water and are able to farm intensively on a large scale. Even Arabs who still have small private landholdings cannot possibly compete. Most of the Arab workforce has been transformed into what might be termed a "village proletariat"—casual labourers who must commute each day to Jewish areas to work on construction sites, in factories or as hired farm hands. In Tamra, large numbers of these day labourers can be seen in the dawn hours waiting in groups on the streets for a minibus to take them to their work. When hard times arrive, they are always the first to lose their jobs. A report in 2004 by Adva, a research centre based in Tel Aviv which monitors inequality in Israel, found that the thirty-six worst spots for unemployment were all Arab areas. But rather than try to help Arab towns and villages out of their desperate plight, the state has been pumping money to Jewish communities instead. Some of this comes via a system of "national priority zones," whose residents and businesses are entitled to extra benefits and grants. At the time of writing, 4 very small Arab villages had priority A status, compared with 492 Jewish communities.

I started to understand the systematic nature of the state's racist employment practices only after meeting Wehbe Badarni, an outstanding individual who is waging a lonely battle on behalf of Arab workers through his small Nazareth-based organisation, the Voice of the Labourer. Scraping for funds and facing the determined opposition of the authorities, Wehbe's Voice, like that of the country's Palestinian minority, has been all but drowned out. "Let's take the jobless figures," he told me. "Arab towns and villages are always at the very bottom of the pile by a large margin, even according to the official statistics. When unemployment is high in the whole economy—say about 10 per cent, as it has been through much of the second intifada—the figures show that the average is about twice as high in the Arab sector. But this doesn't even begin to tell the real story. In reality the jobless total is far higher in Arab communities, but it doesn't look that way because the figures are massaged by the state, which includes in its head count only those receiving benefits—and many Arab citizens are made ineligible for benefits. There is a story of terrible unemployment and dire poverty in Arab communities which is hidden by these figures.

"There are two main ways the state strips Arabs of their entitlement to benefits, both of which are cleverly cloaked so as to make it appear that they are not discriminatory," he continued. "First, benefits are not available to unemployed youngsters up to the age of twenty. This does not affect many Jews—they are being provided for by the state, either as wage-earning conscripted soldiers or as religious students entitled to special grants from the government. But Arabs in this age group are excluded from military service, and most cannot study at university. There are almost no jobs for them at this age, so the great majority are unemployed. The problem continues in a modified form as they get older. Between the ages of twenty and twenty-five, claimants are not entitled to any benefits until they can prove they have worked for at least one and a half years. Many Jews in this age bracket are not yet in the workforce; they are at university, after having completed their army service, or they are still studying Torah at religious colleges. But just about all Arabs are searching for work, most of them unsuccessfully. If Arab youngsters between the ages of eighteen and twenty-five were included in the jobless totals, it would push up the unemployment rates in Arab areas significantly.

"Second, there are severe restrictions on unemployment benefits for people who own land and property. In theory this rule appears to be nondiscriminatory, but in practice it ensures that Arab claimants are treated entirely differently from Jewish claimants. That is because the overwhelming majority of Jews do not own land: they are given long-term leases on some of the 93 per cent of the land owned by the state. Most Arabs, however, are excluded from living on state land and so must build their homes on plots of overcrowded private land—the 3 per cent of land in Israel owned by Arabs. But their ownership of land puts them in the same category as the tiny minority of Jewish private landowners, usually wealthy businessmen, who use their large landholdings for income-generating housing, farming or business projects. The effect of this rule is simple: while almost all unemployed Jews are eligible for benefits, a large number of unemployed Arabs are ineligible."

Wehbe dug out a confidential government document from the 1980s which set out the rules for dealing with claimants who own land and property. Its cover featured a cartoon of a man in a Sherlock Holmes costume peering intently through a huge magnifying glass at a house. The illustration neatly sums up the purpose of the dossier: it is a web of legal regulations designed to make most unemployed Arab citizens ineligible for benefits. A special form issued to unemployment offices in rural areas in 2002 also lists a series of questions that should make it clear to a jobless Arab citizen that he is wasting his time seeking help from the state. If a claimant owns land, has any animals, has more than one apartment in his name or lives with relatives, his application is likely to be rejected.

"These rules are designed to be a Catch-22 for Arab claimants," Wehbe told me. "One has to remember that there are different living patterns in Arab and Jewish society. Traditionally, Arab families live in close proximity. And nowadays, given the chronic shortage of land, most sons usually build their apartments directly above their father's ground-floor home. But because the land is registered in the father's name, he immediately becomes ineligible for benefits if he loses his job. That is because he is effectively treated by the state as a landlord, charging rent from his sons. Even if he registers the land in the name of his sons, he is assumed to have sold the land and he cannot claim benefits for five years. Jews are unaffected by these rules, because they can rely on the state making its land freely available to them."

Wehbe said there have even been cases of Arab claimants losing their benefits after they have had their lands confiscated by the state: "One unemployed man from Kafr Kara lost all his benefits after officials found he still had land registered in his name. It was a surprise to him. The land they were referring to had been taken from him years ago by the state and now has a Jewish settlement built on it. But apparently the authorities never cancelled his tabu [title deeds] to the land, and so he cannot get benefits."

Other Arab citizens who still own a small plot of the land they held before the creation of Israel are also caught in this kind of bureaucratic trap. "The owner cannot build on the land or develop it because the state will always refuse him the necessary permits," Wehbe said, "and he cannot leave it fallow because the state would then have a legal pretext for confiscating it. So what usually happens is he plants an olive grove on it. It would be an exaggeration to say he is farming the land, because he cannot hope to compete with the state-subsidised intensive Jewish farms; he simply harvests the olives on his plot for family use. Nonetheless, the state can treat the land as income-generating and withhold benefits if he loses his job. It is a measure designed to increase the pressure on him to sell his land to the state."

About the time I first met Wehbe, two stories broke in the media that keenly illustrated the problems of discrimination faced by Arab citizens who do work. In the first, in March 2004, the *Maariv* newspaper reported that Arab construction workers building a new wing of the Knesset in Jerusalem were being required to wear white hard hats with a large red cross painted on the top. The story was accompanied by a picture of the branded workers at the site. According to officials, snipers stationed on the Knesset's roof were using the crosses to track the Arab workers' movements while months-long security checks were completed by the Shin Bet. Amazingly, the hats of workers at the site who were not citizens, mainly from China and Thailand, were left unmarked. Apparently the authorities trusted their own citizens less than they did imported workers.

In the second story, a twenty-year-old Arab woman, Abeer Zinaty, was sacked by the manager of her local McDonald's, even though she had recently won an award from the company for being an "Excellent Worker 2003." Zinaty's claim that she had been dismissed for speaking Arabic to a colleague was at first denied by McDonald's. However, a media investigation confirmed her story. In correspondence over the dismissal, Talila Yodfat, the human resources director for the Israeli branch of the chain, wrote that a well-known company directive instructed employees not to speak Arabic "in order to prevent discomfort felt by clients and staff, who mostly speak Hebrew." She was of course forgetting that for 20 per cent of Israel's population—and a similar number of McDonald's potential customers—Arabic is the first language.

Zinaty's case was unusual only because she chose to speak out about the discrimination. Most Arabs are far too afraid to raise their voices against this common practice. For example, Omayma in my family in Tamra, a nurse in one of the biggest hospitals in Israel, told me that she and the other Arab staff had been repeatedly instructed not to speak Arabic while on duty. She was not prepared to take on her employer.

Wehbe knew of similar cases to Zinaty's and told me, "This informal ban on Arabic has always been a problem, but it has become much more severe since the intifada broke out in September 2000. There are many examples of workers being sacked for speaking Arabic, even though it contravenes Israel's equal opportunities law. Getting that law enforced, however, is pretty difficult. For example, I have been dealing for many, many months with the case of an Arab catering manager and thirteen Arab staff at a hotel on the shores of the Dead Sea. The manager was sacked after he refused to fire the Arab staff under him. The hotel bosses told him guests had been complaining about the presence of Arabs in the hotel. They were afraid of bad publicity if they sacked the workers themselves, so they tried to make him do it. They thought that because he is an Arab, it would not look so bad. I have not been able to get any of them reinstated."

Such overt discrimination against Arabs can be traced back to the days well before Israel was founded, said Wehbe, when Jewish immigrants arrived in the area hoping to establish their own state in Palestine. With stiff competition for control of the land and resources, the immigrants developed the concept of "Hebrew labour," favouring Jews over Arabs both in access to jobs and in levels of pay. Whenever possible, Jewish-owned companies, small businesses and farms would try to employ Jews only.

What is shocking is that this Zionist concept has survived to this day in the state of Israel, even though such discrimination should be illegal. Although it is never admitted publicly, racist employment practices and the exclusion of Arabs from wealth-generating sectors of the economy are the bedrock of state planning policies. "There are almost no economic development zones or industrial zones in Arab areas," said Wehbe. "If a factory is built, it is always in a Jewish area. Even if an Arab can get work in the factory, the business rates and development grants it generates go to the Jewish municipalities and not the Arab ones." Wehbe pointed out that for several years there was even a website called Hebrew Work, which promoted businesses that refused to employ Arabs. He and other Arab organisations had to press the authorities repeatedly before they finally agreed to take action against the site in January 2005.

Historically, the main actor in promoting the concept of

Hebrew labour has been the Histadrut, a Jewish trade union federation founded in Palestine in 1920. Although the Histadrut promotes itself as a trade union, early on in its development it became a strange hybrid beast, acquiring control of large sectors of the local economy. Both before and after the establishment of the state of Israel, it merged the roles of trade union and major corporation in a confusing manner. For example, it established the country's biggest national health-care system, Kupat Holim; the Workers' Bank, Bank HaPoalim, which went on to become Israel's largest bank; a giant industrial concern, Koor Industries; a major construction firm, Solel Boneh; a dairy production company, Tnuva; the national bus company, Egged; a national daily newspaper, *Davar;* and most of the cooperatives responsible for the country's agricultural output.

Arabs were excluded from any association with the Histadrut until 1943, when they were allowed to join a special Arab section. They had to wait until 1959—eleven years after the creation of Israel—before they could nominally become members. However, the Histadrut's Hebrew labour ideology was never abolished. "In the early 1990s, when hundreds of thousands of Russian Jews poured into Israel following the collapse of the Soviet Union, Arab workers—even well-qualified doctors—were sacked to make way for the new immigrants," said Wehbe. "The Histadrut never protested those job losses nor the discriminatory policies behind them."

This marginalisation of Arab workers by the Histadrut has severely limited their employment opportunities. In 1971 the state made the Histadrut the sole legal representative of organised labour in Israel, and by the late 1980s Histadrut-related companies were reported to be generating a fifth of the national income and employing more than a quarter of a million workers. But Arab membership of the federation, which at its peak reached about a hundred thousand workers, today stands at only a few thousand. Why the dramatic fall?

"The reason the Histadrut opened itself up to Arabs was that it wanted to destroy the Palestinian trade unions," said Wehbe. "It was determined to grow stronger, both numerically and financially, and it didn't want competition. It attracted Arab members because it offered welfare services, particularly health insurance, which Arabs couldn't afford otherwise. The Histadrut severed its ties to these services in the mid-1990s, and the Arab membership quickly fell away. Today Arab workers realise that the Histadrut has nothing to offer them. Its primary function is to protect the privileges of the tens of thousands of highly paid Jewish employees of state firms like Bezeq and the Electricity Corporation. The income earned by the Histadrut is invested in the Jewish sector, in clubs, education centres and health centres. There is no investment in Arab areas, in training Arab workers or in creating industrial zones in Arab communities. The Histadrut simply became irrelevant to Arab workers."

As things stand, it is unclear to me how Arab citizens can hope to end their exclusion from the Jewish economy. However, a few self-made figures in the Arab community have shown that it is possible to succeed even when the system is designed to defeat them. One of the most inspiring is Sobhi Nakleh, whom I know through my work for his son Amer's Beit al-Musica. Struggling to provide for his wife and children as a taxi driver in the early 1970s, Sobhi sold his cab and opened a grocery shop in Shefaram. He had a passion for Arabic coffee and experimented endlessly with blends until he found a formula that proved a particular hit with customers. Although his business became very successful in Shefaram, he held on to a bigger vision: to make his coffee famous throughout the Galilee and Israel. In the late 1970s he began selling out of the back of a van, and today Nakleh Coffee is the biggest-selling brand of Arabic coffee in the country. He even has a steadily growing export business.

This rags-to-riches story reminds me of examples I knew from my childhood of Jewish entrepreneurs who had succeeded against overwhelming odds. I thought of Michael Marks, who started Marks & Spencer, and Sir Isaac Wolfson, the chairman of Great Universal Stores, who was a close friend of my parents'. One winter in my youth my family made a sea crossing on the mail boat from Tilbury to Cape Town with Sir Isaac and his wife, Edith. I remember him sitting with me on the deck, telling me about his youth in the Glasgow tenements. When he met Edith, he told her that one day he would buy her the biggest diamond she had ever seen. And on that boat she showed it to me.

Sir Isaac Wolfson fought to earn every penny, and so it is with Arab citizens like Sobhi Nakleh. There are no handouts or legs-up for them; they are truly self-made. Although Jews like to celebrate their own success stories, most fail to recognise the same spirit of creativity, imagination and daring in the Arab population. Whenever I hear Israeli Jews talking about Arabs, they almost always refer to them as primitive and lazy or as welfare scroungers. Most Jews have no knowledge of Palestinian entrepreneurs and professionals who have had to battle to educate themselves or build a business in spite of huge obstacles. They fail to understand that Jews and Arabs have known the same sort of institutional racism and that ultimately they share the same dreams. This lack of empathy serves only to make Jews fear their fellow citizens, to encourage them to see their Arab neighbours as alien and menacing.

The need to change Israeli Jews' assumptions about the Arab minority is pressing indeed. I asked Dr. Manna during our long conversation why he believed Israeli Jews found the idea of an Arab citizen's identifying himself as Palestinian so disturbing. "As long as we are called and call ourselves 'Israeli Arabs,' then Jews are not reminded of the history of the country," he replied. "If we are Israeli Arabs, then Jews can feel reassured that we have forgotten our roots and our history before 1948. And if Jews and Arabs are persuaded that the country's history only started in

1948, then Israeli Arabs are really just guests in the country, who can be either integrated into the Zionist project or expelled. But at the same time, in a sort of contradiction, the majority of Israeli Jews believe that Arabs must not regard themselves as full Israelis but as second-class citizens, with no identity or equality. The Arab population disagrees: 'Sorry, but we will define our own identity and we will struggle for equality. You tried to make us forget we are Palestinians, but after a time we have rediscovered our identity—not least because Israel does not give us an alternative identity.' Any Jew in Britain, France or the United States is a full citizen of that country, but in Israel we are not equal even according to the law. On the best view we are second-class, if not worse than that. We are the Other."

Listening to Dr. Manna, I realised how far Israel has to travel before it can confront its past and atone for its sins. It will need much help in making that transition. South Africa is an obvious example to which it can look for guidance, from the work of Desmond Tutu's Truth and Reconciliation Commission to the small-scale initiatives of organisations and individuals whose work is far less trumpeted.

One such person is my friend Mike Abrams, a South African who was active in ending white rule. In 1999, Mike established a nonprofit organisation called Change Moves, which tries to heal the deep institutional and personal scars left by apartheid as blacks and whites find themselves in a society where they must learn to integrate. One of the most impressive programmes he runs helps South African businesses overcome failures of management caused by the lingering trauma of apartheid.

A big problem Mike has identified is that white managers are finding it difficult to adjust to a new reality, where they must work alongside or even under black managers. His team finds that new black middle managers often complain of being unable to work effectively because they do not feel they have all the information they need. When he sets up counselling groups to discuss these issues, it emerges that white managers are withholding the information. Why? "Often it's because there is a deep-seated resentment among the white managers, caused by their lack of confidence in the new political arrangement or because they still cling to the racist ideology of apartheid and don't want black managers succeeding," he says. "Under the new political system, white, black and coloured workers are suddenly thrust together, but they have not had time to address what the issues are that are still separating them, why they still don't trust each other. You can't really move forward until you address those issues."

Mike, who is Jewish and who lived for several years in Israel, says he can see the similarities with South Africa every time he visits. What he tries to do is give people a safe place from which to confront and overcome their fears and prejudices. Just as white South Africans were happy to see a black man cleaning their swimming pool but not sitting across from them on the other side of a desk, so Jews hold irrational fears about coming to Arab areas or working alongside Arabs as equals.

"The state wants our loyalty, but it is not loyal to us; it wants our lands and our resources without also wanting to develop us," Dr. Manna told me. "The state keeps us in our underdeveloped villages because it fears that if one day we are strong enough, we will take revenge for the years of discrimination—just as the white settlers in South Africa were afraid that if power passed to the blacks, they would be decimated. In Israel, what you see is the mentality of the settler who is afraid of what he has done. We remind Israelis that we are the natives."

4

ECHOES OF APARTHEID

For some time I had resolved to visit Ein Hod, the village from which Samira's parents had been forced to flee in 1948, before they found refuge in Tamra. Unlike most of the more than four hundred villages that were depopulated in that war, Ein Hod still stands largely intact, its homes saved from destruction by a group of Jewish artists who were given permission by the new state of Israel to colonise them. Today Ein Hod is an important centre for both art and tourism, the artists drawing inspiration for their work from the dramatic setting of the village and its old stone structures, and the tourists attracted by the sculptures, statues and installation art that grace the village's gardens, balconies and narrow lanes.

Samira had described to me the traumatic experience of visiting Ein Hod a few years earlier to see her parents' home. It had taken a great deal of courage to make the journey, knowing as she did what had happened to the village. She was accompanied by a young friend visiting from Sweden, who perhaps gave her both the resolution and the excuse to venture there. Samira told me that she eventually located the family home and knocked on the front door. When the Jewish owner, a woman artist answered, Samira explained who she was, said that this house had once belonged to her family, and asked, if possible, whether she could look inside. Angry and uncomfortable, the woman refused and told her to leave. She was about to close the door in Samira's face when the Swedish girl stepped forward and pleaded with her: "Please, my friend has brought me all this way to see her family's home. Let us come inside just for a minute." Embarrassed, the woman stood aside and let them look around briefly before she ushered them out. Samira told me she had not returned since.

Samira's experience stood in stark contrast to a story told me by Rabbi Dr. John D. Rayner, the retired head of the Liberal Jewish Synagogue in London and a long-standing family friend. Some years ago he decided to return with his daughter to Berlin, the city in which he was raised until Nazism tragically tore apart his family. As a boy, John was one of several thousand Jewish children moved from Europe to Britain on trains and boats known as the Kindertransport. He left his parents behind; they were eventually caught by the Gestapo and sent to Auschwitz, where they both died. The most emotional part of the trip for John was visiting the family's home with his daughter. The new owners received the two of them warmly, showed them around the house and invited them to sit in the garden, where they drank coffee and listened to the rabbi's memories of the house and Berlin in his childhood. John was assured that he was always welcome to return.

It occurred to me that the difference in the treatment of John and Samira spoke volumes about the difference in the readiness of these two nations, Germany and Israel, to acknowledge their respective pasts and to make amends. Whereas Germany had accepted its responsibility and atoned for the Holocaust, Israel was still pretending to itself and the world that the Nakba had never taken place. Whereas Germany had for decades been paying large sums of compensation to individual Holocaust survivors and to Israel, Israel had yet to apologise for the expulsion of the

Palestinian population, let alone pay money to the victims of its aggression, mostly peasant farmers trying to hold on to their lands.

I hoped to persuade Samira to take me to Ein Hod along with her youngest daughter, Suad. But despite regular assurances to both of us that she would soon make the journey, Samira always found a reason to put off a second visit. Eventually I concluded that she could not face seeing Ein Hod again, so Suad and I arranged to travel there without her.

The old Arab village is in a stunning location. Sitting on the lower slopes of the great Carmel Ridge, which extends southwards from the city of Haifa, Ein Hod overlooks the Mediterranean Sea. The backdrop is the luxurious foliage of the Carmel Forest, a national park of pine and cypress trees that extends over much of Mount Carmel. Official guidebooks and tourist information describe the village in glowing terms, as one of the most picturesque sites in Israel, but carefully avoid referring to its Arab history. The Ein Hod artists' website, which also happily promotes the village's scenic qualities, makes no mention of its past, apart from euphemistic and misleading references to earlier occupants—the generations of Palestinians documented as having inhabited the village since the twelfth century—who, it says, belonged to the Turkish empire:

> Ein Hod is characterised by the special setting of a village sitting on a hillside, surrounded by olive groves, with a view of the Mediterranean Sea, where baroque sunsets end each day. Despite lack of funds and development resources, the village has managed to preserve its original, historic nature and the romantic and simple charm of Israel in its first years of independence. Very few places in Israel have managed to retain the authentic quality of the Mediterranean. One can still discern in the old structures the many textures and architectural forms

of earlier occupants—from the Christian Crusades to the Turkish Empire.

As soon as Suad and I walked from the car park into the artists' colony (as Ein Hod officially describes itself), I could see why Samira was reluctant to make the journey again. The artists had managed to preserve and to transform the village at the same time. They had saved the buildings, simply to reinvent them in a way designed to conceal their original identity as Arab homes. The old mosque in the centre of the village is now the Dona Rosa restaurant, its front wall adorned with a sculpture of a naked woman stretching up her arms provocatively to reveal her breasts; alcohol is served to the patrons. The giant grinding stones that once belonged to the olive press have been propped up against old stone walls to transform them into works of rustic art, deflecting attention from the fact that they once served as tools in a vibrant Arab farming community. Doorways, balconies and gardens are stuffed with sculptures and artworks which obscure the Arab origins of the village.

Despite the claims of the website, I struggled to see what remained authentic in this "Mediterranean village." Rather than an exercise in honesty, Ein Hod is a case study in deception. The landscape has been reinvented to create what appears to be an entirely Jewish space. Clearly impressed at seeing an old village like this—Israel has made sure that very few such examples are left in the country—Suad pointed out the Arabic writing over some of the doorways. But the artworks and sculptures disturbed her. "They make me feel like a stranger here," she said. At one spot we found a decrepit wooden gate and pushed it open to reveal an overgrown garden and, behind it, a neglected stone building. Finally we had found somewhere untouched by the artistic mayhem all around us, and Suad, I saw, could at last connect to the village her grandparents had inhabited, to the generations of ancestors who called this place home and to the earth from which her family had been so violently uprooted.

When we returned to Tamra, Suad and I sat with Samira to tell her of our day in Ein Hod. I could see it made for painful listening. At the end, Samira could find no words, except "Tamra is nothing compared to Ein Hod. It is nothing." For the first time I realised how bitter she felt about her family's displacement and the destruction of her heritage.

The story of Israel and the policies that led to the ethnic cleansing of Arab communities like Ein Hod has two intimately entwined themes: land and people. These are the twin Zionist obsessions, nowadays spoon-fed to almost every Jew on the planet. It is no coincidence that the mantra of the early Zionist leadership was that in settling Palestine, they had found "a land without people for a people without land." I was raised on that slogan and accepted it throughout my adult life until I came to Israel. The terrible tragedy for the Palestinian people is that Israel has succeeded in convincing not only Jews to accept this myth as an article of faith, but the rest of the world too.

According to the most reliable figures, more than 1.3 million Arabs were living in Palestine on the eve of the Jewish state's birth. Zionist writers and organisations have tried to rewrite this historical fact, but one need not even search in the usual Palestinian sources to demonstrate that there had been a long-standing Palestinian presence in the Holy Land.

In 2003, on one of my trips back to South Africa, I was carrying out research in the library of Cape Town University, where my father completed his first medical degree, when I stumbled across a record of a little-known speech made by the former South African prime minister Jan Smuts, an ardent Zionist and one of the country's venerable statesmen. He had visited Palestine in February 1918 on behalf of the British government, which was soon to rule Palestine under a mandate from the

League of Nations and which had recently issued the Balfour Declaration, promising to use British influence to create a Jewish homeland in the Holy Land despite the fact that a well-established Palestinian population was already living there. On his return to South Africa, Smuts addressed representatives of the Jewish community in Johannesburg to tell them about the difficulties of implementing the Balfour plan:

> The problem there is one of great delicacy because a large Arab population is still living in Palestine. You have a minority of Jews there, and the policy that will have to be promoted and fostered in future will be the introduction of larger and ever larger numbers of Jews into Palestine. [Cheers.] It is easy to see that there are possibilities of conflict, of misunderstanding, in a situation like that, between the old Arab population and the new Jewish population. The whole situation will have to be handled with great great delicacy, with great tact.

Smuts was right about the numbers of Jewish immigrants needed to realise the Balfour Declaration's intention, if optimistic about the "delicacy" and "tact" with which that policy would be pursued. During the British Mandate period, more and more Jews found refuge in Palestine, until by the late spring of 1948, David Ben-Gurion, the leader of the Jewish people there, felt confident enough to declare the establishment of the state of Israel on the territory known to a majority of its inhabitants as Palestine. A war between the Palestinians and the Jews was the inevitable outcome.

Dating the first shots in the war of 1948, which was to be known in Israel as the War of Independence, is not easy. Tensions had been simmering between the native Palestinians and the recent Jewish arrivals for many years under British rule. But by late 1947, as the two communities sensed that events were coming to a head with the end of the British Mandate, tit-for-tat attacks became a regular occurrence, and dozens of civilians were killed on both sides. In December 1947 and January 1948 the Haganah, the pre-state Jewish army, raised the stakes, calling up young Jews for military service and ordering large shipments of arms from abroad. Jewish fighters launched a series of harsh retaliatory strikes against Arab villagers suspected of firing on or attacking Jews. In several cases, massacres took place at Arab villages in the western Galilee and in the Tel Aviv area. According to the Israeli historian Benny Morris, the first Arab village was entirely abandoned as early as December 1947.

As in all wars, terrible deeds were committed by both sides. But trying to cast blame for who started the war or who committed the most atrocities serves only as a useful way to distract us from the central issues. The first is that the traditional Zionist account of the 1948 war—the one I was brought up on—is entirely mythical. According to the Zionists, a small Jewish community faced almost impossible odds in defending itself against a sea of hostile Arabs. Its triumph was little short of a miracle. That account hardly seems to square with the historical facts. The Jewish community, though only half the size of the Palestinian one, was far better organised, armed and prepared for war than the Palestinians were. The Jewish immigrants were mostly staunch Zionists with a high degree of commitment to the project of creating a Jewish national home in Palestine. Many Palestinians, in contrast, were poor, isolated rural farmers who felt little personal involvement in the preparations for war. Although the first soldiers of the Arab Liberation Army (ALA) started arriving from neighbouring countries in January 1948, most historians agree that they were disorganised, poorly equipped and often not highly motivated. Almost all the early retaliatory attacks launched by the ALA on Jewish communities were repulsed, often with heavy losses to the Arab side.

The second central issue is the tendency among Zionists to overlook the context in which the war occurred. The Palestinians were defending themselves and their homeland from the aggressive colonisation of their land by Jewish immigrants. Zionists counter that argument by claiming that the Jews were entitled to their state; its birthright was based, they say, both on the Balfour Declaration and on the Palestinians' rejection of a United Nations partition plan in 1947, which would have given the Jewish population 55 per cent of the territory and the indigenous Arab population 44 per cent, with Jerusalem coming under international control. Although most modern commentators blame the Palestinian leadership for making a historic error in rejecting this deal, they choose to overlook several simple facts: the Palestinians at that time still had a large numerical majority (they were estimated to make up two thirds of the total population); most of the 650,000 Jews in their midst were recent and unwelcome colonisers; and, despite a well-funded campaign of land purchases run by an international Zionist organisation called the Jewish National Fund, local Jews had managed to buy only 7 per cent of Palestine. In the circumstances, the offer of 44 per cent of their own homeland by the UN may not have seemed overly generous to Palestinians of the day.

Third, Zionists seek to deflect attention from the outcome of the war. Whatever atrocities were committed by both sides, the result of the fighting was that 750,000 Palestinians—not Jews— were either terrorised or expelled from their homes and beyond the borders of the new state. The majority of them were not fighters but civilians, mostly poor farming families. Plenty of evidence has emerged, including documents concerning a military operation known as Plan Dalet, to suggest that it was probably always the intention of the Jewish leadership to rid the Jewish state of its Arab inhabitants. Even if that was not their intention at the start of the fighting, it quickly became their goal when they sensed their military superiority. Further proof is provided by the fact that the Israeli army demolished in wholesale fashion all the villages from which the refugees were forced to flee, to ensure that they could never return.

Over the course of the ensuing war, Israel won some 78 per cent of Mandatory Palestine, losing only the West Bank and Gaza. With its territorial windfall, the Jewish state had a free hand to rewrite the history of Palestine, in terms of both the people and the land. Having forced out 80 per cent of the 900,000 Palestinians whose homes were located within the new state of Israel—either directly, by forcing them across the borders to neighbouring Arab states, or by frightening them away through a policy of well-publicised massacres such as the one described by Dr. Adel Manna in Majd al-Krum—the army then organised the razing of the homes. The refugees, in exile in camps across the Middle East, had their homes, lands and bank accounts in Israel appropriated by a new official of the Jewish state called the custodian of absentee property.

It was not only the refugees who found their homes and lands taken by the custodian; so did a sizable number of the 150,000 Palestinians who had become Israeli citizens. As we have seen, Israeli bureaucrats, adept at abusing language in Orwellian ways, created a classification of citizen called the "present absentee" (present in Israel but absent from his or her home). To be so classified, a family needed only to have been away from their home for one day during the war. But the consequence was irreversible and permanent: the present absentees were barred from ever returning to their villages. Like my own family in Tamra, they became internal refugees, with no choice but to begin their lives again from scratch. Although there are no precise figures, the number of internal refugees is today believed to be a quarter of a million Israeli Arab citizens, or one in four of the Arab population.

The material and emotional losses sustained by the Palestinians in 1948 are the true root of the Middle East conflict, although no one—not diplomats, journalists or politicians—dares to say so. Instead we are told that the conflict began with the 1967 war, when Israel occupied the West Bank and Gaza. On this view, a solution requires only that the occupation be reversed and a Palestinian state created in the occupied territories, on 22 per cent of the Palestinians' historic homeland. No one, it seems, wants to remember that such a solution would entirely ignore the losses inflicted on hundreds of thousands of Palestinian refugees—and millions of their descendants.

The dispossession of the Palestinians, it is often assumed, may be an unfortunate historical event, but little can now be done to correct it. Left-wing Jewish friends to whom I talked would often tell me not to reflect on this too much. But Israel's dispossession of the Palestinians continues in unremitting fashion. This was brought home to me in an encounter with a man whose family originally came from Ein Hod. While most of the village's refugees ended up either in camps in the West Bank and Jordan or in Galilean communities like Tamra, one expelled family lives only a short distance from the artists of Ein Hod, in a village that goes by almost the same name: Ayn Hawd.

I first heard about Mohammed Abu Hayja through an organisation he founded in the late 1980s, called the Association of Forty. His own family, like that of Suad, was forced out of Ein Hod in 1948, but unlike Suad's, his battle with the state is not over the right to become an equal citizen but over the right to exist at all. His story, and that of tens of thousands of Arab villagers in the same situation, is one of the most dishonourable episodes in Israeli history.

To meet Abu Hayja, Suad and I had to drive through the grounds of a religious moshav, Nir Etzion, that occupies and cultivates the lands once farmed by the Arab villagers of Ein Hod.

We passed through the metal gates of the moshav, past its communal swimming pool and the manicured lawns and neat detached homes that belong to the Jewish inhabitants and through a field containing an enormous milking factory before we reached a winding path that led into the Carmel Forest and onwards over the ridge to Mohammed Abu Hayja's village. As we drove down into the huddle of houses, Abu Hayja was there to greet us, standing on the terrace of his home. His deeply lined face suggested many years spent in the sun, and possibly too many worries for one man easily to bear. I introduced Suad, and in a routine I had grown familiar with, Abu Hayja asked a series of questions to identify which branch of the family she belonged to. When he was certain of who she was, he launched into a short reminiscence. "My father often used to recall your grandfather," he said. "Once, a short time after the war had ended, when it became clear that the state had no intention of honouring its obligations to allow us to return to the village, your grandfather decided to take matters into his own hands and return without permission. The village was empty then, because it was before the artists arrived, in 1954. Under cover of dark, your grandfather left Tamra, stole back into the village and reoccupied his brother's home. Of course, the police soon found out and arrived to evict him."

Abu Hayja's own branch of the family have been living next door to their former homes since they were expelled in 1948. Rather than fleeing from the region, Mohammed's grandfather, Abu Hilmi, took his family a short distance farther up the slopes of Mount Carmel to live in hiding by the village's cattle sheds. There he waited for the fighting to subside and to be allowed back to Ein Hod. But when the war was over, Israel did not restore Ein Hod to its former owners; instead it sealed off the area as a closed military zone in preparation for the destruction of the homes. For several years it was impossible to get to the village. Then, in the mid-1950s, a group of artists led by Marcel Janco, a Romanian painter and one of the founders of the Dada movement, was given permission to settle it.

Aware that he would never be able to return, Abu Hayja told us, his grandfather decided to create a new village where his family was encamped and to call it Ayn Hawd, the Arabic name of his old village before the artist colonisers Hebraicised it to Ein Hod. Ever since, the villagers of the new Ayn Hawd have had to fight to hold on to their corner of the Carmel, a tiny sliver of the land that originally belonged to them, against the unremitting pressure of Israeli officialdom's attempts to dislodge them.

"It is a long and complex story, but I will try to make it as easy as I can," said Abu Hayja. "It began in 1958, when officials from the government arrived at the village to tell my grandfather that they had confiscated not only the buildings of Ein Hod, which we knew, but also all its farmlands, including the spot where we now live. All of it was declared state land. At the time it did not mean much to us, but a few years later, in 1964, more officials arrived, this time to erect a fence tightly around our homes, forcing us into a ghetto. There were a few concrete homes in the village by then, including a two-room school. I can prove it because I still have an Israeli newspaper cutting from 1965 showing the teacher and me and my friends standing outside the school, with the fence visible just in front of us. The fence was a major problem for our parents, because they needed to graze the village's herds of goats, sheep and cattle—that was our livelihood. I remember my father telling me and the other children to pull down the fence so that he couldn't be blamed or punished by the authorities. We pulled it down three times and they re-erected it three times. It was like a game to us.

"Though we didn't know it, our situation grew much worse the following year, in 1965, when the government passed the Planning and Building Law. Under this law, the state decided that there were to be 123 Arab communities. That was it. It didn't matter where you lived or how long you had lived there; if you weren't on that list, you didn't exist. The way they did it was to create a master plan for the whole of Israel. In the case of every community they listed, Jewish and Arab, they set down a border for its development, what they called the blue lines. In the case of Arab communities, these were drawn tightly around the houses, so there was no room left for development. In the case of Jewish communities, they were drawn loosely, so there was plenty of space for them to expand and develop."

This has led to shameful anomalies, as Asad Ghanem had explained to me before. The Arab population of Israel today stands at a little over one million—seven times the number it was more than half a century ago—but the state has refused to create a single new Arab community. The result is chronic overcrowding of the sort I know only too well from Tamra. The land lost to these Arab towns and villages has simply been passed to Jewish settlements for their benefit. Thus, for example, the Arab town of Sakhnin has a population of 24,000 and jurisdiction over 2,500 acres of land, while the neighbouring Misgav bloc of Jewish settlements has a smaller population, 18,000, and control over an area twenty times larger, 50,000 acres. Or take the Arab city of Nazareth, from which land was taken by the state in the late 1950s to build a Jewish city virtually on top. Today the Jewish city, Upper Nazareth, with 50,000 residents, has three times as much land as Nazareth but only two thirds of its population.

"Everything outside the blue lines created by the Planning Law was deemed agricultural land, on which it was illegal to build," continued Abu Hayja. "Our village was not listed among the 123 Arab communities, no blue lines were drawn around us, and therefore we were living on agricultural land. Our homes were retroactively deemed illegal and faced demolition. We were not alone; dozens of other Arab villages were in the same situation, and most of them had been standing on their land for centuries. In many cases the villagers had the titles from the Ottomans and the British to prove they owned the land. None of that made any difference to the state. Of course, in those days none of us understood the game that was being played with our lives, and no one from the state came to explain it to us, either. It took nearly two decades before we realised the extent of the policy we were facing."

More than a hundred thousand Arab citizens, or one in ten of the Arab population, are classified under the Planning and Building Law as living in what the state considers "unrecognised villages." The majority of them, about seventy thousand Bedouins, live in appalling conditions in the Negev Desert region in the country's south, where they are forced to live in tents or tin shacks, because anything more permanent would be demolished by the authorities.

Very few Jews know about the abuses heaped on the unrecognised villages, and in particular on the Bedouin population. I can recall journeys to Beersheba, the capital of the Negev, during my stays in Israel before my immigration, when I saw dishevelled encampments made up of dozens of huts and tents dotted along the landscape. They registered in my mind then, as I am sure they do for other Jews, as the primitive way of life chosen by the Bedouins, who I assumed were resisting the best efforts of Israel to bring them into the twentieth century. Little did I appreciate that the government had pushed them back into a dark age that might have astonished even their forebears.

At least many of the inhabitants of Ayn Hawd have managed to build concrete homes that have not been destroyed. Nonetheless, said Abu Hayja, they have experienced relentless pressure to evacuate the village since the passing of the Planning and Building Law. "No one ever put a gun to our heads—the authorities were far too clever for that," he explained. "Instead they made a series of master plans that none of us understood. The first was the National Carmel Park Law, in 1971, which makes it illegal to build a house inside the park. And where does the park exist? It begins south of Haifa and follows the contours of the mountain till it reaches the last house in our village. We are entirely surrounded by the park. But in the case of our immediate neighbours, Ein Hod and Nir Etzion, the boundaries loop carefully around them."

At this point Abu Hayja said something that shocked me. He pointed to the slopes of Mount Carmel and told me that all the pine and cypress trees I could see spreading in every direction through the national park were planted by Israel after 1948. The state uprooted the natural vegetation of olive, carob and fruit trees, for which the area was renowned and which the villagers had cultivated for generations, and surrounded them instead with the useless pines. "I am sure the point was to prevent us from making a living from our old trees," Abu Hayja said.

I interrupted him to say that many years before I had stayed at the Carmel Forest Spa Resort, which is just visible from the road leading to Ayn Hawd. In those days I had wondered at the glory of the forest and national park; it had never occurred to me that the whole landscape was artificial. Learning that a modern pine forest had been imposed on these mountains at the expense of its ancient and fruitful flora had unsettling parallels. Again I could feel the solid ground on which another of my Zionist assumptions had been built give way. The sensation, which by now was becoming common, was no easier for that.

According to its own figures, the Jewish National Fund (JNF) has planted more than 240 million trees, mainly fast-growing pines, across the country. They have been paid for by Jews from around the world, who have been encouraged to "buy a tree" for Israel. Such schemes exist to this day. On many Israeli and Jewish websites, the JNF has prominent advertisements asking readers to "show you care" by donating a tree. "Give the gift that grows: a gift that lasts for generations!" they say. Jews are asked to donate $18 to plant a tree in Israel for a special occasion, including births, bar mitzvahs, graduations, birthdays and weddings, or as a way to commemorate someone's life. The true purpose of these mass planting programmes, however, is rarely discussed. In the early years of the state, the government claimed that the trees were needed to ensure supplies of wood for fuel and construction. But in fact much of the greenery paid for by the Jewish Diaspora has been planted either directly over the ruins of the Arab villages destroyed in 1948 or on land that Arab communities were once able to farm. It has been used as another weapon in their continuing dispossession.

This point was driven home during several trips I made to destroyed villages in the Galilee. For example, the razed Palestinian village of Lubia, between Nazareth and Tiberias, is now covered with the lush pine trees of South Africa Forest, paid for by Zionist organisations in South Africa. For Israeli Jews, it is simply a pleasant spot to enjoy a picnic or barbecue at the weekends or to go to on organised hiking trips, as I had done in my Zionist days. They are entirely unaware, as I once was unaware, that in 1948, about 2,500 Palestinians were expelled from this site.

In April 2004, during the national celebrations for Independence Day, when Israeli Jews enjoy a day of rejoicing over the founding of their state, I joined a family from Nazareth who quietly commemorated the Palestinians' mirror event, Nakba Day, which marks the loss of their homeland. We visited a Jewish moshav called Tzipori, close to Nazareth, which has been built over the ruins of their parents' village, Saffuriya. I cannot even say that we managed to see their former home: the site of the Arab village is now hidden behind barbed wire and covered by the thick growth of yet another forest planted by the JNF. The only visible clues that Palestinians once lived there are the great mounds of cacti that Arab communities traditionally used as boundaries to separate properties. Despite the best efforts of the JNF to poison and burn these indigenous Middle Eastern plants, the cacti have refused to die or disappear.

The Jewish National Fund website tells visitors nothing of this. Instead it claims in its title to be "the caretaker of the land of Israel, on behalf of its owners—Jewish People everywhere." In July 2004 the organisation announced in a press release that it had been given the distinction of United Nations status: "Our acceptance by other countries into the United Nations legitimizes our award-winning efforts in water, environment and sustainable development." UN status, according to the press release, will allow the JNF to sit on the world body's environment committees and give its advice on sustainability and afforestation programmes.

Abu Hayja told me that more officials arrived throughout the 1970s to warn the villagers that they were sinking ever deeper into illegality. The army created a firing range alongside the village, which extends from the first house to the last. At another point Ayn Hawd was declared an archaeological site. And in 1975 the Black Goat Law was passed, declaring that it was illegal to keep goats in a national park because they posed a threat to the young pine trees. To make sure we understood the plight of his village, he recapped: "By the end of the 1970s, we knew our homes were standing on land that was state-owned and for agricultural use only, although we were not allowed to graze our herds. It was also an archaeological site. It had been declared a military firing range, and it was designated a national park. So by that stage we had lost everything—the land, the goats and cattle, our trees. All we were left with was our homes, and they were all facing demolition." The worst was not over, however. "In 1981 the government passed the Services Law, which stated that no house without a licence could be connected to any public service—to the water and sewerage network, to the electricity grid and to the telephone lines. We were not allowed roads, or to have our garbage collected, or to have mail delivered to our village. And the state had no obligation to provide us with educational or medical services. If we wanted to see a doctor or to educate our children, we would have to send them long distances to recognised communities."

The state was actually just formalising practices that the authorities had used against all the unrecognised villages since the establishment of Israel. As Abu Hayja explained, "We were never provided with water or electricity by the state. Our parents used generators and had to carry water from the river in the valley below. There was no road to Ayn Hawd, apart from a winding dirt track through the forest that often disintegrated during the winter rains. We had to collect our mail from Nir Etzion. We had a kindergarten, but it was illegal. We covered the building with metal sheets so that the spy planes that circled over us and the officials who arrived unannounced would think it was a shack and wouldn't demolish it."

I found it difficult to make sense of the way Israel treats the inhabitants of the unrecognised villages. Despite all the discrimination, the rights to education and health care they enjoy by virtue of their citizenship are honoured. But because they are effectively invisible to the authorities as the inhabitants of the places they actually live in, the state is not responsible for providing them with services in their communities, as it would be if they were living in a recognised village or town. They are like free-floating citizens. Their children can turn up at a school in a recognised locality and will have a place, but the state does not have to take account of how they get there. In the Negev I had heard that the children of a village called Abda had to make a round trip of seventy kilometres each day to go to school.

"As a boy I had to go to high school in Haifa, without help

from the state," Abu Hayja told me. "I would wake at five A.M., walk three kilometres through the woods to Nir Etzion and try to catch a lift from the moshav down to the main road. If no one was around, I would have to walk to the main road myself. Then I would catch a public bus to the central station in Haifa and change onto a local bus to the school. It took three hours there and another three hours back. Sometimes I would get back so late I would have to walk through the forest in the dark. I still remember one night when I hid up a tree, frightened by the darkness and the sounds of animals. My parents found me hours later, past midnight. Such difficulties continue to this day. We still have no water from the state. We built a pipeline from the moshav, which agreed to let us siphon off water in return for voting for their party's candidate to the Knesset. We still use generators for electricity. A few years ago, when my daughter was at school, she made the same journey I had."

Abu Hayja finished his education studying engineering at the Technion in Haifa, and later landed a job with the Interior Ministry in the neighbouring Druse council of Daliyat-Isfiya. Only then did he start to realise that what was happening to Ayn Hawd was being replicated across the country. "Our parents had been farmers. We had no connection to anything outside the village. The limits of my world as a child were the mountain and the forest. The only Jews I knew were policemen and soldiers. None of us realised what all these separate pieces of legislation amounted to. It had been going on so long that we had grown to accept it as normal, as the way our lives would always be."

Recognising the qualities of his young grandson, Abu Hilmi appointed him the leader of the village's committee in 1978. After the passage of the Services Law three years later, Mohammed Abu Hayja decided the villagers should take on the government directly. He told me, "People of my generation in the village said we cannot live like this any longer. 'How can it be that the cows of the moshav are entitled to electricity and water and we are denied them?' they asked. 'Do we have fewer rights than the cows?' We decided to open our problem to the world, even if by doing so we risked retaliation from the government and the destruction of our homes. We organised a demonstration of Arabs and Jews on the mountainside. We managed to recruit one Jew from Nir Etzion and another two from Ein Hod. In those days I believed in the support of these left-wing Jews, but after twenty years of dealing with them, I no longer believe in their good faith."

I asked him why these Jews had come to the demonstration if they did not really support him. "Maybe the three of them were embarrassed that we didn't have water or electricity," he replied. "Who knows? But over time it became clear these left-wingers did not want us to have the same rights that they enjoyed in their own communities."

Two weeks later a demolition order was served on each home in Ayn Hawd. "The authorities were amazed by our cheek. 'You want services! Forget it—you're illegal,' they said. So we had to begin fighting in the courts, not for the services we wanted but so that our homes would not be destroyed." By this time Abu Hayja knew that many other villages were in the same position as his, and he decided in 1988 to form an umbrella organisation, the Association of Forty,* to campaign inside and outside Israel for their rights.

Sitting across the table from Abu Hayja, I marvelled at the quiet, gentle defiance in his eyes. He had been battling for three decades against the emissaries of his own state—soldiers, police-men, planners and politicians, each one determined to deprive him of everything he had ever owned, and yet they had utterly

*So named to commemorate the fortieth anniversary of the 1948 Universal Declaration of Human Rights.

failed to strip him of his most powerful weapon: his incontrovert-
ible belief that no one had the right to violate the dignity of his
family and his village. Abu Hayja's refusal to compromise on his
rights, his ingenuity and his passion have so far saved his village
from the wrecking crews. Many other unrecognised villages have
been far less lucky. Most weeks there are reports of the police entering an Arab community to destroy a handful of homes. In
2003, a total of five hundred Arab houses were demolished inside Israel.

After six years of vigorous lobbying in Israel and abroad, Abu
Hayja's association won a symbolic victory in 1994. The government of Yitzhak Rabin agreed to recognise a handful of the
villages in the Galilee, though the majority of unrecognised villages in the south, in the Negev, were ignored. However, Ayn
Hawd's recognition changed nothing on the ground, as Abu
Hayja explained: "Recognition in itself means nothing. You
need recognition and a master plan from the regional council
before you can get services. For ten years the regional council
did nothing about the master plan, and our situation stayed the
same."

In the summer of 2004, after decades of struggling and campaigning, Ayn Hawd finally won a master plan from Hof
HaCarmel regional council. There have been a few fringe benefits for the 250 inhabitants. The village now has an elected representative on the council, Mohammed Abu Hayja, who sits
with fifty or so Jewish representatives. The council has agreed to
collect the rubbish, and to do so it has had to build a primitive
concrete road over the dirt track so that its trucks can reach the
village. A school bus now collects the children to take them to
Haifa. And there is a road sign to Ayn Hawd, located far from
the main road, at the entrance to Nir Etzion moshav.

Abu Hayja is far from satisfied with these successes, which
have taken more than fifty years to achieve. "Hof HaCarmel

agreed to provide these minimum services on condition we paid taxes to them," he said. "That is the deal. But on the big issues we are no nearer a solution. The master plan the council has approved for us is entirely unacceptable. It simply draws a tight blue line around what is already here, a bit like the fence the state erected all those years ago, leaving us with no room to expand or develop. Where are our children supposed to live? Where can they establish businesses, schools and medical clinics? Where is the room for them to make their quality of life better than ours?" Worse than that, the master plan has not even lifted the threat of demolition from their homes. "I have been telling the other villagers for three decades that our homes will be made legal next year, that we will get services next year. And I am still telling them that today. And maybe theoretically one day we can get licences for our homes and make them legal. And then maybe we can get water and electricity. But before we can do that, we need to own the land on which our homes stand. We have to persuade the government to redesignate this land as ours rather than as state land. At the moment they don't seem even close to agreeing. So we remain a community of criminals living illegally in Ayn Hawd."

Back at the founding of the Jewish state, the land on which Ayn Hawd now stands was transferred, along with the lands of hundreds of thousands of other Palestinian refugees, to the custodian of absentee property. There is not a single case of the custodian's returning property to its former Arab owners. It is hard to imagine how Israel could ever sanction such a move: it would be too concerned that returning land, even to the villagers of Ayn Hawd, would be the first step in conceding the right of return for millions of other Palestinian refugees. That, as all Jews around the world have been told endlessly by their leaders, would make the Jews a minority in Israel and so destroy the Jewish state.

Abu Hayja is no dreamer. As he waved us off, he had a part-
ing word for Suad: "Forget the old Ayn Hawd. You will never be
allowed back." I asked whether he wanted to return to the old village himself. "No, I never think about going back," he said. "Ein
Hod belonged to my parents, not to me. I was born in the new
village, and I will keep on building here." Even this small demand—the return of a tiny fraction of the lands that once belonged to the Abu Hayja hamula—will require a concession
from the state that is inconceivable. Despite the fact that his family never left this hillside, Abu Hayja is as likely to get the title
deeds to the new Ayn Hawd as the refugees in Lebanon and Syria
are to regain the destroyed villages of Majedal (now covered by
a Jewish town called Migdal Haemek), al-Bassa (now covered by
the industrial estate of the Jewish town of Shlomi) or Tantura
(now a Jewish coastal resort called Dor).

The flip side to the Palestinian story of dispossession is the
Israeli story of rebirth, of the "ingathering of the exiles" in a
Jewish state. The Zionist movement argued from the end of the
nineteenth century that the Jews needed a state of their own, a
safe haven from the persecution they had experienced in Europe
throughout their history. The three main Zionist organisations—
the World Zionist Organisation, the Jewish National Fund and
the Jewish Agency—worked tirelessly to encourage Jews to go to
Palestine, both by buying land for them and by easing their passage there. In 1948, with the creation of Israel, these organisations finally achieved everything they had longed for. Filling the
new state with Jews was not difficult: immigrants flooded into
the country, fleeing their experiences and memories of the Holocaust. In the process the myth of "the land without people for
the people without land" was confirmed. Vast empty spaces,
where Palestinian villages had once stood, greeted these immigrants, who had little idea about their new homeland's past.
Recruited to land-hungry farming communities like the kibbut-

zim and moshavim, these pioneers truly believed they were "making the desert bloom."

Now, after more than five decades of aggressive land confiscation policies towards Palestinian citizens, 93 per cent of Israeli land is owned either by the state or the Jewish National Fund. This figure, in itself unremarkable, is significant because the land is held by the state not for the benefit of its citizens, all Israelis, but in trust for the Jewish people around the world. Almost all of it is being used for the exclusive settlement of Jews. The rest of Israeli territory, 7 per cent, is split between private Jewish and Arab owners. Even so, much of the 3 per cent of the land held by the country's Arab population has been put under the jurisdiction of Jewish regional councils, which refuse to give Arab citizens permits to develop it.

Today there are hundreds of settlements exclusively for Jews across Israel, part of what the state terms its "Judaisation" programmes: moving Jews into traditionally Arab areas so that Arab communities can be brought under Jewish dominion. The first such communities to be built—some in pre-state days, but the majority in the 1950s and 1960s—were the collective communities known as the kibbutzim and moshavim, promoted internationally as experiments in communal living. The glorified image of the kibbutz continues to this day. One liberal and widely respected British newspaper columnist, Will Hutton, recently praised the kibbutz as a noble idea. "The kibbutz movement was a living example of how to build a new society based on genuine equality of opportunity and mutuality of respect in collective democratic communes that actually worked," he wrote in the *Observer*. In reality the kibbutzim, which were usually established on the land of destroyed Palestinian villages, have always barred Arabs from living in them. So much for equality of opportunity and mutuality of respect!

More recently, the state has been creating a new model of the exclusive Jewish community known as the mitzpe, or "lookout" settlement. Developed in the 1980s and 1990s, the mitzpim are self-consciously rural communities designed to attract Israel's wealthier Jews, those tired of living in the crowded and congested centre of the country. In contrast to the kibbutzim and moshavim, the mitzpim are usually established next to, and on, land confiscated from existing Arab towns and villages. They are always built on hilltops, and their function is essentially no different from that of the settlements established on the hills of the West Bank: to put Jews in commanding positions overlooking their Arab neighbours. These mitzpim are designed to observe the Arab communities they watch over, to ensure that the Arab inhabitants do not attempt to claim back their confiscated lands by building on them. In Tamra we have our own mitzpe sitting close by, on land confiscated from us: Mitzpe Aviv.

For anyone who cares to visit a town like Tamra, the land policies of Israel are immediately clear, if only because of the overcrowding and squalor that are visible everywhere. But understanding the complex legal edifice on which such policies have been constructed and the racism at the heart of the country's land management system is no easy task. I talked to dozens of Arab families who tried to explain how they had suffered at the hands of Israeli bureaucrats, but I—and I suspected even they—found it almost impossible to unravel the tissue of regulations that was ruining their lives.

My guide in this difficult education was a man I was introduced to soon after my move to Tamra. On my return to Britain in early 2002, I had visited Rabbi John Rayner to tell him about the dramatic new twist in my life. John, ever supportive, suggested I get in contact with Dr. Uri Davis, who had been based in the neighbouring Arab town of Sakhnin for several years. Until that point I had believed I was the only Jew to be openly living in an Arab community, so I was keen to meet him, hoping that he shared my vision of an Israel that encouraged Jewish-Arab solidarity rather than fostering ethnic division and that advocated equality of all citizens. I was not to be disappointed.

Uri Davis is one of the most remarkable individuals I have met. Born in Israel, he spent most of his life here until his political views found disfavour with the government in the 1980s and he was forced into exile in Britain. A lifelong pacifist and defender of human rights, he absolutely rejects the Zionist conception of Israel as an ethnic state. Allowed to return to Israel in 1994 following the signing of the Oslo Accords, he chose to move to Sakhnin to highlight the fact that the state is enforcing policies of ethnic segregation. He has suffered for taking this humanitarian stance: he is shunned by much of Israel's Jewish society and has found it hard to work as an academic in Israel in his chosen field, anthropology. I now consider it an honour to be counted among his close friends.

Uri's offence in the eyes of Israeli society is his conclusion that the Jewish state is really an apartheid state. These are not the musings of an ivory-tower intellectual. He has reached his views after years of detailed examination of the racist laws that underpin life in Israel and much time spent dedicated to fighting human rights abuses through his nonprofit organisation, Al-Beit, which he runs with a successful Arab lawyer named Tawfik Jabareen.

"Let me make a first point, which is that in reaching this assessment [that Israel is an apartheid state], I make a clear distinction between apartheid and popular racism or xenophobia," Uri told me. "I use the term 'apartheid' in a specific sense, to mean the regulation and enforcement of racism and xenophobia in law. Apartheid is a system where the parliament, the judicial system and the law enforcement bodies impose racist and xenophobic choices on the population. To the best of my knowledge, following the dismantlement of the legal structures of apartheid in South Africa, Israel remains the only member of the United Nations that is an apartheid state."

Uri acknowledges that Israel has been careful not to replicate the worst excesses of the notorious apartheid system of South Africa. It has avoided what he calls the "petty elements" of apartheid and has concentrated instead on the core elements of its apartheid project, which concern the control of land. "When a visitor arrives at the airport in Israel, apartheid does not hit him or her in the face in the way it did visitors to apartheid South Africa," he says. "You go to the toilets in the airport and there are not separate toilets for Jews and non-Jews; you go to a public park and there are not separate benches for Jews and non-Jews; you use public transport and there are not separate buses for Jews and non-Jews. And it is this veil over Israel's apartheid that has made it possible to project Israel in the West as an enlightened liberal democracy."

The core element of all apartheid states, according to Uri, is a structure of laws that allows the colonising population to exploit the resources of the state—mainly land—to the disadvantage of the native population. In South Africa, the white population derived grossly disproportionate benefits from the country's land and mineral wealth, particularly diamonds; in Israel, the Jewish population derives grossly disproportionate benefits from the region's land and water resources. As Uri points out, "Looked at in that way, Zionist apartheid is definitely comparable to South African apartheid, and is in fact more radical and devastating. In South Africa, 87 per cent of the territory under the sovereignty of the apartheid government was designated in law for the exclusive settlement, cultivation and development of whites, while 13 per cent was designated in law for non-whites. In Israel, 93 per cent of the land is designated in law as state land for the settlement, cultivation and development of Jews only, and less than 7 per cent is private land and so theoretically accessible to non-Jews. So if we accept that the core of the conflict is the battle between the indigenous people and the colonial settler society for control over the land and the subsoil, then Israeli-Zionist apartheid is in fact more radical than its South African cousin."

The 93 per cent of land owned by the state and the JNF is leased to communities like the kibbutzim, moshavim and mitzpim—the backbone of the apartheid system identified by Uri. He has been closely involved in a long-running fight to open up just one of these communities, a mitzpe called Katzir, so that Arab citizens can live there too. The vehement resistance of the authorities to this campaign reveals everything about the true purpose of these communities. "In the early 1990s, plots of land were being marketed in Katzir by the Jewish Agency to Jewish applicants who wanted to build their own villas," Uri said. "Katzir's location is attractive for anyone who needs to commute to the major employment centres on the coast, either Haifa or Tel Aviv, and it quickly took off among well-established, middle-class families. Today it is an attractive leafy suburb. Like the hundreds of other mitzpim, moshavim and kibbutzim, Katzir is known in Israel as a cooperative association. The advantage of these settlements is that by law they can only be accessed by applicants who are prepared to submit to an interview process. Each community's selection committee has the legal authority to authorise or deny membership. So joining these communities is rather like joining a club. It is true that not all Jewish applicants are admitted. Cooperative associations have developed the features of a closed society: single mothers, people with a physical disability, unmarried couples, elderly people and homosexuals are not usually welcomed. So Jewish applicants are rejected as well as Arab applicants. But at least if you are a Jew you have the right to apply; Arabs don't even qualify for application. If a Jew arrives at the doorstep of a cooperative association, he will be given the application papers. If an Arab applicant arrives, he will be refused them."

I had visited Katzir earlier to hear the story of Adel and Iman Qaadan, a couple living in the nearby Arab town of Western Baqa, who have been fighting for ten years to move to Katzir with their three daughters—so far without tangible success. Katzir was created in the early 1990s by the then housing minister, Ariel Sharon, as part of his scheme to Judaise the small region of central Israel known as the Triangle, which is heavily populated by Arab families and lies close to the West Bank. Perched on a hilltop overlooking Palestinian villages around Jenin, Katzir has been built on a large swath of land confiscated from the neighbouring Arab communities of Umm al-Fahm, Arara, Bartaa and Ein Sahia. The inhabitants of those towns and villages are barred from living in Katzir, as they are from all other cooperative settlements. The Qaadans, however, hoped to challenge their exclusion from tranquil, spacious Katzir and its luxury villas in the courts, and so leave behind the overcrowding of Baqa.

The Supreme Court sat on the case for five years, apparently hoping to delay reaching a decision indefinitely. In 2000, however, after embarrassing international scrutiny, Chief Justice Aharon Barak issued a ruling. Describing it as one of the most difficult decisions he had ever faced, Barak ordered Katzir's selection committee to consider the Qaadans' application. The ruling was hailed by many observers as a revolution in Israel's land laws. But it was never enforced, and for the next four years the Qaadans' application was ignored by Katzir. In May 2004, the day before the Qaadans' appeal was due to be heard, the Israel Lands Authority, a government body responsible for managing state land, announced that it would sell the family a plot of land, apparently concerned that if it lost a second court case, a dangerous legal precedent on Arab land rights might be established.

However, at the time of writing, the Qaadans were still waiting to be allowed into Katzir.

Uri has been actively involved in the Katzir case too. Out of the view of the media, he has been directly helping another Arab couple, Fathi and Nawal Mahameed, to build a home in Katzir. "Fathi started his career as a manual labourer in a small company run by his father that went on to build many of the homes in Katzir," he told me. "But he harboured a dream to build his own home there if he ever made it in the building business. By 1995 he was the proprietor of a successful construction and investment company called the Fathi Brothers, so he presented himself at the door of the Katzir cooperative. Many people there know him—he has built many of their homes—and he is well liked. He presented his ID card and said he wished to buy a plot in Katzir. The person at the desk said something to the effect of 'Sir, you must know that Katzir is meant only for Jews and you are an Arab.' He replied, 'Well, I may be an Arab, but I am also a citizen of the state of Israel and I would like to build my home in Katzir.' The official repeated, 'I am sorry, but Katzir is only for Jews.' "

Fathi Mahameed turned for help to Al-Beit. They were aware that the Qaadan case was stuck in the courts and suggested a different tack, as Uri explained. "We took as our model the 'tester' system used in the United States. There, for example, if a black family wants to buy a home but suspects that reluctance to sell on the part of the vendor is motivated by racism, they can check their suspicions by using a white tester. If the property is offered to the tester, the black family can begin legal proceedings for racism and violation of U.S. law. When Mahameed approached us, Jabareen immediately said, 'Let's send in a tester.' He suggested I act on Mahameed's behalf to buy the plot of land he needed."

Under Israel's Agency Law, Uri was under no obligation to

declare to the Katzir committee that he was acting on behalf of Mahameed. "I was aware that one factor in my dealings with Katzir would assist me: racism makes people blinkered and stupid. The committee would see an elderly, white-haired, middle-class gentleman, an academic and a fluent speaker of Hebrew, and would therefore assume that my decision to move into Katzir was driven by Zionist and settler-colonial motivations. My assumption proved to be correct. I put on the table my ID card, which registered me as a Jew with a home in the Jewish community of Kafr Shemarayhu—at that stage I was not yet living in Sakhnin. Where Mahameed encountered outright rejection because he was an Arab, I was offered the initial paperwork to sign on the day I showed up.

"In order to build a home in Katzir, you have to pass through four contractual stages. The first is an interview with the cooperative association, at which they decide whether to accept you as a member. I sailed through the interview. With a letter endorsing my membership in the association, I went to the next stage. I signed a contract with the Katzir Economic Development Corporation, the body that develops Katzir's infrastructure: the sewerage, road and pavement system, the public gardening and so on. Having signed these two papers, I was then entitled to go to the Jewish Agency and sign a contract with them, a contract which is available only to Jews. And with these three documents I was able to go to the final stage: signing a contract with the Israel Lands Authority, which, unlike the Jewish Agency, is a state body.

"In the contract with the Jewish Agency there is an explicit reference to Jews and non-Jews, but the text of the Israel Lands Authority contract makes no such distinction. However, you can't sign the Israel Lands Authority contract unless you bring the previous three pieces of paper. So representatives of the Lands Authority can stand up in public and truthfully say, 'I challenge you to show me one Israel Lands Authority contract which makes a distinction between Jew and non-Jew.' That is true, but they don't also tell you that you cannot sign a contract with the Lands Authority to join a cooperative settlement like Katzir, or a kibbutz or a moshav, unless you bring these three documents first, which do make such a distinction.

"The hundreds of communities classified as cooperative settlements and governed by these rules are also the settlements that control almost all of the 93 per cent of the territory of Israel. Together their populations represent much less than 10 per cent of the Israeli population. In other words, less than a tenth of the population is sitting on legal communities that control 93 per cent of the territory of Israel. And the primary purpose of these communities is to make sure that Arabs don't get property rights in them, that they can't join them."

Armed with all the legal forms, Uri pretended he was employing Mahameed to build his dream home in Katzir. "Mahameed put all his heart and professional skill into building that house and its garden, and it took time. I applied for a plot in 1995, but it was 1999 before the finishing touches were being put to the house. Shortly before I was officially due to move in, I needed to sort out a technical problem over the boundary between Mahameed's plot and the adjacent one. I attended a meeting at the Katzir Economic Development Corporation with my neighbour. The matter was easily sorted out, but as we were about to leave, the director asked me to stay a moment longer. He said, 'Uri, there are rumours that you are not going to enter the house and an Arab family is going to enter in your place. Is that true?' I tried to fob off the question, saying it was only a rumour. He persevered: 'Can you give me an assurance that you will enter the house?' I said, 'Yes, not only can I assure you that I will enter the house, but I can give you a date.' I didn't lie. It was correct that I would enter the house on the date specified, but I didn't owe him an explanation about what would happen after that. I entered the house, and a few days later we had a house-warming celebration. We invited lots of friends and activists, and at the end of my speech I handed over the keys to Fathi Mahameed."

Uri and the Mahameeds had broken no laws in failing to reveal their true intentions to the Katzir selection committee. Nonetheless, they had achieved a result that the land management system in Israel was designed to render impossible. "Katzir went straight to the courts, and the case has been stuck there ever since. We are demanding that the Israel Lands Authority transfer the property rights registered in my name to Fathi Mahameed. The Israel Lands Authority refuses to do so," Uri said.

Not only have the Mahameeds yet to get their property rights registered, they have also been evicted by Katzir. Uri is now living in the house a few days a week to prevent it from being repossessed. "The bylaws of cooperative associations are such that Katzir can claim the Mahameeds' home is abandoned property if it is not occupied for any length of time," he explained. "It is quite possible that Katzir hoped that by evicting Fathi Mahameed, they would have an excuse to repossess his home. In a cooperative association, one cannot rent a home to someone who has not passed the same interview process faced by prospective buyers. So Katzir can bar Mahameed from renting his property as well as from living there. However, there is one person who can legally occupy the house without going through the interview, and that is me. So I now divide my residence between Sakhnin and Katzir—and make sure the garden looks nice."

I was shocked that the Mahameeds were now allowed to enter their own home only as guests. It was difficult to believe that Katzir could act in such a racist manner with the courts' backing, or at least their complicit silence, and that the other inhabitants of Katzir appeared to be allowing all this to happen without an outcry.

Uri is convinced that eventually both the Qaadans and the Mahameeds will win their legal fights to live in Katzir. But both face a long struggle to achieve it. "There are two possible ways of looking at this story," he said. "The first says, 'This proves that Israel is a democracy. The Mahameeds are succeeding; the Qaadans are succeeding. If you adhere to Israel's democratic procedures, you can win your case.' That's not my view. My view is that it stinks that a citizen of the state of Israel should have to resort to such procedures—to use a tester, to go to the courts, to battle for a decade to get his rights. The Mahameed and Qaadan stories do not highlight Israeli democracy; they highlight the depth of apartheid inside Israel. It should not be necessary for these families to lose years of their lives, their energies and resources to establish their rights, whereas someone registered as a Jew is exempt from all these delays, insults and sufferings. What took me, Dr. Uri Davis, a few weeks to achieve—namely, to get the papers signed and sealed—will take a Palestinian citizen of Israel a decade or more. This discrepancy cannot be recovered. The time that has elapsed cannot be retrieved. The Qaadans and the Mahameeds have been tied up in legal battles for a decade and still do not have their property rights registered."

Both Uri and I have tried to show by our own example that Jews and Arabs can live together in peace and understanding. What Katzir and the hundreds of other cooperative communities in Israel have been designed to do is persuade Jews and the world that precisely the opposite holds true. Perceptions can be changed only when Israel's apartheid system is ended and Jews and Arabs are offered the possibility of choosing where and how to live, including living together in open communities. But how can this be achieved?

The first step must involve the dismantlement of Zionist organisations like the Jewish National Fund and the Jewish Agency, which determine and shape land policies in the interests of Jews rather than in the interests of all Israeli citizens. Both these organisations long predate the founding of Israel. In fact, they were established precisely to bring about the creation of a Jewish state in Palestine by buying land for the settlement of Jews. Once statehood was declared and their purpose achieved, they should have withered on the vine. The sovereign state of Israel should have concentrated its efforts on creating a new Israeli identity open to Jews and Arabs; it should have developed a notion of citizenship premised on equality for all; and it should have provided fair access to its resources.

Instead, as Uri observes, Israel chose the path of apartheid, incorporating the Jewish Agency and the Jewish National Fund into the framework of the state. One of the early acts of the government, for example, was to transfer huge tracts of land to the JNF. By 1953 the organisation had been given nearly 500,000 acres of confiscated land, and that figure continues to grow. Today the JNF owns 13 per cent of the land in Israel, in the main habitable regions, on which more than two thirds of Israeli Jews have a home; none of it, according to the organisation's own charter, can be leased or rented to Arab citizens. Most of the rest of the country's lands are managed by the Israel Lands Authority, but even here the JNF is really pulling the strings. The Jewish National Fund nominates half the members of the ILA's governing council, thereby determining the policies of the ILA too. Such gross discrimination is almost impossible to challenge in the courts or elsewhere, because the JNF and the Jewish Agency are not state agencies. They exist in parallel to the state, as shadow bodies that have the power to exercise great control over the management of resources but cannot be held to account through any of the normal channels. In practice, this means that the JNF can act without penalty as a kind of bullying overlord to-

wards the country's Arab citizens, constantly seeking to confiscate private land on the flimsiest pretext and transfer it to its own
or state ownership for the sole benefit of Jews. There are few re-
straints on the JNF's behaviour, and even fewer recourses to law
open to Arab citizens when it behaves in an arbitrary fashion.

I was aware of all this in theory, but it did not lessen the impact
when I saw the JNF in action against a neighbour in Tamra. Ali
Diab owns the pharmacy at the bottom of my road. Belonging to
one of Tamra's elite families, he is visibly a wealthy man. The reason is to be found in the story of his family's lands. Unlike Samira,
Ali can trace his lineage back many generations in Tamra, and he
has the tabu (title deeds) to extensive private lands surrounding
the town. Whereas my family in Tamra has only the small patch of
land it was able to buy to build a home, Ali is by Arab standards a
substantial landowner. "On the south side of the town I have
twelve dunums [three acres] planted with olive groves," he explained as I waited for a prescription one day. But precisely because Ali is one of the last remaining major Arab landowners, he
has been attracting the less than benign attention of the JNF. He
told me that he and many other members of the Diab family had
been losing their landholdings to the aggressive tactics of the
JNF. I said I would like to see his fields, and we arranged to drive
out to them later that day.

The southern road out of Tamra ends abruptly as one enters
the last neighbourhoods, becoming a rocky track descending
into the valley. Here, in Tamra's most fertile soil, cucumbers are
grown—and reputed by many in the Galilee to be the tastiest
and most succulent in Israel. I could make out on the far side of
the valley, halfway up a gentle hillside, an isolated small concrete
building painted a distinctive pale blue-green. We reached it via
a recently created stone-and-dirt track. "This is my agricultural
store," said Ali, pointing to his glorified shed. It stood in a spec-
tacular location, overlooking Tamra to the north and a forest of

pine trees to the west. Less than half a kilometre to the east, the nearest detached homes of Mitzpe Aviv, Tamra's Jewish neighbours, were visible. Next to the shed were carefully tended olive trees.

The JNF had banned Ali from using his land for business, trade or housing, but nonetheless he is obliged to put it to some use, since fallow land can be confiscated by the state or the JNF. That is the reason he planted the olive groves. By law, anyone who owns and cultivates more than ten dunums is entitled to build an agricultural shed in which to store his tools and machinery. For Ali, the building is also a useful place for him and the family to rest, out of the midday heat in the summer and away from the chill winds of a Galilean winter, and to prepare meals while working all day in the olive groves. Although the JNF could not stop him building the shed, he was sure they did not really want him to be able to use it. "They have tried to get me off this land in every way they can think of," he told me.

I asked him what evidence he had. "Where do I begin?" he said wearily. "My latest problem is that they won't connect the shed up to public services, and particularly to the electricity supply, which I need for my agricultural work. The electricity company has come out here and approved the route of the cables, and I have shown I can afford the connection charges, but the JNF refuses to give the go-ahead." When I wondered why, Ali thrust into my hands a letter from the JNF which stated that his shed was "too isolated for any infrastructure." It seemed a strange reason, given that we were standing only a stone's throw from the houses of Mitzpe Aviv. But then again, Mitzpe Aviv is a cooperative association just like Katzir, and serves only Jews. Maybe there was a law that electricity cables from a mitzpim could not be redirected to help an Arab like Ali.

Lack of electricity, it soon became clear, was the least of Ali's worries. He pointed to the thick forest of pine trees to the west and told me they had been planted thirty years ago, on the land of a relative of his. "The JNF accused him of failing to cultivate his fields regularly enough, so they established the forest on them," Ali said. "I am determined not to make the same mistake." Nonetheless, the JNF had made it clear that it covets his fields too: on several occasions a representative had offered him money for them. "The sums were always far below the market price," he said. "The first time they came they offered me $2,000 per dunum. On the last occasion I had already planted the olives you can see, so they doubled the price. I refused. There is no price they can offer me for this land that I will accept."

The JNF, however, appears unwilling to accept Ali's no. Recently they confiscated part of his lands, arguing that he had not been cultivating them. "They produced aerial photographs which they said showed that the soil was rocky and that therefore I was not tending the ground. Other pictures they said they took a few years earlier showed the same. This was proof, they said, that I wasn't working the land. So they took that part of my fields," Ali said. The JNF lost no time in transforming his land in the way it knows best: it planted young pine saplings all over the recently confiscated land, rendering it unusable. Looking back down into the valley from Ali's shed, I saw a swath of young pine trees taking root in his most fertile soil.

The loss of fields that had been in his family for generations spurred Ali to stake an even stronger claim to his remaining fields, and he planted olive trees on every available bit of land. The increased workload of tending to these groves required him to build his shed. "The JNF understood my predicament very well, so they have been trying to prevent me from getting to both the shed and my fields," he said. The only way to reach Ali's land is via an access route whose coordinates are plotted on a local survey map of the area. Checking it closely with a surveyor, Ali found that having land confiscated by the JNF also deprived him

Me aged about eighteen
months, with my father.

My parents on the beach at Blouberg
Strand near Cape Town, April 1976.

A view of the street from my terrace in Tamra. The people are gathering for a wedding.

View of Tamra from my apartment.

My street in Tamra. Note the
telephone and electrical cables
strung from pole to pole.

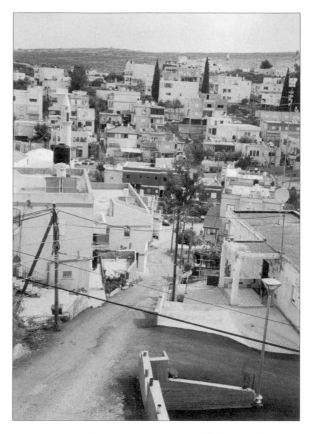

Election poster for the Hadash
party—for which I voted—in
Tamra, 2004. The successful
mayoral candidate, Adel Abu
Hayja, is in the centre.

A home with a farmyard of sheep, goats, and chickens in the garden. Such houses are common in Arab communities inside Israel, which have been stripped of most of their farming land since the creation of the Israeli state.

My neighbours in
Tamra during an
engagement party.

A Tamra neighbour
making traditional pitta.

Engagement party
in Tamra.

Street scene in
Tamra during
the festival of
Eid al-Adha

Surrounded by all that is left of their furniture, a Palestinian family stand on the site of their former home in the Galilean village of Beaneh, where five houses were demolished by the Israeli authorities in February 2004. Five hundred Arab homes inside Israel were destroyed in 2003, usually without warning.

The Dona Rosa restaurant in the Ein Hod artists' colony, which before Israel's creation in 1948 was a mosque in the Palestinian village of Ayn Hawd. The mother of my family in Tamra was expelled from the village in 1948.

At an event held to mark the Palestinian "nakba" (catastrophe) on 27 April 2004—Israel's Independence Day—an Israeli Arab boy distributes signs naming some of the four hundred Palestinian villages destroyed by the Israeli army in the 1948 war that founded the Jewish state.

Eitan Bronstein (in baseball cap) of the Israeli Jewish lobby group Zochrot (Remembering) helps erect a signpost in Hebrew and Arabic alerting local residents in the city of Haifa to the fact that Arab neighbourhoods existed there before they were cleared during the war to found Israel. Such signs are invariably removed shortly after they have been put up.

of his access track; the JNF had planted trees over the only route by which he could reach his fields. If he could not get to the olive groves, he could not tend them. In a few years the JNF would have the pretext to confiscate them too. Ali consulted lawyers and found that he was entitled to restore the access road and to destroy any trees planted over it, as long as they were still saplings. So a few months earlier he had taken a bulldozer and carved a path back up the hillside to his shed.

Ali's problems are far from unique, even in this small valley. His cousin faces exactly the same problem on his neighbouring fields, as Ali explained. "The JNF planted trees over a two-metre strip of land they confiscated from him that cuts across the only access path he has to his olive groves. Then they put up a barbed wire fence. When he argued that they were blocking the only access to his land, the officials offered a compromise: they would give him back his two metres on condition that in return he gave them two dunums of fields, including the olive trees. So far he has refused, but he is too frightened to tear down the fence and the pine trees. He sits at home wondering what to do next. I keep telling him that if he doesn't act soon, the JNF will be able to say he hasn't cultivated his fields, and they will take them."

The JNF has used these tactics against the country's Arab population for more than fifty years. Every dunum of land coveted by the JNF, every hillside needed for a new Jewish settlement, every fertile valley needed for a kibbutz, has been won in a struggle in which the JNF has had a free hand to write and rewrite the rules. No Arab citizens can cry foul, because the JNF is not subject to the normal procedures by which government and public bodies are held to account. Ali managed to keep hold of some of his land by sheer force of will, by his quick-wittedness and by his refusal to be intimidated or worn down. But my guess is that eventually either his stamina will be exhausted or he will find he cannot match the resources of the JNF, with its battery of well-trained officials and legal advisers.

I had one more question for him. "How does the JNF keep track of what you and your relatives are doing in this valley?" I asked.

"Look over there," he said, pointing to the largest house on the edge of Mitzpe Aviv, the building closest to Tamra. "That house is owned by a representative of the JNF. He is the one who used to come to me offering me money for my land. Nothing happens here that he doesn't know about."

I knew several Jews living in Mitzpe Aviv from meetings arranged by coexistence groups promoting dialogue between Jews and Arabs. Mitzpe Aviv is considered one of the more left-wing communities in the Galilee. Ali's story was a disturbing reminder that the true purpose of these mitzpim, however well-meaning many of the inhabitants are, is to spy on their Arab neighbours. And as Uri had explained to me, the mitzpim are designed to sit on as much land as possible, to occupy it on behalf of Jews while denying access to Arab citizens. It does not matter that some of the residents of Mitzpe Aviv see themselves as enlightened and liberal; the purpose of their community, and of the Jewish state, is to enforce an apartheid system of land tenure.

Mitzpe Aviv was founded many years ago on land confiscated from Tamra and from the Diab hamula by officials of the JNF, using tactics like those being used against Ali now. Today, 500 Jews live there, occupying 1,000 dunums of land, while the 25,000 Arabs of Tamra are squeezed into 4,600 dunums. Each Jew in Mitzpe Aviv has access to more than ten times the land that is available to a Tamran. That explains why they have large detached homes and private gardens, while we in Tamra are trapped in suffocating apartment blocks, without gardens, parks or public spaces.

"Each time the man from the JNF came to me," said Ali, "he

pleaded with me to sell my land. He said Mitzpe Aviv desperately needed more space so that it could grow and so its children would have room to build their homes. He told me, 'Without the land, what kind of future will the next generation have in Mitzpe Aviv?' "

5

THE MISSING LEFT

After I had been living in Tamra for slightly less than a year, my presence here finally registered on the radar of the Israeli media. A reporter, Sara Liebovitch-Dar, rang me from *Ha'aretz*, saying she had seen an article about me in Britain's *Guardian* and wanted to interview me and learn more about my views. It seemed like a breakthrough. Maybe now I would get the chance to tell ordinary Israeli Jews about what life is really like for the country's Arab population.

Ha'aretz is by far the most progressive of Israel's dailies and during the intifada has even dared to give a flavour of life as it is experienced by Palestinians in the occupied territories. It employs two highly distinguished, if unpopular, journalists, Amira Hass and Gideon Levy, who have made it their job tenaciously and bravely to uncover abuses by Israeli soldiers enforcing the occupation of Palestinian land. Hass, living in Ramallah in the West Bank, experiences the army's atrocities first-hand, while Levy regularly ventures into dangerous areas to give a voice to ordinary Palestinians and expose their daily suffering and misery at the hands of soldiers. In doing so, both are breaking the law, which bans Israeli journalists from entering Palestinian-controlled areas.

Nonetheless, *Ha'aretz* scarcely even attempts to report as fairly on the Palestinian minority living inside the country. While Amira Hass and Gideon Levy have recounted in heartbreaking words the disaster that befalls Palestinian families when, for example, an army bulldozer razes their homes, neither is apparently allowed to write about the same actions when they are carried out by the Israeli police against the country's Arab citizens. The irony is that the abuses inflicted on Palestinians under occupation are far better reported than the same abuses inflicted on Israeli citizens who are also Palestinian. This failure is compounded by the Hebrew media's almost total exclusion of Arabs from their ranks of journalists. At the time of writing, *Ha'aretz* has only one Arab on its staff, a sports correspondent. In effect, this policy is given legal sanction by the Israeli Broadcasting Law, which defines the media's role as representing Jewish society, reinforcing Jewish, Hebrew-speaking culture and establishing a bond between Jews living in Israel and those in the Diaspora.

So when I received the phone call from *Ha'aretz*, I knew there was little point in asking the paper to send an Arab reporter to interview me. But I recognised the name Sara Liebovitch-Dar from the Friday features supplement, where she writes sympathetically about social issues, including discrimination against women and many of the marginal Jewish communities inside Israel, such as Jews originally from Arab countries, the Mizrahim, and the Ethiopians. She is one of the more socially aware correspondents, and I assumed she would give me about the best hearing I could hope for from the newspaper.

From our initial contact, however, there were clues that I should be on my guard. When Sara called, her first words, uttered in irritated exasperation, were "Is that Susan Nathan? I've been looking for you everywhere!" I immediately felt reduced to the status of a wayward toddler. After I assured her that she had indeed found me, she followed the first enquiry with an accusing question: "So, where are you living?" As she had read the *Guardian* article, I had no doubt she knew exactly where I lived. "I live in Tamra, Sara. It's near Acre." She was not placated. "But where *is* that?" I told her to get a map of Israel and look for it. "So Tamra's an Arab village, is it?" she said, in what appeared to be an attempt at clarification but was in reality the expression of a common Israeli prejudice: that Arabs do not live in towns but only in villages, the assumption being that these are primitive places, out of touch with the times. The idea of a modern town of twenty-five thousand Arabs inside the state of Israel is possibly too threatening for most Israeli Jews to contemplate. "No," I said firmly. "We are a town, and we are twenty minutes from Acre."

Despite her bravado, she sounded nervous and uncomfortable. I asked if she had ever been to an Arab town before. "Well, I've been to Ramallah," she said, referring to the Palestinian city in the West Bank, close to Jerusalem, where Yasser Arafat was effectively imprisoned for much of the intifada by Israeli military forces. A few Israeli journalists had made the pilgrimage there to interview him, but I think it more likely that Sara ventured there in more conciliatory times, before the outbreak of fighting, as part of one of the regular delegations of Israeli journalists who met with the Palestinian leadership. Her reply suggested that she was familiar neither with the nature of the occupation of the Palestinians nor, more important, with the issues facing her fellow citizens in the country's dozens of Arab communities. I ended the conversation by giving her directions to the mosque in the centre of Tamra and suggesting she call me when she reached it.

No one had ever before got lost following my directions, but Sara managed it. In the morning I waited for her call; when it finally came, she was in a near-hysterical panic. "I can't find you! I can't find you!" she shrieked. "I'm at the top of the hill and they are all looking at me!" Although I knew she could be in no danger, her voice sounded so strained that I found myself starting to panic too. I rushed down the hill from my house, but she was nowhere to be seen. The phone rang again. Finally realising that she had driven past the mosque and on up the hill to the far end of the town, I told her to turn back and follow the main road downhill. But she wasn't listening. Instead, all I could hear was her wailing: "I've gone up! I've gone up!" I tried again to calm her down: "Turn back, Sara, and come down. You can't miss me. I'm blond. I'm the only one who doesn't look like an Arab." Then at last I saw her in the distance, at the steering wheel of a rental car coming down the hill. (It occurred to me that a *Ha'aretz* feature writer would need to own a car for her line of work, but maybe Sara felt it would be unwise to bring her own car to an Arab area.)

She pulled up outside the mosque, trying to look as unflustered as possible. I climbed into the car and we exchanged brief greetings. In her late thirties, she was clearly ignorant of or insensitive to local Muslim culture; she was wearing a crop-top that showed her navel, something no Muslim woman in Tamra would ever do. She seemed suitably unnerved by the steep ascent along the potholed road to my neighbourhood, but as we turned left into the narrow street where I live, she tried to lighten the mood, saying, "Oh, it's very pretty." The comment made me smile. Did she really imagine that this was pretty? Maybe she was simply making small talk, or desperately trying to ignore the visible poverty, overcrowding and filth and convince herself that she was driving down a narrow village lane in Tuscany or Provence. Or was she hoping to conceal from me any trace of her true thoughts: *Why on earth would any sane person choose to live here if they didn't have to? Why would someone move from Tel Aviv to* here?

Sara came up to my apartment and surveyed it with some interest. I could see she was surprised. Though my home is not the best in Tamra, it is a nice, clean, airy space with a fine view from the balcony. She asked if it was like this when I rented it. I told her that structurally it was the same but I had furnished it with my belongings. It was obviously not quite the mud hut she was expecting.

I had assumed that a journalist from a paper like *Ha'aretz* would arrive with some sense of what avenues she hoped to explore in the interview, or some idea of the framework she wanted to impose on our encounter. But once seated, Sara simply leaned forward with her huge notepad on her lap and said, "Well . . . begin." At this point I realised that the woman before me had failed to internalise any of the things she had read about me. She didn't know where to start or what issues to raise. As far as she was concerned, I was the star of a freak show, and she was intrigued to see my act. I was expected to perform for her, to horrify and appall her.

A more experienced interviewee, I suspect, would have bailed out. That was what my instincts were telling me to do, but I suppressed them and began telling her my life story. I told her about my difficult childhood, my obsession with the Holocaust, and my Zionist upbringing. But her interest was engaged only when I mentioned an incident in South Africa when I was sixteen. My family was dining at my wealthy aunt's home when she rounded on a black servant in his early twenties and severely rebuked him for serving us without wearing white gloves. The meaning of her comment registered with me as "We don't want to see your black skin. You're good enough to serve us, but you aren't good enough to touch our food." I had already secretly befriended this young man and felt his pain and humiliation as she addressed him. I literally couldn't swallow my food. I excused myself from the table and followed him to the kitchen. There we talked. Feeling a strong mutual attraction, we then put our arms around each other and ended up having sex on the kitchen table.

Sex between a white woman and a black man in apartheid

South Africa was not just a physical act, it was an act of the most powerful political dissent. In breaking the ultimate racial taboo, we were also breaking the law. Both of us, but especially him, were taking a huge risk. At the age of sixteen, I felt both exhilarated and empowered: I was sticking two fingers up to apartheid and to members of my racist family in South Africa. I was separating myself in every way I could from what was going on on the other side of the door.

Sara, it was clear, was far more interested in the act itself than she was in the political circumstances in which it took place, or for that matter in the motives that lay behind my decision, forty years later, to move to Tamra. I suggested to her that Zionism was a colonial ideology that might have made sense when it was first developed in the nineteenth century but that now stood in opposition to the spirit of the times. I argued for the abolition of the Law of Return. I questioned the viability of a Jewish state, especially when Palestinians would soon form a majority of the population.* None of these arguments surfaced cogently in her report, published in September 2003 under the title "Living with Them." The "them" presumably referred to the country's Arab citizens. The racist headline reflected the tone of the article, which opened with a sensationalised account of my having sex with the black servant in South Africa.

I should have expected no less. Sara spent all day in my apartment, but her questions were always punctuated with the same despairing assessment: "I don't understand you, I just don't understand your life." The interview descended into a series of confrontations in which she tried to question my credentials as a Jew and as an Israeli citizen and thus my right to criticise my newly adopted state. She asked, for example, if I had other passports.

---

*Israeli demographers believe that within ten years the Palestinian population will outnumber Jews inside Israel and in the territories it occupies.

Like many Israeli Jews, I do: I have a British one and a South African one. She then said, "If you don't like it here, why don't you use those passports and go home and leave it to us Israelis?" I wondered which "us Israelis" she was referring to—presumably not Israelis who are Arabs. But I was astounded by her nerve. After all, she was not the one protesting about the Law of Return, which uniquely privileges Jews from anywhere in the world to come to Israel and receive automatic citizenship. "Sara," I snapped back at her, "don't tell me one minute that you want Jews like me to come from the Diaspora, the ones who have money and are well qualified, so that we can increase your demographic strength against the Arabs, and then tell me to take my passports and bugger off out of here when I start criticising the way you run the country." There was an uncomfortable silence.

Next she began delving into my background, concentrating her questions on the fact that my mother was not born a Jew but converted from Protestantism after marrying my father. I knew where she was leading the interview. "Listen, Sara," I said impatiently, "this is not an inquisition into my parents. You came to Tamra to interview *me.*" In halakhic law—the theological edicts of the Orthodox rabbinate—only the children of a Jewish mother are considered Jews. This is still the official position in Israel, where the state gives official standing only to the Orthodox stream of Judaism, to the exclusion of the other two main streams, Reform and Conservative. It does not have to be this way. In the United States, for example, the majority of Jews belong to the more enlightened Reform stream, which makes conversion much easier. In Orthodox Judaism, being a Jew is a little like belonging to a closed society, the membership of which is highly restricted. The Orthodox rabbinate's long-standing stranglehold on the bureaucracy of the Israeli Interior Ministry means that no civil marriage is allowed in Israel, and it is impossible to identify oneself as an atheist or agnostic. By law, all Israeli citizens must be classified along confessional lines—be it Judaism, Islam or Christianity—and can marry only members of the same sect. (Couples from different confessions are forced to marry abroad, usually in Cyprus.)

The inconsistency that Sara Liebovitch-Dar was trying to tease out was that in the official Israeli view, the Jewishness of a Jew like me is suspect, even if, according to the Law of Return, I am considered Jewish enough to make aliya. Under that law, a Jew is defined as anyone who has one Jewish grandparent. The Law of Return has such generous terms because the state has taken the pragmatic view that it cannot prevent large numbers of people who identify themselves as Jews and who are classified as such by Reform and Conservative rabbis from claiming citizenship in a country that defines itself as the state of the Jews. In any case, Israeli governments decided long ago that they needed to recruit all the Jews they could find in their battle to keep a Jewish majority ruling over the Palestinians. Thus, despite my non-halakhic status, the Jewish Agency approved my application to immigrate to Israel in just a week. Nonetheless, as far as the religious authorities inside Israel are concerned, I am a sort of pseudo-Jew, or second-class Jew. Hundreds of thousands of Israeli Jews are stuck in this identity limbo, especially the one million Russian Jews who arrived following the collapse of the Soviet Union. Many were the children or grandchildren of a marriage between a Jew and a non-Jew. Today they are unable to marry "proper" Jews inside Israel. They and I cannot be buried in Jewish cemeteries. And their children will inherit this official "flaw" in their Jewishness.

Sara was truly baffled by how I could fill my time in Tamra. "But what does your life here consist of?" she kept asking. The facts that I supervise the local branch of Mahapach, that I am involved in women's empowerment projects, that I help promote a local music conservatoire and that I teach English were apparently not enough. "But what else? What about your personal life?" she asked. I said that in the evenings I visited friends and neighbours. She was genuinely astonished: "You mean you have friends here? You walk on the streets at night and go into people's homes?" She looked perturbed. "Maybe I will understand all this better after I have read my notes," she said, as if she were a doctor trying to piece together a particularly problematic case study.

Finally she suggested that maybe I should move to the West Bank and live with the Palestinians there. I had an inkling of what she was really saying: "Go live with Amira Hass—then we can pigeonhole you as a Palestinian-lover." That way my criticisms would be less dangerous. I could be dismissed as a "self-hating Jew" by right-wingers and recruited by left-wingers as another Jew who advocated the creation of a Palestinian state to solve all our problems. But as long as my attention was focused on the discrimination against Arab citizens of Israel, my criticisms threatened the identify of Jews like Sara Liebovitch-Dar, who believe they are the only and eternal victims of this story.

Sara drank half a cup of tea that day, and managed a couple of mouthfuls of the salad I had prepared for lunch. At the end of the interview, as she got up to leave, I pointed out that she had not been to the toilet once in all the time she had been here and it might be sensible to go before she set off on the long journey back to Tel Aviv. "Oh, yes," she said, as if jolted back into reality.

Sara's interview was published in Hebrew but was never translated for the paper's English edition, even though its subject was a British citizen, it concentrated on my schooling in England and, in touching on matters of discrimination against Arabs, it should have been of interest to an international audience. I suspected, however, that the piece was meant only for a domestic audience, and to place me outside any consensus Israeli Jews could understand. I wrote a reply, which the paper's editors refused to publish. But despite the distortion of what I had said, a number of Jews understood the point of my criticisms. It was most gratifying to receive supportive calls from Holocaust survivors. One eighty-year-old man called to say, "You know, what we do to the Palestinians was what was done to us in Europe. We Jews have to realise that we do not have a monopoly on suffering, we don't have to be special in everything." He added that despite his failing health, he was considering going to live in the West Bank. He and other survivors said they felt the memory of the Holocaust was being cheapened.

This episode was a wake-up call to me in many ways, but perhaps most important, it accelerated my rapidly growing disenchantment with what is known in Israel as "the left." This vague term is used by many Israelis as a withering criticism of anyone who doesn't uphold the exclusive claim of Jews to the Holy Land or who is committed to the idea that Arabs should be entitled either to some level of rights or to a state. Politically, however, the label is almost meaningless. The Labour Party, which has ruled the country for most of its five decades, is usually considered left-wing but has overseen the most aggressive periods of settlement activity in the occupied territories. One disillusioned Israeli journalist, Daphna Baram, summed up the party's sham philosophy: "Labour tradition is mostly about pragmatism, which translates into pragmatic expansionism or pragmatic moderation, according to changing circumstances. Its goal is to grab the most land with the fewest Arabs on it, while maintaining a measure of international acceptability for Israel. The means: building a large number of settlements in the occupied territories, not too near Palestinian centres of population—thus asserting facts on the ground while maintaining a constant soundtrack of peacemaking."

The left encompasses a broad band of opinion that is equally pragmatic, from Israel's mainstream left-wing parties, Labour and Meretz/Yahad, and their peace-campaigning offshoot, Peace Now, to a handful of what are considered by most Israelis as extremist, if not possibly subversive, organisations, such as Gush Shalom. In truth, the position of Gush Shalom, led by the veteran peace campaigner Uri Avnery, is moderate in the extreme: it supports the end of the occupation and the creation of a Palestinian state on less than a quarter of historic Palestine. It is prepared to recognise in theory the rights of the Palestinians expelled in 1948, the refugees, but in practice it rejects any Palestinian return that might threaten the demographic superiority of Jews or compromise the state's Zionist mission. It also, of course, has little to say about the injustices perpetrated on the country's Palestinian citizens.

The number of Israelis who adopt positions more left-wing than Gush Shalom's can be counted on the fingers of a few hands. If I had any doubts of that, a series of encounters with people who considered themselves left-wingers, even radical left-wingers, soon settled the matter for me. My first taste of the racism at the heart of the left-wing and intellectual establishment came in my first days in Israel. I had befriended a leading Israeli academic during his regular visits to Britain, and after my arrival in Israel I spent a lot of time at his home. I vividly recall one day watching a programme about the intifada on Israeli TV with him. We saw footage of a young soldier in Ramallah shooting in the leg an old man who had approached him with his hands in the air. I was appalled. "What is going on?" I said. My friend replied, with the air of a man who can find endless excuses for such behaviour when it is perpetrated by Jews, "Susan, he is young and he is under pressure. That is why he shot him." On another occasion, while crossing the campus of his university, we walked past a flight of steps where Arab students like to congregate. "Can't you smell them?" he said as we passed. I wondered what kind of ideas a man like this was inculcating in the young minds he was responsible for.

Many middle-class Israelis introduce themselves as left-wing, but their conversations soon give them away. In the days when I taught English to professionals, I talked with an official of a well-known Israeli bank who often boasted of his left-wing credentials. Because he dealt with financial issues, I made the observation that wherever I went, I could see wonderful housing developments for Jews and advertisements for government-approved mortgage schemes to encourage Jews to buy their dream home. "That tells me very publicly how much my state values me as a citizen," I said. "But if I am an Arab citizen, I don't see such developments open to me, and I don't qualify for the mortgage schemes, or even in the rare case that I do, I will get a much lower discount. What does that tell me about how much my country values me?" His reply was disdainful: "So what? They can look after themselves. I want this country for me and my children." While he was at it, he might also have admitted that his bank refuses to employ Arabs in the most senior positions. (Worse still, the Central Bank of Israel, which has more than eight hundred staff members, employs no Arabs at all.) "Why is there no Arab on your board of directors?" I asked him. "Well, it's not just down to me," he replied feebly. I found his answer morally repugnant. If someone in his position cannot begin the process of change, who can?

There have been innumerable disheartening moments like this. Another that I find hard to dislodge from my memory occurred in the wake of my move to Tamra. About the only Israeli friend who supported my decision to live in an Arab town was a middle-aged archaeologist at one of the Israeli universities, who is in charge of major digs in northern Israel, where she supervises Jewish and Arab students. She told me constantly about her interaction and friendships with Arabs, and how it made her heart sing to drive all over the West Bank in the days before the intifada because of her love of wild open spaces. Just before I moved to the Galilee, when I invited her to visit me, she replied, "Try keeping me away." She always talked about visiting Arab areas as though it were some adventure, like going on safari.

After I had settled into Tamra and started understanding much better the trauma inflicted on Arab society by the war of 1948 and the ongoing suffering of the internal refugees, I explained my new thinking to her during a phone call. I told her I now realised that there could not be peace until Israel recognised the right of the Palestinian refugees to return. "You are an extremely intelligent but naïve woman!" she exploded. "If we let them back, they will be everywhere!" Suddenly the Arabs she had spoken of so fondly were a contagion, an outbreak of smallpox that threatened to wipe out the Jews. She continued an angry rant, which I finally interrupted by saying, "I'm sorry I raised the subject." "Yes, I'm sure you are," she said, closing the matter. A few days later, I opened my e-mail to discover that she had sent me a link to an offensive Zionist website that monitors the rantings of obscure Muslim clerics against Israel. She never made contact again.

I soon came to understand that these so-called left-wingers were hypocrites of the worst kind. The fact that they are to be found everywhere in Israeli society, in the government, in academic institutions, in charge of major companies and even of Jewish and Arab coexistence groups, makes this realisation all the more depressing. Is it any wonder that Jews in the Diaspora have almost no understanding of what really goes on in Israeli society when these people, the country's brightest and best, are responsible for projecting its image abroad?

The most disturbing moment came during an encounter from which I had expected a great deal. I was introduced to a former businessman who is a leading figure in more than one of the most prominent Jewish-Arab coexistence groups in Israel. This man has a huge influence on the establishment left in the country, and several people suggested that there might be ways we could work together. When we met in his office in Tamra, he opened the conversation by saying, "I think you are a brave woman." I couldn't help thinking that if he shared my views, he would not find my behaviour so brave, but I let it pass. He asked me what had prompted my decision to move to Tamra. I told him I was disturbed by the direction I saw Israel taking and that I was pessimistic about the chances for peace unless we started to be more honest with ourselves. I could see that he was barely able to control his anger. When I described the lack of equality, the failure to invest in Arab areas and the sense that Arab citizens had no future, he leapt in to interrupt me: "Well, you in Britain can't speak. Look at the way the British government treats asylum seekers. Look at the way you put them in holding centres. You can't speak—you don't treat them so well."

As he spoke, the obvious flaws in his argument struck me. Since when had I become a representative of the British government? I was speaking to him as a concerned Israeli citizen about official Israeli policies, yet he wanted only to categorise me as a Briton and restrict my criticisms to British policies. And although I hold no brief for the British government on its treatment of asylum seekers, how was the analogy fair? The Israeli Arabs are not immigrants trying to gain entry to a foreign country on humanitarian grounds, they are citizens whose rights are supposedly enshrined in law. But faced with his rising ill temper, I kept my mouth shut on these points. Instead I asked him how he could justify the fact that Israeli educational institutions had such an appalling record of employing Arab academics (according to reports, fewer than 1 per cent of the country's university lecturers are Arabs). "Oh, that was an oversight," he said dismissively. I raised the subject of my experience in South Africa, but he swatted that away too: "I am familiar with South Africa." I mentioned the problems I had had at the airport. "You remind me of my daughter," he mocked. "You have principles." I had assumed that he had principles too. "Are not principles what underpins civilised life?" I asked.

Exasperated by my interjections, he launched into a speech about how a Zionist state requires as its core principle that it be a Jewish state. One could play nice games about helping the Arabs, he said, but at the end of the day Israel had to be a Jewish Zionist state. He concluded, "I know what I have just said is elitist and Ashkenazi." There was a silence which seemed to last an eternity. He sat on the other side of the desk looking at the wall, because he could not bear to look at me directly, while I sat staring at him. Eventually I stood up and said, "Yes, it is." I offered him my hand; it was a long time before he took it.

The lesson I learned from this meeting was that many prominent left-wing Jews are not really interested in justice or the suffering of the Arab population. They engage in left-wing activity, I suspect, either because they feel it gives them and their country a more presentable face or because it helps them sleep a little easier at night. When I told Asad Ghanem, who has worked closely with this man, about our conversation, he could hardly believe it. "But he's the left," he said. "I've known him for some time, and he's the left." "Exactly," I replied.

The problems faced by Arab academics who want to promote equality at Israeli universities were revealed to me in a conversation with the head of the Jewish-Arab Centre, Faisal Azaiza. At the beginning of the academic year, he told me, he had printed a banner to hang above the entrance to the centre's office. On each side it said innocuously in Hebrew and Arabic, "Welcome to the students of Haifa University. Feel free to use the Jewish-Arab Centre." When the university's management heard about the sign, they were indignant, and they demanded that it be removed. They wanted it printed only in Hebrew, as are other official signs at the university. Dr. Azaiza had to appeal to the dean of the university to get special dispensation to print the sign in two languages.

His story left me speechless. Arabic is one of Israel's two official languages, and a fifth of the students at Haifa University are Arabic-speakers. What could possibly be the objection to including both languages on a sign for a Jewish-Arab Centre? But what astounded me even more was that no protests had come from the university's lecturers' association or from the Jewish students' union. What message does that send to the Arab students from what is supposed to be one of the more enlightened educational institutions in Israel?

Despite these incidents, I hoped to find in my area Jews who thought a little more like me. The Galilee, because its population is almost equally divided between Jews and Arabs, has more coexistence projects than anywhere else in the country. My experience with most, however, was far from reassuring. I attended a couple of meetings with one of the most left-wing, the Alternative Voice in the Galilee, whose Jewish and Arab members are active in the area around Tamra. My friend Dr. Uri Davis introduced me to the group, feeling that I would find it helpful to meet other left-wing Jews who wanted to alleviate the discrimination faced by their Arab neighbours.

The first meeting I attended was in Mitzpe Aviv, the luxury Jewish settlement right next to Tamra, built on land that was confiscated from our town. When I was introduced to the group as "Susan from Tamra," the Jewish chairman stared at me in bewilderment and asked, "From *where?*" I repeated that I lived in Tamra. He was not satisfied: "But where were you from before that?" I told him Tel Aviv. He had an uncomfortable smirk on his face that I had seen many times before from left-wingers. It said, "You have gone too far. You are embarrassing us. You are making us look bad."

The next meeting was a short distance away in the Arab town

of Sakhnin, where I struck up a conversation with a regular Arab participant. I asked him what he thought of these gatherings. He replied with an air of resignation: "Any contact with the Jews is better than none."

I soon realised that I had little to offer these groups, which pay mere lip service to the notion of coexistence. They concentrate on coffee mornings and getting-to-know-each-other sessions, but the Jewish participants generally refuse to allow any talk of what they term "politics." That approach can never work, because the problems faced by Arabs in the Galilee are profoundly political. The Jews who belong to the Alternative Voice enjoy their privileges in land, housing and economic allocations because of government policies that disadvantage their Arab neighbours. If Jews in these coexistence groups refuse to face that simple fact, how can they help the Galilee's Arabs?

This was illustrated in very stark fashion by the case of friends of mine who live in Sakhnin. Ali Zbeidat is married to a Dutch woman, Terese, and the couple have two delightful teenage daughters, Dina and Awda. For the past six years they have been living in a Kafkaesque world in which their beautiful home overlooking the olive trees that Ali's ancestors have farmed for generations is under constant threat of demolition. Their house is built on land owned by Ali's family, it lies inside Sakhnin's municipal boundaries and the Sakhnin municipality believes that they should be allowed to live there in peace. But neither Ali nor the municipality has any say over what happens to his home. A Jewish regional council called Misgav has been given jurisdiction over the land by the government, and it wants the house demolished. Thousands of Arab families have been caught in this kind of administrative trap created by the state to prevent Arab families from building homes and expanding the spaces they live in.

Ali and Terese are victims of the Judaisation of the Galilee. They have been paying endless fines to the Misgav council to try to fend off the demolition order, but Misgav is determined to enforce the destruction of their home through the courts. Ali was even arrested in a late-night police raid on his home and jailed for not paying a fine on time. Sakhnin has suggested to Misgav that the Jewish council return the small area on which Terese and Ali's home is built to Sakhnin's jurisdiction. Ali showed me the response from Misgav, which reveals everything about its policies. "We refuse to give even one centimetre of our land," it says. "In fact we want the opposite: we need more land and we want to take more of it into our jurisdiction."

Terese is scathing about the tepid support she has received from Alternative Voice, many of whose members belong to Jewish communities inside Misgav. She said, "At a personal level most of them are lovely people, but they really don't begin to understand what the problem here is. They don't want to get involved in what they call the politics of it. One told me, 'Don't worry, if the bulldozers come we will be there.' But by then it will be too late. We don't need solidarity visits, we need them to be lobbying their councillors, picketing Misgav's council offices, producing banners saying 'Stop demolishing homes' or 'Give Sakhnin back its land.' They must put pressure on their own leaders—that is the only thing I want from them."

I could not agree more. The Jewish members of Alternative Voice have to be ready to take on the government and the Jewish regional councils in a public showdown, but there is not the faintest sign that they are prepared to do it. Why? Because it would make their own lives too uncomfortable. Do I hear any of them saying, "Tamra is desperately overcrowded. The government has been promising for three years to return land to Tamra but has done nothing to make it happen. We in Mitzpe Aviv are on the land of Tamra, and if our government won't act, we will give the land back to Tamra ourselves"? Not a chance!

I did make one lasting friendship through Alternative Voice.

Harry Finkbeiner, a German non-Jew who moved to Israel after marrying an Israeli, Hannah, many years ago, lives on one of the most left-wing kibbutzim in the country, a short distance from me. Harduf is situated a kilometre or two from another Arab town, Shefaram, in a superb location high on a Galilean hilltop, where it enjoys commanding views of the coast and Haifa. Unlike most kibbutzim, Harduf was not built on the ruins of an Arab village. The state allocated the lands to it in the early 1980s. Harduf, like other kibbutzim, benefited from the generosity of the state because its members are Jewish. Today it is a wealthy community, with each family owning a lovely detached house with a neat garden. It has a flourishing farming business, including a deal with the dairy company Tnuva to produce organic food, and high-tech dairy sheds. The kibbutz has a large communal swimming pool, two playgrounds, a hostel, a kindergarten and one of only five Waldorf schools in Israel.* It is a truly wonderful, peaceful place to live. And it is committed to the principle of living in harmony with its Arab neighbours.

But even at Harduf, the practice of coexistence, as opposed to the principle, seems more than a little hollow. I was invited to see the kibbutz's Jewish-Arab meetings at first hand by the group's organiser, Yaakov. At a planted forest on its eastern side, the kibbutz has created what in less politically correct times would have been called a Red Indian camp, with a large, billowing awning tied between the trees and a campfire at its centre. There we congregated, but as is typical at such meetings, the Jewish members sat on one side and the Arabs on the other. I sat with the Arabs. The two sides got together only when photographs of them holding

---

*Waldorf schools educate children according to the principles established by the German social philosopher Rudolf Steiner, who believed that they should be given as much opportunity and creativity as possible in order to develop their personalities fully.

hands were needed; apparently these pictures are sent to left-wing Jewish organisations overseas as part of fund-raising drives.

By the campfire, each participant spoke in turn about the need for love, understanding and mutual respect. When it came to my turn, I talked of my reasons for moving to Tamra, such as to show Jews that most of the views they have of Arabs are based on emotion rather than fact. I asked the Jewish participants, "Why do you find it so difficult to come to Tamra, when we in Tamra have no problem coming to you?" The Jews looked stunned. (The question had been prompted by an earlier comment from Yaakov. Despite having lived in Harduf for twenty years, he admitted to me that he had never visited Tamra.) I also suggested to the group that coexistence could not work unless Jews and Arabs first had equality of citizenship. As the meeting broke up, the Jewish members either ignored me or said good-bye looking at the ground. It was as if I were holding up a mirror to them and they were too embarrassed or too appalled to look at the reflection. The Arabs, from Tamra, Shefaram and Sakhnin, came up and offered warm support. I decided that these campfire photo opportunities were not for me. They were intended to make Jews feel better, to let them believe they were doing their bit. I could not see how they were helping to end discrimination against Israel's Arab citizens.

The message of love and brotherhood promoted by the Jews of Alternative Voice and Harduf—to the exclusion of all political discussion—echoed an interesting analysis I had read by a British Jew, Paul Eisen, who is the director of Deir Yassin Remembered, an organisation committed to commemorating one of the worst massacres perpetrated by Jews on Palestinians in 1948. He argues that as the immorality of the Palestinian dispossession has become clearer to Jews in Israel and the Diaspora, they have fallen back on ever more convoluted moral justifications for their behaviour. One that appeals particularly to left-wingers is what he calls the "sin of moral equivalence," which claims that the core of the problem between Israelis and Palestinians is not the brutal dispossession of the Palestinian people but a tragic clash between two conflicting and equal rights:

> In this new narrative Israel is not guilty, because no one is guilty, and Israel is not the oppressor, because there is no oppressor. Everyone is an innocent victim. Variations on the theme include the "I've suffered, you've suffered, let's talk" approach, and what has been called the psychotherapy approach to conflict resolution, "You feel my pain and I'll feel yours." Proponents of this theory say that the two sides are not listening to each other. If only each side would hear the other's story a solution would surely be found. But it is not true that neither has heard the other's story. Palestinians have heard the Zionist story ad nauseam, and they have certainly heard enough about Jewish suffering. It is not, then, both sides that need to listen: it is Israelis, and Jews, who need to listen.

I regularly visited Harry Finkbeiner at his chiropractor's clinic in Harduf, where he was treating a problem in my back. He told me that his wife, Hannah, was curious to meet me and see how I lived in Tamra, so we arranged a date. Arriving with a bunch of flowers she had picked from her garden, she was at pains to point out to me that she was left-wing despite coming from a well-known military family. She asked me about my views of Israel, and I expressed my well-worn criticisms about the rampant discrimination and the lack of equality for its Arab citizens. She sat there silently and listened. Then she said with concern, "Susan, do you hate Jews?"

I could not quite believe what I had heard, and it took me a few moments to recover. I had to tell myself, *Susan, the problem is hers, not yours.* I assume Hannah had never heard her society examined in this way, except possibly by Arab or foreign critics, whom she could easily dismiss as anti-Semitic. In a less direct way, that was how she was trying to label me too. Her comment revealed to me very clearly the inability of most Jews to see what kind of society Israel has become. We expect Arabs to be self-critical, but we do not require the same of ourselves. Hannah's reaction was ludicrous—as ridiculous as that of those who accuse other Jews who are critical of Israel of being self-hating—but unfortunately, it is all too common. What she could not understand is that it is precisely because I take human rights so seriously and want to treat others the way I expect to be treated myself that I speak out.

Harry also introduced me to David Lisbona from Harduf, a Londoner who came to Israel twenty years ago. He is the coordinator of Middleway, a group of Israeli Arabs and Jews who visit Palestinians in the occupied territories in an attempt to promote peace. David came to have coffee at my home, and we had a difficult if amicable conversation. His assumption—one I come across all the time—was that my decision to move to Tamra was related in some strange way to the peace process. It is not just Jews who think like this; plenty of people in Tamra made the same assumption when I arrived. It disturbed me that they found it so hard to understand why a Jew would want to protest against the discrimination they, rather than the Palestinians in the occupied territories, experience.

I suggested to David that he would do better to deal with problems on his own doorstep than to charge off to the West Bank to give support to the Palestinians. "We are Israeli citizens, we pay our taxes to Israel, not the Palestinian Authority, so should we not see it as our first duty to take responsibility for the injustices that happen here? How can we cure injustices over there when we are blind to them here?" I asked.

David's answer was evasive. In Umm al-Fahm, he told me, an

Arab town which has earned a reputation for Islamic radicalism, no one was talking any longer of injustice. All the shopkeepers wanted now was for the Jews to come back on Shabbat and eat hummous again. I could not dispute the fact that the Arab population has been crushed in the past five years; since the start of the intifada, the community's most important political and religious leaders have been put on trial or jailed. There is little mood at the moment for confrontation. But even so, I warned him that the teenagers in Tamra are not going to accept what their parents and grandparents accepted. They want equality; they demand the same rights from the state as those given to Jews. "David, you want them to accept second best, to accept that they don't need to be equal citizens," I said. I told him Arab citizens would not remain resigned indefinitely to having their rights ignored and trampled on by the state. "The issues you are raising are not even in the Israeli consciousness," he said. *Well,* I thought, *they are not there because supposedly left-wing people like you are not putting them there.*

At the end of the meeting, David suggested I see Middleway in action and come on their next trip, a peace walk in the West Bank. Intrigued, I agreed.

I am not the sort of person who easily dons a white sash and a badge bearing the emblem of a tree and the slogan "The Middle Way." On the day of our peace walk, I kept wondering, *The middle way between what?* It is no clearer to me now. Maybe it was meant to convey only a sense of the participants' reasonableness and moderation.

As a group we drove to an army checkpoint—a gated section of the wall Israel is building in the West Bank, and the official crossing point into occupied territory—close to the Arab town of Bartaa. On the other side we were to meet a Palestinian delegation. As we passed through Bartaa, we had a chance to see for ourselves the insane folly of Israel's "security barrier." Until the completion of the wall in this area in the summer of 2004, Bartaa had been a thriving town straddling the Green Line, the border between Israel and the West Bank which was erased with Israel's conquest of the latter in 1967. Technically, Bartaa has existed in two halves: on one side of the line is the Palestinian town of Eastern Bartaa; and on the other the Israeli town of Western Bartaa. In practice, however, for nearly forty years the two sides have been indistinguishable from each other, and most residents have only a vague idea of where the official dividing line lies.

The inhabitants of both towns are ethnically Palestinian, though on the western side they hold Israeli IDs and on the eastern side Palestinian IDs, and are drawn from the same network of families and hamulas. Until the wall was built through the town, brothers and sisters, aunts and uncles lived on either side of what was just a theoretical border. They mingled freely in Bartaa's well-known market and could visit each other's homes without hindrance. That was still the situation when we visited in April 2004. But shortly afterwards the market, and with it the centre of life in Bartaa, was demolished to make way for the wall. Now the same families are effectively living in different countries, separated by razor wire, military guntowers and "sterile approach zones" protecting the wall from infiltrators.

At the crossing point I could feel the tension in the air. It was rather like approaching a high-security prison: there was razor wire everywhere, soldiers with machine guns and camouflaged watchtowers. These checkpoints have been built in deserted locations, surrounded by open ground to ensure a good line of vision for the soldiers. On the nearby hills, the scrub has been burned to improve visibility still further. On the Israeli side, some distance from the gate, was what I can only describe as a Third World bus stop. A small patch of corrugated iron sat atop four metal posts: this was the sole shelter from the sun provided by Israel for those waiting to cross. There were no seats, not even upturned crates; no toilets or refreshments. Nothing.

And because only Arabs are usually waiting to cross at these checkpoints, the wait can be long indeed. You are allowed to cross only when a soldier decides it is your time. It can take half an hour, or two hours, or most of the day, for him to crook his finger in your direction. You have to watch silently while he drinks from a can or chews on a sandwich or chats with a friend. However urgent your business, you must wait till he is ready to deal with you. At one point we saw an old man bent nearly double, who could walk only with the help of a stick, hobbling futilely towards a soldier, who shouted at him, "I didn't say you could approach yet." A young man propped up on crutches as he stood under the corrugated iron shelter told me that he had been waiting three hours to cross. He had not been told why there was a delay. Uncertainty like this hangs in the air all the time. A feeling pervades that control over your life, your fate, has passed to a stranger, a teenager dressed in an army uniform. It is not a pleasant feeling.

I could see across to the other side of the checkpoint, where the queue of cars and pedestrians waiting in the late-morning heat was even longer. Getting permission to enter Israel is always much harder than leaving it. Nearly all of the people I could see on the other side were probably Israelis, as Palestinians are rarely allowed to come into the country. But of course they were not Jews; they were Arab citizens returning from visits to relatives, from the weddings of cousins or the funerals of uncles, or from business trips.

Israel has made visiting the West Bank a maze of bureaucratic complications. Strictly speaking, Israeli citizens, whether Arabs or Jews, are not allowed to enter Palestinian territory. But one of the few surviving legacies of the Oslo Accords is the different security zones, called Zones A, B and C, into which the West Bank has been carved. Zone A, which covers the main Palestinian population centres, falls entirely under the control of the Palestinian Authority, while Zone C, the largest area of the West Bank, falls entirely under Israeli military control. Zone B is a grey area of supposed cooperation. Although Israeli citizens are banned from entering Zone A, it is possible for them to receive permits to enter Zones B and C.

Our group had permission to enter a Palestinian village called Yabad, not far from Jenin, which is in Zone C and so under Israeli military authority. David Lisbona had received written permission from the army for us to cross over that day, and the soldiers at the checkpoint already knew our details. I could see that our peace walk had taken a fearsome amount of organising. If we had been Jewish settlers, we could have passed effortlessly to the other side of this wall on special bypass roads that connect Israel with illegal settlements deep inside Palestinian territory. But Israel appeared to have little interest in making life easy for peace campaigners, even if the soldiers were not heaping on us the humiliation reserved for Arabs. Whether it is the army's intention or not, the menacing atmosphere at the checkpoint would be enough to put off all but the most committed peace activists.

After we crossed over, we were greeted by a Palestinian delegation that included Abdullah Barakat, the assistant to the governor of Jenin. The delegation escorted us to an olive grove close to the checkpoint, where we stood in a big circle and introduced ourselves. Several of the Jews made short speeches about how much they wanted to come to Palestine and how they brought with them love and understanding. I felt an impulse to shout out that the situation had long since passed the point where what was needed was love and understanding.

The Palestinians, in contrast, spoke about their desperate situation. They described how they did not have enough water or food and how when they were under curfew, they had no access to hospitals or to schools for their children for long periods. The dissonance between the Palestinians' explanation of how they were being stripped of their basic rights and the Jews' reply that their hearts were full of love was jarring. David's group appeared to have brought with it exactly the same flawed thinking that had been so visible by the campfire at Harduf. They were telling the Palestinians to keep politics out of this encounter and to concentrate on the belief that we were all one big happy family.

When it was my turn to speak, I said that I had come to witness the Palestinians' lives at first hand and that I did not believe there could be peace or coexistence until there was a full recognition of rights for the Palestinians. "When you are equals in every sense of that word, then we can live together," I concluded. Again I saw the hushed disapproval from the Jews that had been so obvious at the Harduf meeting. Afterwards the Palestinians came up to me and thanked me for what I had said. Abdullah Barakat told me, "You are welcome with us any time. Any time we can help you or you want to learn about our lives, or just visit us, you are welcome."

Among the Israeli group was a Sufi sheikh from Nazareth, Abdul Salam Menasre, who warned me to be careful of the other Jews on the walk: "My dear, they will hate you for what you have said." I asked him why. "Because you have come to the crucial issue—and that is of rights," he replied. "They have not even begun to reach that point."

It was noticeable how desperate the Palestinians, like Israel's Arab citizens, were for any contact they could have with Israeli Jews, whatever the terms. And just how unequal these meetings were. The Palestinians and Israel's Arab citizens kept their mouths shut, because they knew that the Jews would withdraw their contact and their support if they were to express their true feelings.

From that moment I felt an outsider, an observer of the day's proceedings. The Jewish members' hostility to me was apparent. It was made clear to me that most of the group did not agree with me when I said the Palestinians were entitled to equal rights by virtue of their being human. I was told in no uncertain terms that the Palestinians would get their rights when they had quietened down and started to behave themselves. In a subsequent e-mail forwarded to me by David Lisbona, Maya, one of the participants, said she had gone as an "emissary of love" and commented about the day's peace walk: "I heard words of political agendas and requests to help promote statehood . . . This is not my understanding of our purpose in visiting. Some of us found ways to express that we are here for a social spiritual foundation." I am not sure what "a social spiritual foundation" is, but whatever the group's intentions, the experience was yet more proof of the faultiness in the thinking of the left. Rights were being treated as though they were to be earned for good behaviour, like gold stars to be added to a child's name on the class register. There appeared to be no concept among these left-wing Jews that rights are basic and universal.

One exception was an ultra-Orthodox rabbi from Jerusalem, a young American named Eliyahu, who sought me out. "What you are doing is the most extreme form of Judaism," he said. "It encapsulates the very essence of what Judaism is about." Also in the group was a Swiss woman, Dominique Caillat, a non-Jew whose father had been active in the Swiss diplomatic corps. She had been commissioned by the German government to write a play about the conflict. Later in the day she came over and said, "I don't understand the Israeli left. Is this really it?" I told her it was, and about as far left as she would find. "It's appalling—they are so out of touch with the real issues," she said.

Jeeps arrived to drive us to Yabad, a village in bad shape after it had been damaged by a series of army incursions. We were taken to a courtyard where a wonderful lunch of barbecued meats, salads and fruits had been prepared. The villagers were poor but desperate to welcome us and show us that normal contact with Palestinians was possible. I found it heartbreaking and humbling to sit there and have them supply us with this feast, and I ate at some distance from the other Jewish members of the party, sitting among the local children, who wanted to practise their English. An Arab man in his mid-thirties came over and told me he had seen me on Al-Jazeera TV, which had interviewed me in Tamra some months earlier. He said, "I know why you are here. But tell me, why are *they* here? Have they come just to make their consciences feel better?" My impression is that many Arabs privately feel like that. There is huge resentment, anger and bitterness.

Israelis often criticise the Palestinians for lacking a proper peace camp, saying there is "no partner for peace" on the other side. But this is a grossly unfair interpretation. Many Palestinians are anxious to work for peace and want to join like-minded Israeli activists. The welcome given to the peace walk group I accompanied is confirmation of that. But when Palestinians meet Jewish peace activists, they find they are speaking an entirely different language. Discussion of strategies for nonviolent protest or campaigns of civil disobedience rarely comes from the Israelis; they talk only of love and understanding. Israelis also forget that the risks of taking part in peace activities are far greater for the Palestinian population than they are for Jews. Israeli soldiers have shown little compunction in shooting unarmed Palestinians who violate military orders, even if their actions pose no threat to the army. Palestinians also risk being arrested and held in Israeli jails for months or years, often without a trial or even a charge. All of this is well documented but is largely forgotten by Israeli peace activists, who take none of these risks when they stage officially approved peace walks.

After lunch we were driven back to the checkpoint. I noticed that two petrol pumps close to the olive grove where we had met, the only source of fuel for many kilometres around, had been crushed by a tank in the few hours we had been away. Why? Apparently the army had decided that Palestinian vehicles should not be allowed to refuel at the site anymore. It was an illustration of how quickly and unpredictably things change here, from day to day, from hour to hour, without warning or explanation. The result, if not the purpose, of such constant "reorganising" of Palestinian life is to make any attempt at establishing a daily routine unbearably stressful and difficult.

In Yabad I had gone walking in the old alleyways and had caused quite a stir. Women peering from their windows had shouted out, "Al-Jazeera, Al-Jazeera!" as I passed underneath. The people of Yabad, as in other Palestinian towns and villages, have spent much of the time in the last months and years under curfew, locked inside their homes. The only available entertainment is the television. This is the best explanation I could find for why everyone seemed to have seen me on the channel.

I asked many of the people I met, "If next time we could bring just one thing to help you, what would it be?" The answer was always the same: "We need more water." This was not surprising. The West Bank sits atop the biggest aquifers in the Holy Land—one reason given by some observers for why Israel is so reluctant to end the occupation and return the territory to Palestinian control. Most Palestinian water is taken by the Israeli water company, Mekorot, and sold to Israelis. While Palestinians in the West Bank have their water cut off at frequent intervals (and, I noticed, didn't even have enough water for flushing toilets), the Jewish settlers who live nearby splash around in private swimming pools and have sprinklers to keep their lawns green.

At the checkpoint, while we were waiting to cross back into Israel, I told David of the conversations I had had with the Palestinians, and added, "If you really want to help the people of Yabad, then arrange for tankers to deliver water to them." Looking uptight, he replied, "I will have to look into what the real problems are here." I thought, it's not as if it's a secret that there are huge water shortages in the West Bank. And if he doesn't know what the main problems are, why has he not asked the local inhabitants? His reply seemed like an evasion.

At the checkpoint I was spotted by a friend, Tamar, from Kibbutz Hazorea. She volunteers for Machsom Watch, one of the few left-wing groups that is doing something practical and positive to mitigate the worst effects of the occupation. The women of Machsom Watch stand at the checkpoints observing and noting down the behaviour of the Israeli soldiers. Their very presence there, they hope, deters some of the young soldiers from committing the worst human rights violations, but sometimes they try to intervene if a soldier is behaving in a particularly unreasonable manner. Tamar came over and threw her arms around me, causing great annoyance to the soldiers, one of whom shouted, "Move, move, I want this area sterile." I asked Tamar what she had seen while she had been on duty that day, and she said it had been relatively quiet. However, just before we had arrived, she said, a soldier had lost control and started shouting wildly at the queuing Palestinians, "We have to teach you bastards a lesson! You need to be taught a lesson!" She had gone over to ask him precisely what lessons he intended to teach the Palestinians. A commander quickly intervened, separating them and telling the soldier he would not tolerate that kind of behaviour.

I later told Harry about Tamar's account, and he said, "You know, Susan, I see it from all sides." I asked what exactly he saw from the occupying soldiers' side. "You have to understand the terrible compulsion in Israeli society to conform. These soldiers feel the pressure of the peer group," he replied. His answer reminded me of a question I often asked my parents about the Holocaust, to which I never received a satisfactory reply: "Why did so many German soldiers say they were only following or-

ders?" Harry's response served only to confirm my fears that we
have become a nation of soldiers simply following orders. That is
what our young people are being trained to do.

That afternoon two queues were trying to cross back into
Israel. One was a long tailback of cars, each of which was being
searched while its driver was questioned. The other was a line of
pedestrians, often the passengers of the cars, who had to pass
down a narrow alleyway separated from the drivers by razor wire
and a fence. Both male and female soldiers were on duty, and
the women were noticeably more aggressive than the men. One
blond soldier with a gun slung over her shoulder was screaming
obscenities and abuse at the Palestinians trying to cross. I could
see no reason for her behaviour apart from the fact that she
wanted to demonstrate to them and her male comrades her absolute power. I was reminded of an account by a prisoner in
Dachau in which he described the particular brutality of the
women guards.

Then the girl turned round to deal with the human traffic going in the other direction, and her gaze fell on me. "Where are
you from?" she demanded. It was as if she was saying, "What the
hell do you think you're doing over there with the Palestinians,
wasting my time?" I took out my ID card and handed it to her.
"So you are an Israeli." Yes, I said. She made me pass through the
metal detector, and the alarm sounded. I went through again
and set it off again. She was getting angrier and angrier, shouting at me. Finally a young male soldier told her he would take
over. He asked me to remove my earrings and watch, but I still
set off the alarm. Then it occurred to me that I was wearing a special belt for my back which included metal rods for support. I
lifted up my top to show it, in a farcical mimicry of the Palestinian men who are made to take off their shirts to show that
they are not wearing suicide belts. In the only moment of hu-
mour, the two of us laughed as I said, "If you don't mind, I pre-

fer not to have to get totally undressed here." He searched my bag and let me through. The female soldier was glowering at me the whole time. The next member of our party to be searched was shown even less respect. A woman from Fureidis, an Arab town close to Haifa, was taken off to a room for a strip search.

Although I had been deeply unimpressed by the peace walk, I continued my friendly contacts with the members of Kibbutz Harduf. Only later did I discover, almost by chance, that the criticism I had levelled at David Lisbona and his group during our first encounter—that he should take more notice of what was going on in his own backyard before chasing off to the West Bank—was closer to the truth than I could have imagined.

I was being treated at Harry's chiropractic clinic when I heard the familiar wail of the muezzin as he called Muslims to prayer. I knew there was no mosque in Harduf, so where was the sound coming from? Harry told me a Bedouin tribe lived right next to the kibbutz, in a village called Sawaed Chamera. The residents of Harduf and Sawaed, he said, were on excellent terms, and several of the Bedouins were employed on the kibbutz. The two communities loved each other like brothers, he remarked, in a phrase I would hear several times more when the people of Harduf and Sawaed spoke of each other.

Later Harry took me to Sawaed to meet the inhabitants. I was surprised by the village's proximity to Harduf. Just a small olive grove separated them, and from the last houses on Harduf's western flank you could make out the top of the mosque's minaret. Harry appeared to be right about the good relations between Harduf and Sawaed, especially compared to the usual dismal standards of dealings between Jewish and Arab communities. The kibbutz had even refused a special grant from the government to build a fence to "protect" itself from Sawaed. In contrast, neighbouring Jewish community, a moshav called Adi, had taken the money and built a fence to separate itself from its Bedouin neighbours. Although it is never reported outside Israel, countless such fences and walls separate Jewish and Arab communities. They go entirely ignored while the world concentrates on the much larger wall being built across the West Bank.

In Sawaed I met Taha, the village's sixty-four-year-old mukhtar, or leader, and one of his sons, Amin. Taha told me the history of his tribe, which had arrived in Palestine many generations ago from Syria. They had not owned land but had moved around the area, grazing their herds of cattle, camels, goats and sheep. In the summer they would move to an encampment on the "sand area," the shoreline by Haifa, and in winter they would move up into the Carmel hills in search of food for their animals. Taha said that Haifa had grown much busier following the First World War, as Jewish immigrants arrived from Europe. The sand area became increasingly developed, leading to tensions between what he called the "animal people," the Bedouins, and the "land people," the Jews.

The village of Sawaed was founded close to the town of Shefaram because of the vision of Taha's grandfather, Faizal Hussein Mohammed Sawaed, who foresaw a time when the Bedouin way of life would no longer be possible. He spotted the land on which the village now stands one day in 1920, when he was out riding his horse. It was owned by a Moroccan tribe known as the Mjirbin, and he negotiated to buy it from them. Taha said his grandfather chose this piece of land because of its beautiful location, overlooking the coastal plain towards Haifa, and its rich pastureland. The village also had easy access to the waters of the River Tzipori.

In 1942 Faizal died, and his son Faiz was recognised by the British Mandate authorities as the new mukhtar. During the war that founded Israel in 1948, Faiz decided the tribe would not flee to Lebanon or Syria, as the populations of many other villages did, but would remain close to its land. They therefore relocated to a site a little north of Karmiel, which Faiz thought would be safer. They encamped there for a few weeks, waiting for the fighting to subside. When they returned, they found their village untouched; it was too far from the main highways to be considered a threat by the advancing Israeli army.

Taha inherited the mantle of mukhtar from his father in 1965, at the age of twenty-four. That year was to prove fateful for his village. The Israeli government passed the Planning and Building Law, which, as Mohammed Abu Hayja of Ayn Hawd had explained to me, zoned all the land inside Israel, listing only 123 Arab communities as recognised by the state. That list sealed Sawaed's fate, just as it did Ayn Hawd's. Sawaed was not included, and it has been fighting ever since for proper recognition. Taha still has the tabu for his village, which dates from 1941, before the founding of Israel. The Jewish state implicitly recognised the legality of the document when it offered him money in exchange for the land, but he refused, and his village has been under threat of demolition ever since. On several occasions, he said, the authorities came to Sawaed and destroyed houses to try to intimidate the 250 villagers into selling. They have, however, refused to budge. "I am going to keep the land that my grandfather bought, and no one will force me off it," he said.

Taha's son Amin told me that Jewish land officials used to come after the demolitions, hoping the villagers had been softened up. On one occasion, he said, his uncle, Taha's brother, agreed to sell his share of the land to the state representatives. "He told the official to bring some scales and they would close the deal. The official asked why he wanted the scales. My uncle replied, 'We will put each lump of earth on one side of the scales and a similar weight of gold on the other, and then you will know how much this land costs.' We have not seen another official since that day."

But Amin says the villagers have to be on their guard at all times: "Once an old man from Shefaram came to my father, telling him he had no land left to build a home for his sons and asking if he could buy a plot of land from us. My father took pity on him and gave him the land at a low price. Only later did he find out that the man was really working for the state as a land buyer. This is the way the state hopes it can slowly take our land and homes from us." It made me wonder whether the members of Harduf knew how the land that had been given to the kibbutz was originally acquired by the state. In all my conversations with them, no one had ever told me. My impression was that none of them ever asked such questions. Maybe they were afraid to hear the answers.

As with other unrecognised villages, Sawaed receives no public services. It is not connected to the electricity or water grids, it has no sewerage services, it does not have proper roads. All the houses are illegal and under constant threat of demolition. Sawaed is invisible as far as the planning authorities are concerned, so they make no allowances for the villagers in terms of the provision of schools or doctors. The village's one recent success is a kindergarten building funded by the German government, which the state has promised not to demolish.

I asked Taha what he felt he had achieved for his village. "In reality I have nothing except the words of some of my Jewish friends that things will get better," he replied. When he told me that, it reverberated in my mind as a shameful indictment of Harduf. *I* could not live in the kibbutz and know that my neighbours were enduring these kinds of conditions. Why was Harduf not challenging the authorities to do something? Why were its members not picketing the government until the state agreed to give Sawaed the same privileges it gave Harduf? I strongly suspect that if Harduf publicly refused electricity or water from the state until it was also supplied to Sawaed, the ensuing media storm would win overnight the Bedouin village the rights for which it has been pleading for the past forty years.

Instead, the main debate inside Harduf about its relations

with Sawaed concerns the kibbutz's newly built swimming pool. After much discussion, Harduf has decided that it wants the pool to be open to its Arab neighbours, but there is much agonising about what that will entail in practice. Almost all of the men I spoke to expressed their concerns about the local Bedouin boys being able to watch the kibbutz's young girls at the swimming pool. "I am not sure I want my daughter being looked at by the boys of Sawaed when their own sisters are covered up," said one. This seemed to me a sort of soft, or liberal, racism. So what if the boys want to ogle their daughters? That is what boys do. Are Jewish boys not ogling these girls when they wander around the kibbutz wearing their crop-tops and skin-tight jeans?

My conversations in Harduf, I think, reflect in microcosm the problem of the Israeli left. The feeling that dominates in the kibbutz is, "The Bedouins must adopt our values and beliefs before we can allow them access to our community and our standards of living. We are superior to them because their lives are primitive." That approach can never lead to coexistence. One has to accept that differences exist. In mixing together as equals, the inhabitants of Harduf and Sawaed will find their own common ground. If the members of Harduf are right and the kibbutz's ways are superior to those of Sawaed, then the Bedouin youngsters will be influenced and changed by exposure to them. Maybe what really frightens the members of Harduf is the thought that actually they have as much to learn from Sawaed as Sawaed has to learn from them.

I do not want to sound overly critical of the members of Harduf. They have been trying to alleviate the worst injustices experienced by Sawaed's residents. For example, they paid for one of Sawaed's brightest children, Taha's son Amin, to go to Britain to complete his higher education as a sports teacher, and they now employ him at the kibbutz's prestigious Waldorf school. Harduf has also supplied a single pipe of water to the village, though many members of the kibbutz complain bitterly about the fact that a large number of the villagers in Sawaed do not pay them for the water. When I spoke to people in Harduf, they seemed to have no understanding of the economic pressures on their neighbours. Running your own private generator for electricity is not cheap. And all the villagers have to pay regular, heavy fines to the authorities to prevent their homes from being demolished. Fines can be as high as a thousand shekels (£120) per square metre. As a result, the people of Sawaed are constantly in debt to the state. Surely a wealthy and successful kibbutz like Harduf could afford to be a little more magnanimous in sparing the piped water.

Many of the inhabitants of Sawaed do not conform to the stereotype of the Bedouin that Israel likes to present to its Jewish citizens. One, for example, is a sociologist who has been forced to work far away, in the Negev, because there is no work in Sawaed. Another of Taha's sons, Amel, is a doctor who qualified in Italy. But Amin's achievements stand out. In his early forties, he is a bright, articulate, handsome man who speaks fluent Arabic, Hebrew, English and German. His early schooling was in Germany, paid for by his parents because of the difficulties of educating him properly in the Israeli system. The question of identity must be far more complicated for Amin than it is for me or for the kibbutzniks of Harduf. When I asked him how he saw himself, he replied, "I am Bedouin, Muslim, Palestinian and Israeli—in that order." He added, "Part of me feels proud to say 'I am Israeli,' but in a way this identity is imposed on me by the Jewish state." His behaviour as an Arab and as a Bedouin, he said, was always under scrutiny from Jews; he felt he had to be perfect, to prove himself, to be better than the Jews, to refrain from dissenting or being argumentative.

I had the strong sense that Amin did not really feel free to speak his mind or demand his rights, despite being better informed and better educated than most of the other villagers. I asked him if he felt pressure, given that Harduf had paid for his education, to be the model Arab. He skirted the issue: "You have to understand that we need to look in our own backyard before we blame others." He said some in Sawaed were even afraid of the village's being recognised, in case they would have to pay taxes for street lighting and garbage collection when they didn't have the money. "We don't serve in the army, so many of the villagers can't get proper work. They worry about how they can ever pay for services if the state provides them." The villagers appeared to be stuck in a circle of despair.

I felt that in some sense Amin's compliance had been bought, as he depended on Harduf for his education and his employment. When I heard the members of Harduf and the villagers of Sawaed refer to each other as brothers, it sounded like an evasion of the real issues that need to be addressed between them. The people of Sawaed know that the members of Harduf are the only allies they have in a system that abuses them at every turn; they know they cannot afford to upset the left-wingers who call them brothers. And I can understand how tempting it would be, if you lived in Harduf, to persuade yourself that there was a real brotherly love between you and the Bedouins. But the truth is that it is a romantic illusion, and neither side has the courage to admit it.

6

A TRAUMATISED SOCIETY

The first time I met Bar she was wearing army fatigues and had a rifle slung casually over her shoulder. Sitting with me overlooking the golden beaches of Herziliya, a little north of Tel Aviv, she was at pains to explain that she was not allowed to let the gun out of her sight. I had made contact with this twenty-year-old soldier through her parents, who live on a moshav close to Tamra. This Ashkenazi family and thousands of similar ones across the country were once the backbone of the Jewish state. They belonged to the pioneering rural cooperative communities, the moshavim and the kibbutzim, whose members toiled the land in the belief that they were making the desert bloom and who unquestioningly sent their children to fight a series of wars against the Arabs. These families produced the earliest leaders of Israeli society—the generals, the diplomats and the politicians. Their ethos was one of service and unwavering loyalty to the state.

But those days of Zionist certainty are coming to an end for privileged families like Bar's. Her mother is a left-wing extremist, or at least an extremist by Israeli standards, who wants an end to the occupation and the right of return for the Palestinian refugees. Her father, a former high-ranking officer in the army who is now in the security services, once took the establishment's view of the Palestinians: that they needed to be crushed and contained. Today he is a reluctant reader of *Ha'aretz* and in particular the columns of Gideon Levy. Most Israelis despise Levy and regard him as little more than a traitor for his reports of Palestinian suffering at the hands of Israeli soldiers. But Bar's father affirms that everything Levy writes about the occupied territories is true. "This is what the army does," he says despairingly to her. Bar describes her father as an increasingly irascible man living in a bewildering world, torn between his need to be a patriotic, loyal citizen and his understanding that Israel is committing grave war crimes. Unlike her parents, however, Bar is not opposed to the occupation. She believes both that it is needed to ensure Israel's survival in a hostile Middle East and that she has the same obligation as her friends from school to defend, and possibly die for, her country. Every state needs an army to protect it, she says, and Israel should be no different.

When we met, Bar was coming to the end of her six months' intensive training for a combat unit. She had yet to see any action in the occupied territories; indeed, she had never visited either the West Bank or Gaza. She had barely met a Palestinian, even one from inside Israel. Bar knew from her parents and from newspaper articles that the army does terrible things in ruling over the Palestinians. She also knew about the refusal movement—hundreds of soldiers have refused to serve in the occupied territories—but she said that path was not for her. "Why should I not serve when all my friends are in the army?" she said, before adding, "Anyway, it is too easy to refuse."

But there she was wrong. The refuseniks' numbers have remained low in part because it is so difficult for teenagers barely out of school, especially boys, to refuse to serve in their country's army. All male Israeli Jews are drafted at the age of seventeen or eighteen for three years of military service, except for religious Jews studying in special schools called yeshivas. (The country's

Arabs are also excluded from military service, except for the small and vulnerable Druse community and a tiny number of Bedouins—Israel's most deprived group—who are encouraged to volunteer, normally as desert trackers.) The state will usually do a quiet deal with the families of youngsters who simply want to avoid fighting, agreeing to give them a desk job well away from the occupied territories. But true conscientious objectors—either pacifists or nonpacifists who selectively refuse to join an army that is occupying another country—are hounded mercilessly by the state. They face spells in military jail, not just for refusing their initial conscription but also every time they refuse the call-up for their reserve duties, which they must continue to perform intermittently well into their forties. The refuseniks are effectively criminalised for much of their adult life.

Worse than the prison terms are the social pressures. Objectors are shunned by Israeli society, including their school friends and in some cases their parents and wider families. Their treatment is little different from that of those conscientious objectors in Britain during the First World War who received a white feather; the assumption is that they are cowards and happy to leave their country open to invasion. That is a heavy burden to endure when you are a teenager.

Economic pressures exist too. The refuseniks are excluded from a sort of secret society the Israeli military represents. Soldiers form powerful friendships with the other men and women in their battalions, and later in life these connections can help them win jobs, particularly in politics and the security services, as well as admittance to the more prestigious communities in Israel. In practice, refuseniks find themselves in much the same position as the Arab minority: because they have not served, they do not qualify for a whole basket of financial privileges, such as mortgages and government grants, as well as for many jobs for which military service is a precondition.

For Bar, at least, the pressures were less strong. A determined young woman can usually find excuses for forgoing military service: she can ask the family doctor for a certificate exempting her on medical grounds without too many questions being asked. As a last resort, she can even get pregnant. The ideological conflict is usually less acute too: women are not sent into combat units in the occupied territories unless they volunteer, so it is easy to keep away from the fighting. More than 1,300 men had refused to serve in the army by the time the first female objector, Laura Milo, was jailed in the summer of 2004 for refusing on grounds of conscience. She was not a pacifist but opposed serving in what she called an occupation army.

Bar saw things very differently from Laura. She said the stories she had heard of the atrocities and regular abuses by soldiers made her all the more determined to serve. And not just in a cushy job behind a desk well away from the frontline—she wanted to be in a combat unit enforcing the checkpoints, the blockades placed all over the roads of the West Bank and Gaza to allow or prevent Palestinian movement at Israel's unchallenged discretion. "If I am at the machsom [the checkpoint]," she explained, "I can show the Palestinians that there is a human side to Israelis, and not just the inhuman side they are used to." As well as hoping to prove to Palestinians that not all Jews are bad, she said she would show other soldiers by example that it is possible to be polite and civil at the checkpoint. She believed she could change the army from within.

I was concerned about how a young woman, still unsure of what she should be doing, of where her true moral responsibilities lay, would cope with the demands of enforcing an occupation that is illegal under international law and that daily forces soldiers to make immoral choices. I asked her whether she knew that while thirty Israeli soldiers were killed in combat in 2003, another forty-three killed themselves, mostly using their own guns. That was a 30 per cent increase in the army's suicide rate on the previous year. Although it is not widely discussed, reports show that mental health problems are rife in the army, especially among young conscripts doing their early military service. According to Brigadier General Eitan Levy, the head of the army's personnel division, between 30 and 40 per cent of conscripts seek referrals to a mental health officer during their first year of service.

I asked Bar to tell me about her training for checkpoint duty. She told me that she and her fellow conscripts spent most of their time with a senior officer who had served in a combat unit in the territories, who provided them with a series of scenarios they might face. One she recalled was the following: "What if you have been on guard duty for eight hours in hot and dusty conditions, and you are tired and irritable and want to sleep? There is a long queue of Palestinian pedestrians and vehicles that need searching. Then an ambulance arrives, and the driver tells you that someone is critically ill on the other side of the machsom. You want to tell the driver to go straight through, to reach the ill person on the other side, both because you are tired and because the person needing help is very ill, but you also know you should search the ambulance in case a suicide bomber is inside. What do you do?" Bar looked at me in bewilderment: "What *do* I do?" I wish I could have offered her an easy answer, but there was none. "Look, Bar," I said, "you have chosen to go into the army. You will face this kind of situation every day, several times a day."

I could see that this young woman was filled with doubts and questions. She said towards the end of our meeting that she was not sleeping well because such questions were tormenting her. The army, I thought, would not be able to help her resolve these issues. I asked her how she was getting along with the other soldiers in her unit. Usually soldiers form intense friendships during their service, bonds that last a lifetime. They become blood brothers and sisters. But Bar said she felt a distance: "Many of them just talk about how much they hate Arabs. They are filled with hatred. They say they can't wait to get behind a gun and show who is boss."

I wondered where such hatred sprang from at the age of eighteen. The only answer I could imagine—one confirmed by the accounts of left-wing Jews of their upbringing in Israel—was that these young people had been fed a diet of stories by their teachers and the media suggesting that the Palestinians want only to kill Jews, to drive them into the sea; that the Arabs are Nazis trying to replicate the Holocaust. Such ideas are reinforced by TV images of the aftermath of suicide bombings in Jerusalem and Tel Aviv. Of course, these youngsters had never been to Jenin or Nablus to test whether such stories were true. And when they did have the chance to visit these Palestinian cities, they would be there not to talk with Palestinians but to enforce the occupation behind the barrel of a gun.

Most Israeli youngsters have been brainwashed into fearing an amorphous enemy that wants to exterminate the Jews, and its only identifying feature—or so they are told—is that it is Arab. Such fears last beyond childhood, dominating reasoned argument among Israeli adults. So what checks are placed on the behaviour of an eighteen-year-old armed with a gun and licensed to behave as he or she thinks best? Soldiers are rarely punished when Palestinian civilians are killed because of their actions. Israel could, of course, wait till its youth have finished university and gained a little maturity and insight before recruiting them to the army. But the state wants them young, impressionable and angry. I admired Bar for thinking she could change this culture from within, but as we parted, I could not help thinking the attempt would prove futile.

It was a month before I saw Bar again, when she was on leave from her unit. She had just completed her first tour of duty, ten days manning a checkpoint in the volatile Palestinian city of

Hebron. Postings don't get much worse than Hebron. Here some 150,000 Palestinians live besieged by a few hundred fanatical armed Jewish settlers, who have taken over the city centre. Hundreds of soldiers are there to protect the settlers, effectively bringing life in much of the city to a permanent halt. The Hebrew media carry regular stories of the settlers, many of them Jewish fundamentalists from America, being guarded by soldiers as they attack local Palestinians, either with stones or with their own weapons. The settlers' children are taught to spit at Palestinians and to curse them as animals.

Bar arrived at my home in Tamra in the evening, telling me that her mother had been worried about her coming to an Arab town after dark. I did not know whether to laugh or cry at this misplaced concern. She sat in my living room in a floral summer dress, her dark hair tied up in a Bavarian-style bunch at the back of her head, wearing clumpy schoolgirl shoes and short white socks. Her innocent appearance combined with her pretty young face somehow made what she had to tell me even more disturbing than it would have been if she had been in uniform and armed. She was pale and nervous. I asked her how she felt about being in Hebron. Defensively, she replied, "I want to start by saying that there are some good people in my unit." She looked close to tears, so I didn't press her on what she meant by "good." She continued: "But when we start to talk about 'the Problem'—the situation with the Arabs—they become totally different people. I feel totally alone in my unit, because they all hate Arabs. If we don't talk about that subject, I get on with them like the best of friends. But as soon as that subject is raised, it's me versus them."

She said it was a real test of her principles to be on the checkpoint. The week before, on the day of a suicide bombing inside Israel, her unit had been given orders to shut down the checkpoint so that no one could pass. "We were told it was being closed for twenty-four hours and no one could cross for any reason—not to reach hospital because a relative had died, nothing," she said. But this was also the first day of the Palestinian school year, and in the morning hundreds of parents arrived with their children to cross the checkpoint to register them for classes. When their way was blocked, the parents grew increasingly angry and began shouting at the soldiers that the people of Hebron had nothing to do with the suicide bombing and that they should be let through. "It was terrible to see the little children standing there with their new school bags, waiting to go through, and us refusing to let them cross," Bar said. Then some of her friends in the unit approached the crowd with their guns levelled at them, shouting, "Fuck you! Get back!" Bar said she tried to be polite, telling the parents that she was sorry but they were not allowed to pass today because those were the orders. "And because I was nice to them, they just laughed at me and pushed past." I thought, what the hell did she expect? She was enforcing an occupation that was illegal under the Geneva and Hague conventions and carrying out immoral orders to punish the local Palestinian population, including small children, collectively. But I was more interested in how she had coped with their response. "I think this a test. I must learn to be firmer," she said.

Another incident troubled her. A few days earlier her unit had been sent on an operation to enter the homes of four Palestinian families to find if they had any materials that might be useful in making explosives. After the soldiers had forced their way into the homes, they were instructed to divide the men from the women and children and to keep them in different rooms. They were supposed to separate the Palestinians by pushing them apart at gunpoint. The message they were supposed to give to the Palestinians, Bar said, was simple: "Our guns are watching you at all times." The soldiers did not ransack the homes themselves, as happens in some units, but in each one they ordered a Palestinian captive to empty the drawers and wardrobes while a soldier stood close by with a gun pointed at him. Bar said she could not level her gun at the Palestinians and held it down at her side while she directed them with her hand, rather like a traffic officer. I asked her why she couldn't raise the gun. "I felt too uncomfortable," she said.

I suggested that maybe the reason she felt so uncomfortable was that she knew deep down that what she was being asked to do was immoral, that she knew it was wrong to invade these people's homes. I said, "Bar, has it not occurred to you that the whole occupation is illegal and is putting you in a position in which you are forced to make illegal and immoral choices?" She agreed, but said that was all the more reason that she had to be there. "I am there to show that there is a human face to Israel, that there are decent human beings here," she repeated. It appeared that she did not understand that she was already not behaving decently, that just by participating in the occupation she was compromised. She had been at the checkpoint for less than a fortnight, but the tension implicit in being a good soldier of the occupation was already almost too much for her to bear. As she continued her service, I suspected, she would come to appreciate that she had only two choices: to join the refuseniks or to slip into the same hardened behaviour she so criticised in the other soldiers. It would be a traumatic experience whichever way she went.

Bar told me that her unit had found nothing in the Palestinians' homes, and on their return to base they were called in by the commander for a debriefing. He asked if they had any questions. Bar asked, "Did you have prior information that there would be bomb-making equipment in these homes? What was the point of the operation?" The commander hemmed and hawed for a while before saying to her, "You have to remember that it is important that we show them who is in control." His answer seemed to trouble her as much as it did me. I asked her how she felt about the operation. "I saw these terrified children clutching at their parents and saw how we create hatred. If the children grow up seeing their parents being humiliated and abused at our hands, won't they just want vengeance?" I said she could always leave. "I hate the army and hate what it does, but I have to be part of it," she replied. I could only think, *God forbid she kills someone, or is killed herself.*

Bar had been a serving soldier in the occupied territories for only ten days, but already the moral dilemmas of trying to be good when one is ordered to do something essentially bad were tearing her apart. She looked close to a breakdown. The idea repeated as a mantra by Israeli society—that its army is the most moral in the world—had vanished into thin air for her. I hoped she would soon have the courage to refuse to serve. She was only beginning to see what serving in an occupation army entailed. If she carried on much longer, she would see far worse things.

For too long, a wall of silence has shielded many Israelis and the rest of the world from knowing about the abuses committed against Palestinian civilians in enforcing the occupation. Glimpses into this reality have occasionally been provided by the women of Machsom Watch, who issue monthly reports of the soldiers' behaviour at the few checkpoints they are able to observe. But almost no one apart from a few hardened activists reads those reports. Very occasionally, the Israeli army itself has admitted that things are not quite as wholesome as it would wish to convey. A handful of soldiers has been put on trial, revealing yet more clues as to what really takes place. One such trial began in September 2004. The accused was the commanding officer at the notorious Huwara checkpoint near Nablus, and the trial came about after the Israeli army's education division accidentally filmed him beating a handcuffed Palestinian and assaulting another man as he stood at the checkpoint with his wife and children. A subsequent investigation revealed that this officer had imposed a reign of terror at the checkpoint, including smashing the windscreens of cars waiting to cross. No fewer than seventy-two paratroopers, however, came to his defence, signing an affidavit presented to the court that the use of force at checkpoints was standard behaviour and was necessary if they were to carry out their assignments. The soldier's battalion commander, Lieutenant Colonel Guy Hazut, said in his testimony that he had often seen similar behaviour from ordinary soldiers but was disturbed to see an officer commit such abuses. Nevertheless, he called the defendant "an impressive officer in the battalion. He is cut from the same cloth from which we wish our officers to be made."

The self-enforced silence of ordinary soldiers, however, is finally coming to an end. For the first time combat soldiers are talking publicly about what they are doing—and not just in Hebrew for a local audience. A series of officers in elite combat units have submitted letters criticising the Israeli army for its immoral activities in the occupied territories. In the autumn of 2003, for example, twenty-eight reservist pilots issued a letter warning that they would no longer carry out attacks on Palestinian residential areas from the air. They were all suspended from duty, and two active pilots were dismissed. A year later, the *Maariv* newspaper revealed that four team commanders from the air force's undercover commando unit Kingfisher had written a letter to the chief of staff, Moshe Yaalon, saying that bulldozing houses was "immoral" and that the army "harms innocent civilians." None of the commanders, however, said they would refuse to carry out such immoral orders.

The personal accounts of less senior soldiers have had more impact. The first group to put on an exhibition of photographs and personal videotaped accounts of life in the army was a unit of soldiers who had recently finished a tour of duty in the

Palestinian city where Bar was serving, Hebron. Called "Breaking the Silence," the show was staged for a month in Tel Aviv and caused a storm of outrage in the Hebrew media. Military police raided the exhibition, claiming they were searching for evidence that might later be used in the prosecution of soldiers. Then, shortly afterwards, four of the soldiers who organised the event were interrogated on suspicion of having taken part in illegal actions. One of them, Micha Kurtz, observed of the police operation, "They're not going to shut us up, because we have a lot to say, and they're not going to scare us off."

Much of the sensation concerned the photographs, many of which depict the hatred felt by the Jewish settlers for Arabs. One shows a wall inside the Palestinian city spray-painted with the words "Arabs to the gas chambers." In another, settler children tear down the wall of a Palestinian shop brick by brick. Sixty sets of car keys were also on display, evidence of the common army practice of confiscating the keys of Palestinians caught driving in a forbidden area. They are supposed to be returned later to the driver, but often aren't, as the exhibit proved.

Just as powerful as these visual exhibits are the video accounts recorded by the soldiers. They vividly describe the hypocrisy of the occupation:

> Our job was to stop the Palestinians at the checkpoint and tell them they can't pass this way anymore. Maybe a month ago they could, but now they can't. On the other hand, there were all these old ladies who had to pass to get to their homes, so we'd point in the direction of the opening through which they could go without us noticing. It was an absurd situation. Our officers also knew about this opening. They told us about it. Nobody really cared about it. It made us wonder what we were doing at the checkpoint. Why was it forbidden to pass? It was really a form of collective punishment. You're not allowed to

pass because you're not allowed to pass. If you want to commit
a terrorist attack, turn right there and then left.

One soldier, a teacher in civilian life, explains how easy it is to
slip from the good intentions of someone like Bar into the barbarity of an occupation soldier:

> I was ashamed of myself the day I realised that I simply enjoy
> the feeling of power. Not merely enjoy it, I need it. And then,
> when someone [an Arab] suddenly says no to you, you say,
> What do you mean, no? Where do you get the chutzpah from
> to say no to me? Forget for a moment that I think that all those
> Jews [the Jewish settlers in Hebron] are mad, and I actually
> want peace and believe we should leave the territories—how
> dare you say no to me? I am the law! I am the law here!
>
> Once I was at a checkpoint, a temporary one, a so-called
> strangulation checkpoint blocking the entrance to a village.
> On one side a line of cars wanting to get out, and on the other
> side a line of cars wanting to get in, a huge line, and suddenly
> you have a mighty force at the tip of your fingers. I stand there,
> pointing at someone, gesturing to you to do this or that, and
> you do this or that, the car starts, moves towards me, halts be-
> side me. The next car follows, you signal, it stops. You start play-
> ing with them, like a computer game. You come here, you go
> there, like this. You barely move, you make them obey the tip
> of your finger. It's a mighty feeling.

Another soldier imagines how he would feel if the tables were
turned, if Palestinian soldiers were coming to search his parents'
home:

> I try to imagine the reverse situation: if they had entered my
> home, not a police force with a warrant but a unit of soldiers,

if they had burst into my home, shoved my mother and little sister into my bedroom and forced my father and my younger brother and me into the living room, pointing their guns at us, laughing, smiling, and we didn't always understand what the soldiers were saying while they emptied the drawers and searched through the things. Oops, it fell, broken—all kinds of photos, of my grandmother and grandfather, all kinds of sentimental things that you wouldn't want anyone else to see. There is no justification for this. If there is a suspicion that a terrorist has entered a house, so be it. But just to enter a home, any home: here, I've chosen one, look, what fun. We go in, we check it out, we cause a bit of injustice, we've asserted our military presence and then we move on.

Many of these accounts question what the point of having the soldiers in Hebron is. One soldier tells of a day when he was ordered to protect a visiting group of fundamentalist Jews:

That morning, a fairly big group arrived in Hebron, around fifteen Jews from France. They were all religious Jews. They were in a good mood, really having a great time, and I spent my entire shift following this gang of Jews around and trying to keep them from destroying the town. They just wandered around, picked up every stone they saw and started throwing them in Arabs' windows and overturning whatever they came across. There's no horror story here—they didn't catch some Arab and kill him or anything like that—but what bothered me is that maybe someone told them that there's a place in the world where a Jew can take all of his rage out on Arab people and simply do anything. Come to a Palestinian town and do whatever he wants, and the soldiers will always be there to back him up. Because that was my job, to protect them and make sure that nothing happened to them.

These testimonies are now being supported by the accounts of soldiers from other units. The refuseniks are seeking out disillusioned or troubled soldiers who are ready to speak up. One of the bloodiest places where Israelis are enforcing the occupation is Nablus, where much of the Palestinian population has been under curfew for dozens of days at a time, allowed out of their homes for only a few hours once a week to stock up on food. One soldier interviewed by the refuseniks explained how his combat unit, which he described as having an exemplary discipline record, operated in the city. Stationed in Nablus between December 2003 and May 2004, the unit scored sixteen *X*'s, meaning Palestinian deaths. Eleven of those killed were armed, and four were children. He said, "At some point they told us that since we took down only four kids, they [would] give our company tasks, because we are known as a company that doesn't hit innocent civilians." Some soldiers take killing a child very hard, he added, but others just laugh: "Yes, now I can draw a balloon on my weapon. A balloon instead of an *X*. Or a smiley."

Anyone who doubts the ease with which some Israeli soldiers shoot Palestinian children should consider the case of Iman al-Hams, a thirteen-year-old schoolgirl who was shot dead in cold blood in Gaza in late 2004 by an officer identified by the Israeli army as Captain R. The incident came to light only after soldiers under his command went to the Hebrew media on discovering that the army was trying to hush up the killing. On a taped radio conversation about the incident, Iman was identified as a "girl of about ten" who was "scared to death" when she was shot in the leg from an army position. According to the statements of other soldiers, as she lay bleeding on the ground, Captain R approached her to "confirm the kill" and shot her twice in the head. He walked away, then returned to empty his magazine into her body. Doctors found that she had been shot at least seventeen times. Shortly after the incident, Captain R is recorded saying, "Anything that's mobile, that moves in the zone, even if it's a three-year-old, needs to be killed. Over."

The Nablus soldier's unit was often allowed to go on shooting sprees in Nablus, he said, using live ammunition indiscriminately: "No one would ask why, no one would ask anything." If a child was killed, there would be no investigation or trial; the unit's commander would be fined a hundred shekels (£12). Out of his unit of nine soldiers, only three didn't behave "like retarded kids"; the rest enjoyed hurling stun grenades at children who threw stones at their armoured vehicles, even though the soldiers were in no danger. "There's no need to throw stun grenades at them, making them deaf for a month," he said.

The soldier confirmed suspicions aroused by widely seen TV footage of Israeli army tanks driving over parked Palestinian cars and electricity pylons; these were attempts to cause as much damage as possible, he explained. In some cases, during curfews, his unit's armoured vehicles would chase "live cars"—cars being driven by Palestinians—and crash into them. The driver would be beaten when he was caught. In other operations, if soldiers suspected they were closing in on a terrorist, they would take a neighbour as a human shield to knock on his door. That way, if the suspected man decided to resist arrest, the neighbour was more likely to be hit in the crossfire than a soldier. "It's obvious to me that this is wrong, but not strange," he said. "This is something that happens all the time. A well-known procedure." After a kill, the soldier said, his friends would prop up the corpse and take photographs with it. The pictures are "of people with a V sign over [the corpse's] head. They don't touch the corpse . . . There was no mutilation . . . but they took photos like twenty-year-olds in a normal world do." His account appeared to be substantiated a few months later, in November 2004, when the Israeli army began investigating reports of such incidents.

The soldier said that at the time, they had no sense that they were doing something wrong. "I mean, you don't have the awareness. I don't know. It sounds stupid, but you don't know how what you're doing is bad. Only later, maybe after two years, maybe after you become a commander and you become more balanced, grown up, you start realising what you did there."

I met one such reformed soldier by accident. I was returning from Herziliya by taxi when the driver, a Jewish man in his thirties named Eitan, asked me why I was heading for Tamra. When I told him I lived there, he asked, "Are you married to an Arab?" I said no, I had chosen to live there to challenge the way Jews see Arabs. "Then maybe I can talk to you," he said. He told me that he had just completed a two-month term in military prison for refusing to do his reserve duty in a tank unit in Gaza. "I realised over a period of time that we are crushing other human beings, and one day I just decided I couldn't do it anymore," he said. "I could no longer justify it to myself."

I had never been to the tiny Gaza Strip. It is almost impossible for Israelis other than soldiers and a few thousand Jewish settlers to enter the area, which is home to 1.2 million Palestinians. On the land the strip is entirely sealed off by an electrified fence, and its short coast is constantly patrolled by Israeli gunboats. It is the nearest thing imaginable to an open-air prison. To enter the strip, even diplomats and journalists must sign a waiver saying that in the event they are shot, they will not hold the army responsible. For this reason, the horrors that occur in Gaza are reported far less widely than they should be. The Israeli army has been carrying out some of its harshest operations there, particularly around Rafah. It has demolished hundreds of Palestinian homes in the usually fruitless search for tunnels built to smuggle cigarettes and weapons under the strip's southern border, shared with Egypt. During the course of the intifada, hundreds of Gazan children under the age of fifteen have been shot dead.

When Eitan told me that he had served in Gaza, I was interested in hearing his version of what was happening there. It is one thing to read about these things, quite another to meet a man who has seen it with his own eyes. What was it like? I asked. "You are in the tank and all you can see around you is hundreds of children aged between eight and fourteen, throwing stones at you," he said. "But to be honest, you don't feel threatened. You know you are in the tank and they can't hurt you." What happens while you are sitting in the tank? I asked. "You receive orders." What kind of orders? There was an uncomfortable pause before he replied, "Sometimes, orders to fire." I said, "Let us be clear, so there is no mistake. You are telling me that you receive orders to shoot at children who are unable to protect themselves and who don't pose any threat to you." There was total silence, which lasted several minutes, before I heard an almost inaudible whisper from the front seat: "Yes."

As we drove on in silence, I felt as if the whole weight of the country was falling on my shoulders, just as it had on Eitan's. I could no longer doubt that Israel was committing serious war crimes. I asked whether it had taken a long time for him to reach the point where he could refuse to serve in the army. "Yes, it was gradual," he said. "First of all I refused to serve in the tank, and so they put me on guard duty at the gate to Kfar Darom [an illegal Jewish settlement in Gaza]. But eventually I realised I could not carry on serving." Why had it taken so long? "I suppose peer pressure and the general pressure in Israeli society to conform. One is expected to be part of the herd, to stick together in times of trouble." He said that carrying out orders had pushed some of the people he served with over the edge, and that they were having psychiatric treatment or taking strong medication. Use of illegal drugs, particularly marijuana, was rife, just as it had been among American soldiers in Vietnam. "Is it safe to have soldiers on drugs behind guns?" I asked. "Probably not," he replied.

The psychological trauma inflicted on these soldiers does not affect their behaviour only when they are in uniform and serving in the occupied territories. As a notice at the entrance to the "Breaking the Silence" exhibition observed, "Hebron isn't in outer space. It's one hour from Jerusalem." These soldiers bring their dysfunctional behaviour back to Israel with them when they are on weekend leave and when they finish their tours of duty. They return to parents, partners and children living anything from a few minutes to a couple of hours from where they are enforcing the occupation. This may in part explain the reports of rocketing levels of domestic violence in Israel, as well as the high death toll on the roads.

But even more important, these soldiers return from their service with all their racist attitudes towards Arabs reinforced. Many pursue careers as policemen or security officers, where they work within a professional culture that treats all Arabs, including Arab citizens of Israel, as the enemy. This was the verdict of a Supreme Court judge, Justice Theodor Or, in his commission-of-enquiry report into the security forces' killing of thirteen unarmed Arab citizens in the Galilee in October 2000, at the start of the intifada. One of his central recommendations held that "it is important to act in order to uproot phenomena of negative prejudices that have been found regarding the Arab sector, even among veteran and esteemed police officers. The police must inculcate among its personnel the understanding that the Arab public as a whole is not their enemy, and that it is not to be treated as the enemy."

Israel feels and behaves like a traumatised society. How could it be any other way? Three Israelis whose paths have crossed mine during my time in Israel, however, have given me some hope for the future. They have demonstrated, in their different ways, that the traumatised society can be healed, slowly and patiently, from within. All three emerged from their military service deeply scarred but subsequently rebuilt their lives in ways that offer a vision of how Israel can begin to reform itself. Unlike most Israelis, they have understood and come to terms with the fact that the army corrupted them morally. They have also realised that it is within their power to seek in the mistakes of their past some of the solutions for the future. Each is trying to breathe life into another Israel.

I met Irit one evening in Kibbutz Harduf, where she is the principal of the community's Waldorf school. A small, delicate, soft-spoken woman in her mid-thirties, she is someone whom it is hard to picture ever serving on the frontlines of the army. But that is exactly what she was doing during the first Palestinian intifada, which erupted in the dying days of 1987 and stretched on for five years. Like Bar, Irit is from one of the established left-wing kibbutz families, the sort of family that once supplied the army with its leaders and best fighters. But by the time she received her call-up papers, the star of the kibbutz children was already waning and their place was being usurped by the sons and daughters of the more fanatical national-religious communities, many of them settlers in the occupied territories. "As a teenager," she told me, "I remember our teachers asking us, 'What's going on? Why aren't we producing the outstanding soldiers anymore?' There was a real sense of crisis. It was as though we weren't fulfilling our duty to take care of the country."

Irit had doubts about serving in the territories from the outset, but given her upbringing and the sense of national responsibility she was raised with, she never questioned that she would put on the uniform of the Israeli army and serve in one of its elite units. Almost immediately, however, she found herself being sent to the West Bank. "I have an uncle who was very senior in the army and could pull strings. He helped me to get out of the West Bank, but that didn't really solve the problem," she said. "I was still uncomfortable serving the occupation. I found myself facing a crisis: either I could refuse to serve and go to jail, or I could put off the problem a little longer by opting for the officers' course. I chose the officers' course. When I finished it, I got my new posting: I was being sent back to the West Bank. I cried for about forty-eight hours and then packed my things and went. I was an officer and could no longer get out of my responsibilities."

Irit was sent to Jenin, where she spent fourteen months as an operations officer, responsible for planning military missions in the town and its neighbouring refugee camp. As she recalled those days, her voice faded to barely a whisper. She alluded to the terrible things she had seen, often without managing to bring herself to describe them in words. "For the first four months I tried to escape the reality by planning all kinds of things in my mind, like destroying the whole of the [Jenin] camp," she explained. "I was suffering terribly. I couldn't sleep from what I was seeing and what I was doing. It wasn't even as though I was out on the battlefield. I was in the war room. But I saw enough . . ."

She was given a month's leave to visit her mother, who lived in Ireland, and she seriously considered never returning to Israel. But then, she says, she decided to go back and try her best to be a good officer and to be as humane as possible. "It was an important stage in my life. No one can come to me and say, 'You don't know what is going on there.' That is a common put-down from men in Israel. 'You have never been there, so you can't speak.' That is how they try to silence you. Nobody can tell me that I don't know what is going on there. I know very, very well."

Irit told me that she saw outrages committed by both sides. "There was a Palestinian woman with a broken bottle in her stomach because she was believed to have collaborated with the Israeli army. I saw the Palestinians' poverty, and I saw the Israeli soldiers destroying houses, taking women and children out of their homes and onto the streets so that they could bomb their homes . . . After fourteen months I felt like I had lost all my skin, that there was no skin around me anymore."

By the time Irit left the army, she said, she felt as if she needed twenty years to recover. That was twelve years ago, and it was clear that she had not entirely laid to rest the ghosts of those brief years in the army. Her military service had left her, she said, with a question she had been trying to answer ever since: what are the moral principles that should guide the relationships between individuals? Perhaps unsurprisingly, she has ended up in education and is now teaching citizenship classes in the kibbutz's high school. One of five Waldorf schools in Israel, Harduf's school is driven by a philosophy that children's learning abilities can best be developed by encouraging their natural talents to feel, create and think for themselves. The school is full of art and craftwork, which is how the children first explore the world around them, and only later do they slowly come to think about the meaning of things and make judgements.

"We try to be as free as possible, free from government interference and from economic constraints," says Irit. "We decided to let the state fund us, because otherwise only the rich could afford to send their children—which is the case with Waldorf schools in most other countries. Nonetheless, the parents have to contribute something, because the government never gives us enough. There is a constant fight for more money and more freedom. The freedom bit is key. In other Israeli schools, teachers can't really teach what they want to. Sometimes it's because the Ministry of Education interferes, and sometimes it's just because teachers don't realise that they are allowed to teach a much wider range of things. Too many are given the textbooks and simply assume they must teach what is written in them."

Israel's citizenship curriculum, which is taught only to children in the last years before their matriculation exams and their military service, is less dishonest than that of subjects such as history, she says. "In history it's pretty easy to manipulate the facts, but in citizenship classes it's a little harder. The citizenship textbook we use is the same in both Arab and Jewish schools, which is very unusual. Equality is at the core of the concept of citizenship, so it has to be the same book. When they wrote the curriculum, the officials knew both Jews and Arabs would be using it, so it's a little bit more balanced than normal, but still . . . it's a Jewish country. That's even the title of the textbook: *Being a Citizen in Israel: A Jewish Democratic Country.*

"I have to teach what is in the book, and the students need that to pass their bagrut [matriculation] exam. However, most Israeli teachers understand that there is a contradiction at the heart of what we teach: something is clearly not right with the concept of a state that is both Jewish and democratic. But that is the basis of the whole subject; it's the theme of the whole course of study. I know most other teachers don't ask questions in class about how it can be both a Jewish and a democratic country. OK, they will admit to the children that there are differences of opinion: some Israelis, for example, think we should live in a religious state, and others think the settlers should leave the occupied territories. It's widely agreed that the Jewish holidays should be the formal holidays. You can tell lots of nice stories about these things. But as to its being a Jewish and a democratic country—that can't be questioned."

In her classes, Irit tries to expand the subject beyond the strict bounds of the curriculum, encompassing topics rarely touched on in Israeli schools, either Jewish or Arab. She takes her students on a journey through Israeli society, beginning with the Ashkenazim, the WASPs of Israel, the white, mainly European pioneers like her own family who founded the state. Socialists and nationalists, they built the country and still hold most of the key positions in the army, academia, the media, the judiciary, business and politics. Then she discusses the rise of the national-religious, the first group in Israel to challenge the pre-eminence of the secular Ashkenazis. Drawing their strength from a literalist reading of the scriptures, they found their moment with the capture of the Palestinian territories in 1967 and the vision of a Greater Israel. Ever since, they have been working to take the West Bank and Gaza from the Palestinians through an inexorable process of settlement-building, backed by government funds. Next she examines the difficulties posed by the swelling ranks of the Mizrahim, the Jews who were encouraged or forced to leave neighbouring Arab countries and move to Israel after the establishment of the Jewish state. Their arrival posed a difficult question for the state's Ashkenazi founders: was Israel to try to remain a cohesive society of one colour or to open itself to becoming a more fractured but pluralistic society? The same tensions have been exacerbated by the arrival of other, later Jewish immigrant groups, such as the Russians and the Ethiopians.

Irit also discusses the failure to integrate into Israeli society the Haredim, ultra-Orthodox Jews who place their allegiance to God well before their loyalty to a Jewish state and its secular laws. In fact, Israeli leaders have done their best to avoid confronting the contradictory impulses of the secular and religious communities inside the country. They even abandoned the attempt at drafting a constitution, as promised in the Declaration of Independence of May 1948, after recognising that it would break the fragile Jewish consensus holding together the new state. Instead, Israel has failed to enact important legislation on human rights that would upset the ultra-Orthodox and has given wide-ranging jurisdiction to Orthodox rabbis to determine personal-status issues governing births, marriages and deaths and deciding who is a Jew. Secular and religious laws therefore exist in uncomfortable parallel.

The hardest part of the course comes when Irit's lessons cut through the country's founding myths to discuss its real history and the situation of the Arab minority. She says, "I teach the students about the country before 1948 and about the war in 1948. I tell them, 'Most of the people here used to be Arabs, do you know that?' I tell them the numbers and I show them the maps. They can see that before 1948 there were hundreds of villages that are no longer here, and that after 1949 the maps show fifty or sixty Jewish villages in the same place. There is no mention of the Arab villages having ever existed. They can see it with their own eyes for the first time. For many of them it's like jumping into deep, deep water, and they are very afraid. They go home, they sleep, and they come back the next day and say, 'Was it the same in the Holocaust? Did we suffer the same in the Holocaust?'

"As a teacher I find these thoughts troubling. There is no need to equate the Holocaust with the Nakba, but that doesn't make what happened in 1948 all right. The Holocaust was bad enough, and what the Arabs suffered was bad enough. To lose your village and lose your land is bad enough. It creates an ideal atmosphere for breeding hate and violence and war. And the combination of their hate and fear and our hate and fear is lethal. To heal this problem, we have to notice and understand the Other and to stop thinking about our own suffering all the time. My grandmother's family died in Auschwitz, but if you are stuck in your suffering all the time, you can do nothing positive with it. Better to look into the mirror and tell yourself, 'I am afraid of them, I am afraid of losing my country and my land. I am afraid they are going to kill me.' Even inside me I know there is a layer of this fear which warns me that one day there will not be a Jewish majority here, and maybe there won't be democracy either. There is a fear, and it's all right to admit that I'm afraid, because then I can do something with that fear. I can educate other people, I can meet and share my fears with other people. To ignore it and say it is not there is a lie. But if I can work with it, at least there is hope."

If Irit still struggles with her own fears after years of confronting them, her students find it far harder. "During these classes I see fear, resistance, shock. And great shame. They tell me they don't want to belong to this society. They say, 'It's not mine. I'll go to India, or live in Europe.' I feel the same sometimes. My husband and I start asking ourselves why we don't move to Switzerland, where my sister lives and where it's green and quiet. Or New Zealand."

Compared to Irit, who is quietly trying to change the way young Jews passing through her school view their citizenship, Daphna Golan has enjoyed a much higher profile and more notoriety. A law lecturer at Hebrew University in Jerusalem, where she teaches human rights, she is also one of the founders of Btselem, possibly Israel's most famous human rights organisation. Btselem has been working tirelessly since the first intifada to document abuses by Israelis in the occupied territories and to educate the Jewish public and the international community about the human rights violations that are common there. Its reports regularly embarrass the Israeli government and the army. Daphna is also a former director of Bat Shalom, a women's peace group opposed to both the occupation and the militarisation of Israeli society.

Daphna and I have become good friends through another aspect of her work. Like me, she is heavily involved in Mahapach, helping to advance social rights and create local leadership in deprived communities, Jewish and Arab. Both of us are committed to a greater role for civil society in Israel, and to trying to strengthen it against the encroachment of the military that we see all around us. I admire Daphna for her determination to fight on all fronts against prejudice, racism and discrimination.

At her home in West Jerusalem, she told me that it had dawned on her only slowly that much of what she had been told since her childhood about Israel and its history was untrue. "All through my life I had heard things on the radio or been taught things at school that seemed hard to believe. But the turning point came for me during the war in Lebanon," she said. Israel's invasion of Lebanon in 1982 was a turning point for many Israelis. Until the early 1970s, only about a hundred Jews had resisted the national draft. Although the numbers crept up after the occupation of the West Bank and Gaza in 1967, refusal remained a minor phenomenon. But the invasion of Lebanon severely tested the patriotism of Jews raised on the doctrine of Israel's "purity of arms." Personally directed by Ariel Sharon, the march into Lebanon included an attempt to install a puppet regime in Beirut that would be sympathetic to Israel, the horrors of Sabra and Chatilla, two Palestinian refugee camps where many of the inhabitants were butchered by Lebanese Christian militias under the watch of the Israeli army, and eighteen years of Israeli occupation of south Lebanon. The death toll from the invasion is estimated at nearly 16,000 Arabs, most of them civilians, and 650 Israeli soldiers.

For the first time the principle of limited refusal gained legitimacy among sections of the Jewish public. A senior brigade commander, Colonel Eli Geva, refused to lead his troops into Beirut and later resigned his post in protest. A letter signed by 86 reservists, including 15 officers, stated their opposition to the war and requested military service only within Israel. And a new refusers' organisation, Yesh Gvul (There Is a Limit), argued for a border beyond which Israeli soldiers should not serve. By June 1983, some 1,700 soldiers had joined. Fifteen months after the invasion, in September 1983, 86 Israelis had been jailed for refusing to serve. Probably many more were dealt with quietly by the army to avoid publicity.

Daphna recalled a formative moment in her own decision to oppose the invasion: "It was a rainy winter's day, and I heard the radio presenter announce that our planes had bombed south Lebanon and returned home safely. It was a line I had heard hundreds of times before, but that day, maybe because of the rain and the cold, it sounded like too much of a lie. I thought, 'What do they mean, the planes "bombed"?' All sorts of questions flooded into my mind. Where did those bombs fall, whose homes did they destroy, where are those families now, how are they coping without a home on this cold, wet night? I had images of Lebanese families standing amid the rubble of their bombed homes, and I asked myself, 'Why are we never told what happens to the people we bomb?' Afterwards I became very active in Yesh Gvul, which defined a border that soldiers should not cross.

"Another moment came with the birth of my daughter. I thought, 'What am I going to tell her when she grows up? That I did nothing?' " The geographical proximity of Palestinians to Israel also made their plight difficult to ignore. "I think there is no way we can say we are a democracy without taking into account what happens to the Palestinians. That feeling is even more pressing when you live in Jerusalem, which is so close and yet so far from the Palestinians. During the first intifada we could hear the helicopters and the bombing going on, so it was very difficult not to get involved."

Today, however, with the system of checkpoints and the erection of the wall, Daphna fears that it is harder for Israelis to connect with and understand what is happening in their name in the occupied territories. She told me, "I want my students to see what is going on, but the university won't let me take them into occupied territory. In fact, it is now usually illegal for Israelis to enter the West Bank or Gaza except as settlers or soldiers. But I do take them to the checkpoints between Israel and the West Bank, particularly those in East Jerusalem." She says few parents know what their soldier children are up to in the occupied territories. "I talked with some of the mothers of the soldiers who organised the 'Breaking the Silence' exhibition, and they all said they had no idea that their sons were behaving that way. 'We were sure that our boys were not like that,' they said. But I thought, no way. The moment you send them there, that is what is going to happen. Some soldiers behave worse than others, but you are forcing them into an impossible situation, one they will never be able to cope with."

Daphna worries that the minds of both Israelis and Jews in the Diaspora are profoundly closed to the idea of acknowledging Palestinian suffering. As she says, "We are a people who, because of our history, have attached so much importance to memory and the act of remembering, and yet we refuse to allow another people, the Palestinians, their own memory and their own feelings about the past." She gave me an example of that kind of psychological and emotional blockage: "We had a visit from a delegation of the Canadian Friends of Hebrew University, and several of my law students spoke to them. All my students are working for human rights organisations, and the stories they were telling truly confused the Canadian visitors. One student, a Palestinian who works with Rabbis for Human Rights, explained that she was involved in interviewing families whose homes had been demolished in East Jerusalem. The delegates came up to me afterwards, saying, 'What does she mean? Israel isn't demolishing houses in Jerusalem.' I tried to explain that master plans were never approved for East Jerusalem, so the Palestinian inhabitants could not get building permits. They had no choice but to build illegally, and the authorities responded by demolishing their homes. The Canadians were shocked, but not in a positive way. My impression was that they still went away with closed minds. It was information they were not ready to hear. One said, 'Do you teach them about human rights in Arab countries?' Another said, 'How can you teach them about rights when we are facing suicide bombers?' They could not begin to see that the Israeli army was terrorising Palestinians."

There are glimmers of hope, however. "There has been some

progress," Daphna acknowledges. "For fifteen years I have been saying the same things about the occupation, but it sounds much more legitimate now than it did then. When we tried to talk about the occupied territories in the late 1980s, people would deny that the West Bank and Gaza were even occupied. They would get really abusive. I think a big change has come about because the information is so much more accessible now. In many ways, the big issue in Israel has shifted away from questions about the occupation to questions about the nature of Israel as a Jewish state. Nowadays that is a much more contentious issue than the idea of a Palestinian state. The majority of Israelis understand that the occupation cannot go on. But if a Palestinian state is created, it will throw the question back to us about what kind of country we want Israel to be: should it be a Jewish state or a state of all its citizens? That is a debate most Israelis are not ready to have, because it would signal the beginning of the end of Israel's being a Jewish state, and it would open the door to the Palestinian refugees' right to return. It is a given for 99 per cent of Israeli Jews that the country must be a Jewish state. To an outsider it probably sounds bizarre to object to the idea of a state for all its citizens. But I teach at a law school, and everyone there thinks I'm nuts even to consider the idea. You'd think that university students and lecturers would be all in favour of a state for all its citizens, but my guess is I'm alone in supporting it."

Daphna believes we will see the establishment of a Palestinian state in the coming years, and that we must wait till that day before beginning a discussion about the status of Israel's Palestinian citizens. "Most Jews realise that there should be some kind of political negotiation of a Palestinian state—not by this government, but maybe by the next one. Eventually there will be a Palestinian state, and then the real discussion will start about what happens here in Israel. We can't begin discussing our future as citizens here unless there is a solution in the occupied territories. Once there is a serious negotiation about two states, then the position of the Arabs in Israel will have to be raised. This internal discussion can be seriously confronted only when a Palestinian state exists. Until then the Arabs will always be seen as the enemy. That is the only way I can understand the racism towards Arabs. Why do we have it? Because in the imagination of Jews, Tamra, Jenin, Nazareth, Ramallah—they are all enemy territory."

I am not convinced by the final part of Daphna's argument. Why is she so sure that Israel will be ready to make the sacrifices necessary to create a Palestinian state in the occupied territories when it cannot bring itself to do something that should be far easier: recognise the rights of its Arab minority and the equality of their citizenship? My feeling is that all the elements of the equation will have to be dealt with together, and a just solution for the Palestinians in the occupied territories will require a similar settlement for Palestinians who are citizens of Israel and Palestinians living in exile as refugees. Israel appears so reluctant to create a viable Palestinian state precisely because it will open up the question of what constitutes justice for these other two long-overlooked groups. It will reopen the debate about what really happened in 1948, a history that has been overshadowed by what happened following Israel's conquest of the West Bank and Gaza in 1967. It will bring the war crimes of 1948 back into the spotlight, and that is what really frightens ordinary Israelis.

Irit and Daphna have been trying to effect change by educating Jews about the issues of citizenship and human rights. But however important these issues are, they are not in themselves enough. Israelis also have to face the tough moral questions raised by the way Israel was founded. They have to be reconciled to their past and prepared to apologise for it. Only once they have recognised the historic injustices done to the Palestinian people as a whole in 1948 can they begin to make amends today.

I was under the impression that no organised attempt was being made to address such difficult questions in Israel until friends in Tamra told me about Eitan Bronstein, the founder of a small pioneering organisation called Zochrot (Remembering). Later I heard that he was one of the organisers of a right-of-return conference in Haifa which I was due to attend in the spring of 2004. At the conference I sought him out, only to discover that he had been trying to meet me too. He had read about me in *Ha'aretz* and was pleased to find that we held the same views about the need to educate Jews about the Nakba.

Eitan's participation in the conference, which addressed the rights of some five million Palestinian refugees to return to Israel, revealed everything about the bravery of this man. The right of return is the ultimate taboo for Israelis, because it threatens to end the demographic superiority of Jews and thus the state's pretensions to being both Jewish and democratic. Simply put, the existence of the Law of Return, which encourages Jewish migration to Israel, and the ban on a right of return, which would enable Palestinian refugees to reclaim the homes stolen from them in 1948, constitute together a sophisticated way in which to skew the numbers inside the state to ensure Jewish dominance. Israel is a democracy made to measure: the majority will decide, but only after we have first made sure that Jews are the majority. The conference was the first time a major debate on the right of Palestinian return had ever been held inside Israel. Zochrot's participation alongside several Arab groups was the key to ensuring that the event took place.

Zochrot, which counts a few hundred Israeli Jews among its members, was founded in 2002 and has since been developing a programme to teach Jews that the war they celebrate as their independence is also the Palestinians' Nakba. A website database called "Remembering the Nakba in Hebrew" offers historical information about what took place in 1948, including maps showing the destroyed villages and personal accounts from those who lost their homes. Zochrot stages study days on the Nakba and the plight of the refugees. But most important, it arranges tours of the villages that were destroyed, including regular ceremonies at which a signpost in both Hebrew and Arabic is erected at the site, giving the village's name and basic details about its inhabitants. Such signposts provoke extremely hostile reactions from any Jews who see them. Eitan says they rarely survive more than a few minutes or hours before being torn down.

I have huge admiration for Eitan and his brave stance in the face of so much hostility. The extent to which he is brushing against the grain of his society was revealed in the summer of 2004, when a commentary in *Maariv* denounced him and his organisation in libellous terms under the headline "Hamas Among Us." The paper equated Zochrot's objectives with what it described as the goal of the Islamic fundamentalist group Hamas: to drive the Jews into the sea.

Sitting in a café in Kafr Shemaryahu, outside Herziliya, Eitan told me that the transition from being a loyal Israeli to being a dissenter had not been easy. "I was raised on a kibbutz near Tulkaram to be both a good citizen and a good soldier," he said. "In those days there existed between the various kibbutzim a sort of competition for which would produce more combat soldiers and pilots and which would have more soldiers in the elite units. I joined an artillery unit in November 1979 and finished my service in November 1982. I think it would be true to say that by the yardsticks of my society, I was an excellent soldier."

But Eitan reached a moment of personal crisis when the government decided to invade Lebanon, five months before his military service finished. "From the very start I was against it," he explained. "All of us in the army knew that the real plan was to reach Beirut, despite the lies [Prime Minister Menachem] Begin told about us not going within forty kilometres of the city. The others in my unit were very excited about going, but I was at the end of my three years and I did not want to get involved. At the outbreak of the war I was away on a course for tank commanders. On Saturday night our commanders started calling each of us by phone to order us to return to base. I was at home on the kibbutz and managed to avoid the calls. So the next day, on Sunday, I went to the place where the course was being held to find it completely empty. I had no choice but to go back to the base, south of Beersheba. When I arrived, my friends were very angry. 'Where have you been?' they said. I played dumb, as though I didn't know what was going on. It was before the arrival of cellular phones.

"In fact we weren't called up to the fighting, which disappointed everyone else. However, by October, when the main battles were over, we were sent to Lebanon for one week. I had never disobeyed an order in my life, so I went for the week. A month later I was released from the army, but I had only postponed the problem. I knew that within six months I would get my reserve call-up. I talked to other reservists on my kibbutz, but while they didn't support the war, there was no way they were going to question an order. By then Yesh Gvul had started, and I decided to join them and refuse to report for duty. I was jailed for one month. It was a moment of profound personal crisis: I had crossed the red line from being a good citizen-soldier to a refuser. Later, when the first intifada came, I already knew that I was going to refuse to go. I was jailed twice. But by then it had become something routine and was not a dilemma."

Eitan began a new career, at the margins of Israeli society. For the past ten years he has worked as a teacher at the School for Peace at Neve Shalom/Wahat al-Salam, a unique community north of Jerusalem where Jews and Arabs live in a cooperative environment on an equal footing. Built on private land that belongs to the Catholic Church, the village is, according to its website, regarded by the state as a threat to the status quo: "The government tolerates the existence of the village and gives the minimum of support required by its municipal status." As a director of the school's youth programme, Eitan has facilitated hundreds of encounters between Jews and Palestinians.

"What I found out was that a huge gulf of understanding about the past, about 1948, existed between the two peoples," he says. "If you compare their respective positions concerning the 1967 occupation of the West Bank and Gaza, you won't find this gap. Even Jews who are in favour of the occupation understand that the Palestinians don't like it, that it harms them in some way. And many Israelis oppose the occupation and want to find a way to end it. Even [Prime Minister Ariel] Sharon says the occupation is not OK. So there is some sort of consensus on this issue. But I started to understand that 1948 was the key period, rather than 1967, and that it was determining relations between the two peoples in this land.

"I also realised that there was a huge gap in terms of the understanding of the two sides about what had happened. One side, the Palestinians, was completely defeated, exiled and dispossessed—and that is how they see it. The other side, the Jews, won an incredible victory, but they don't therefore concede that the other side was the loser. Instead they say things like 'It was the Palestinians' fault that they chose to fight us,' or 'We didn't start anything,' or 'We just wanted to be free and have a state.' When they do admit that their victory came at the expense of the Palestinians, such as in the case of terrible massacres like the one at Deir Yassin, a village where more than a hundred Palestinian civilians were butchered by Jewish militias, these events are seen as exceptional incidents. 'That was carried out by a few bad apples,' or 'That stuff happens in any war,' they say.

"So there is this huge gap in the understanding of both sides about what took place. To be honest, neither side has much idea about what really did happen. Even the Palestinians mostly rely on their own families' personal experiences of 1948 for their understanding of these events, largely because they are not taught about them in school. They don't have a wider view of what happened. It seemed that it was an important task to deal with this lack of understanding on both sides; that until we deal with it, there is no chance of a reconciliation."

A personal turning point came for Eitan while he was taking groups of Jews on an "alternative tour" around an area close to Neve Shalom called Canada Park, an Israeli tourist attraction just inside the occupied territories. It has been built over three Palestinian villages destroyed after 1967: Yalu, Imwas and Beit Nuba. Before the development of my own understanding of Israeli history, I, like thousands of other Jews, had enjoyed hiking through Canada Park, with its forests and views.

"Canada Park was established in the 1970s by the Jewish National Fund, using $15 million in tax-deductible donations from all over Canada," Eitan told me. "The JNF created a very beautiful and different sort of park. Many parks in Israel are built over destroyed villages. South Africa Park is built over the village of Lubia in the Galilee, for example. There you have wooden tables and a space to have a barbecue at the weekends or on holidays. But Canada Park is more like a museum or an educational space. The money has been invested in re-creating the traditional ways of agriculture. Through a series of signs and notices, visitors learn about the old methods of farming and about the area's Jewish, Roman, Byzantine and Ottoman history. All its history is there, apart from any reference to its Palestinian history. Despite the destruction of the Palestinian houses, two of the cemeteries remain, as do the water wells, but there is no information about who built them. It's as though the Palestinian heritage has been made not to exist. It is invisible.

"I was working for the School of Peace, guiding tour groups, mostly Jews, through the park and giving them a critical appreciation of the landscape that the JNF refuses to tell them about. I would show them the destroyed villages and explain that I thought they revealed something about the poor state of relations between the two peoples. These were intelligent and curious people, but what I said was entirely new to them. They would be shocked, and would say, 'All my childhood I came here, but I never knew that there were three villages with five thousand people here.' I would show them pictures of the villages, including photos of the destruction and expulsion as it took place. By accident a kibbutz photographer was working in the area during the 1967 war, and he captured it all on film. After one of the tours I said to myself, 'Although it's important to tell these groups about the villages, we can do more. We can post signs indicating where to find Imwas cemetery and Yalu mosque. And if they are removed, we can post them again.' Other people I told liked the idea."

Zochrot performed the first signposting in March 2002, at the remote site of the destroyed village of Miska, near Kafr Sava, on behalf of the Shbeta family, refugees now living some distance away in the Israeli Arab town of Tira. The sign was promptly removed, probably by the inhabitants of a kibbutz which now sits on Miska's land. Then, in 2003, Zochrot and Neve Shalom commemorated thirty-six years of the occupation in Canada Park. About two thousand people attended, including ten refugees from the original three villages. Zochrot posted a big sign, one side in Hebrew and the other in Arabic, at the centre of what was once Yalu village, saying "Welcome to the Village Centre" and giving details about the size of the village, how many mosques and schools it had, the number of people who lived there and where they were now. "Afterwards we posted two signs at Yalu and Imwas cemeteries, and intentionally I left some Zochrot brochures lying near the signs, which included my telephone number," Eitan explained. "After two days I got a call from someone named Mr. Cohen, the maintenance manager of Canada Park. He asked why we had posted the signs. I said so that people would know what had been there. He replied, 'But it's not legal.' I laughed and said there were hundreds of thousands of illegal signs all over the country and no one cared. 'Yes,' he said, 'but your signs are political.' So I retorted, 'Are your signs which tell the Jewish and Roman history of the site but exclude its Palestinian history not also political?' 'Ah,' he said decisively, 'but they are legal.'

"Mr. Cohen said he would remove our signs but that we could write to the JNF to ask for permission to post new ones. So that's what we did. We wrote a letter to the JNF, and after a month I got a one-line letter from the head of the organisation: 'The JNF does not deal with political issues, so please address the relevant body.' Our lawyer found out that because the park is in the occupied territories, we had to write to the military authorities in Beit El, to the Higher Planning Commission. So we wrote asking to post the signs. Under the law, anyone can post a sign with permission, but you have to promise to maintain it and pay the relevant taxes and so on. We told them we were ready to do all that. We sent several letters over a six-month period, but they never replied. Eventually we threatened action, which frightened them a little, as they understood that to mean we would go to the Supreme Court. By law they have to tell us something, so they sent a letter apologising and saying they were working on a reply. But their lawyer admitted to ours that his commanders could not decide what answer to give us. They knew that they would be setting some sort of legal precedent. If they allowed us to post a sign in the park, we could start doing it everywhere. So far we have still not heard anything, so we are challenging them in the Supreme Court.

"It was a strategic decision to start posting the signs before we had permission. We could be held up writing letters to the authorities for years before we got any response. Our strategy is to post signs and start a debate. For us, it doesn't matter that people remove the signs. If they tear them down, it means we are touching something in them. Maybe it would be worse if they just left them there and ignored them. These signs are not provocative in any obvious way. They simply state that people once lived here; they don't say those people were expelled or terrorised, just that there was once a village here. In one place, Ijlil, where Cinema City now stands—a great mall of cinema complexes near Herzliya—we brought a Palestinian family who once lived there and posted a large sign on a raised hillock overlooking the car park. If you parked there, you could see the sign telling you that an Arab village once existed there. It stood for three weeks before someone removed it. They had to scramble through a wire fence and up over rubble to reach it."

Eitan says he sees his responsibility as educating Jews, not Arabs, who must deal with their own history. "We are not a coexistence group—we are dealing only with raising Jewish consciousness. Teachers often come to our meetings, and I hear them saying, 'We teach the children lies for the bagrut, and we know they are lies.' It's remarkable to me that these teachers know they are teaching lies. That is positive, in a way. We want to start taking a special Nakba curriculum package to schools."

Although Zochrot is a young organisation, its message is already striking a chord. Eitan says, "At our first events we had to call our friends and persuade them to come. Maybe there were twenty people there. Now I don't call anyone. We have an evening and people come of their own accord. Always there are new faces. And if they keep coming, something will change in them. If you keep hearing the other side's story, you have to think and feel differently. I think if Israelis said tomorrow that they had a large responsibility for the Nakba and they apologised for it, 90 per cent of the problem would be solved. When you acknowledge your responsibility in front of a Palestinian, something in the air changes—I've seen it. The relations between the people change. From my point of view, I think I can do things to change my society from within, to prepare it for the future. If the change comes tomorrow, if there are suddenly different international circumstances, it's important that organisations like Zochrot have prepared people for the shock, that the change doesn't come out of nowhere."

Most of Zochrot's members, Eitan says, are not drawn from the traditional left wing. "Some of us come from very mainstream families and backgrounds. One of my colleagues is the son of a general who is head of the army's Central Command and a close friend of [former prime minister Ehud] Barak. Another is the daughter of a combat pilot, and she was raised in pilots' bases and married to a pilot. We deal with the Nakba, the memory of the other side, and our responsibility for what happened. We are not a political movement in the narrow sense: we don't prescribe a particular course of action or a solution to the conflict. Our initiative is something much wider. If, for example, there were ever to be an agreement on a one-state solution and the right of Palestinian return, Zochrot's purpose would not come to an end. We are dealing with the suffering of the other side, and we are trying to understand our responsibility for that suffering—that is a role that will continue to be needed for a very long time. There has been change in South Africa, but the reconciliation between the black and white populations and their acknowledgement of the past is a process, a process that is eternal."

Eitan understands how difficult it is for Israeli Jews to alter their understanding of the past, because it is something he had to face up to himself. "I was raised on Kibbutz Bahan, near Tulkaram. Close by the kibbutz was a place called Qaqun, which

I was always visiting as a child. It was a barren hill, and one of the places most dear to me as a boy. My friends and I would ride our bikes there, and later we would drive the kibbutz's tractor to it. On the top of the hill were still standing the remains of several big buildings, which we had always been told were part of a Crusader fortress. This is what I knew all through my childhood and my adult life. Then, about four years ago, when I started my personal adventure of looking for other histories, I was surfing the Internet looking for sites on the Nakba. I found a website which listed among the destroyed villages in the Tulkaram district a place called Qaqun. I was shocked, and to be honest I was even a little offended. I thought, *What does it have to do with you? This is my childhood, why are you putting it on your website?* I clicked the mouse on the link to Qaqun, and I was amazed to find that there had been a village of two thousand people living there. It was really a great shock.

"But this click on the mouse is what Zochrot is all about. This process of clicking and opening our minds to another history. I feel like a child moving inside the space of the Israel I think I know and discovering that there is also another landscape I have never seen before. For me, Zochrot is like reliving my childhood."

7

WHERE NEXT?

The walled Old City of Jerusalem was conquered, along with the rest of East Jerusalem and the West Bank and Gaza, by Israeli soldiers in the 1967 war. For Jews around the world, it was Israel's most glorious moment since its founding two decades earlier. What excited them was the thought that for the first time in two thousand years, the heart of Jerusalem had been brought back under Jewish control. Israel was now master of the Old City and its prized Jewish religious sites, including the Temple Mount, a raised section of land where the Second Temple, built by Herod, once stood. The temple had been destroyed in A.D. 70, but ever since, small numbers of devoted Jews had been going to the Old City to pray at the only remaining part of it, a retaining wall known as the Western Wall, or the Wailing Wall, which was constructed, it is believed, with stones from the First Temple, built by Solomon.

Since the seventh century, when Jerusalem fell under Muslim rule, Jews, Muslims and Christians maintained an accommodation in the Old City. Each of the three groups lived in its own quarter, close to its holiest sites. The Jewish district was near the Western Wall, the only place at the destroyed temple site where the rabbinical authorities allow Jews to pray; the Christian quarter encircled the Church of the Holy Sepulchre, built over the site where Jesus is believed to have been crucified and resurrected; and the Muslim quarter, the largest, was a jumble of crowded buildings around the eastern and southern sides of the Temple Mount, which for centuries has belonged to Islam and is known to Muslims as the Noble Sanctuary (the Haram al-Sharif). This compound includes the Aqsa and Dome of the Rock mosques, the latter a building whose golden dome is the centrepiece of most pictures of the Old City. The Dome of the Rock is built on the spot where Muslims believe the Prophet Mohammed ascended to heaven on a winged animal.

However, the centuries-long status quo started to break down during the British Mandate, as the local Arab population grew increasingly unhappy at what they rightly saw as British attempts to transfer a large part of their homeland to the Zionist immigrants, Jews who had arrived in Palestine not because of their devotion to Judaism but because of their commitment to creating a secular Jewish state there. Jerusalem was at the very centre of these clashes. For the Palestinians, it was the traditional confessional, commercial and geographic hub of their lives, with a profound religious significance to the wider Arab and Muslim worlds; for the Zionists, the city and its possession represented a chance to underpin the foundations of their new state with a powerful symbol that united both religious and secular groups. The war of 1948, though, had an inconclusive outcome from the point of view of the Zionists. Rather than falling under Israeli sovereignty, Jerusalem was divided: the western half was captured by Israel, and its Palestinian inhabitants were mostly expelled, while the eastern half, including the Old City, was occupied by Jordan, and the small Jewish community was forced out. Only in the 1967 war did Israel manage to occupy East Jerusalem and so begin to realise its dream of "unifying" the city. It annexed the Palestinian half of Jerusalem to the Jewish state, in violation of international law, and began consolidating its hold by building a ring of Jewish settlements around the eastern neighbourhoods. Jerusalem's municipal boundaries were expanded to include these settlers, to bolster Israeli claims that the city truly had been unified as the capital of the Jewish state.

While Israel waged a demographic battle for political control of the whole of Jerusalem, it also wanted to stake a claim to the city's main Jewish holy site, the Temple Mount, which was located deep in the Muslim quarter of the Old City. It had to proceed more carefully here, as it feared provoking international opposition to its plans as well as worldwide Muslim anger. Nonetheless, it soon demolished dozens of Palestinian homes near the Western Wall and evicted their owners in order to build an impressively large plaza that hosts the many visitors to the wall.

The waqf, the Islamic religious trust that is the guardian of the Noble Sanctuary mosques, was left in charge of the compound, but Israel made repeated symbolic attempts to encroach on the site. The most notable were Binyamin Netanyahu's decision to build a tunnel under the compound of mosques in the late 1990s and Ariel Sharon's now notorious visit to the Temple Mount in September 2000 to assert Jewish sovereignty there, which ignited Palestinian rage. The next day the Israeli police violently cracked down on the protests, leaving several Palestinian youths dead and triggering the second intifada.

Israel's symbolic assaults on Islamic sovereignty over the Noble Sanctuary have been overshadowed by an uglier, creeping physical annexation of the Muslim quarter around the holy site. Messianic Jews have replicated the tactics of fanatical settlers in the West Bank and Gaza by occupying Palestinian homes around the Noble Sanctuary. According to their leaders, they hope soon to be in a position to blow up the mosques and build the Third Temple, heralding the coming of the Messiah. They have derived some of their inspiration from Ariel Sharon, who on 15 December 1987 committed the provocative act of buying a house in the Muslim quarter of the Old City. He was quickly followed by dozens of young religious extremists. Today, Sharon's house (he has never lived there) stands incongruously in the midst of Palestinian homes, with an elongated Israeli flag draped from an upper window.

This illegal physical annexation of the Muslim quarter by Jewish extremists has been continuing for nearly twenty years, and its extent was revealed to me in striking fashion one day as I wandered on the normally busy streets of the Old City. Most visitors probably pass through the quarter without noticing what is happening, but if you look closely, the signs are there for all to see. For example, at a junction between three narrow alleyways close to the Noble Sanctuary, I found half a dozen armed Israeli soldiers standing below protective wire mesh fixed across the width of one of the alleys. The mesh was littered with objects, from lumps of concrete to bottles and rubbish.

From my conversations with Bar, the young soldier I had befriended, I had an idea of why the protection was needed. In the centre of Hebron, extremist religious settlers had taken over the upper apartments of buildings in the city centre and had been terrorising the local Palestinian traders by hurling objects at them. The army had erected the same kind of mesh I saw in Jerusalem to protect the Palestinian stallholders below. However, the settlers had simply switched tactics, pouring boiling oil on the shop owners instead. Even before the intifada, when a supposed peace reigned under the Oslo Accords, large sections of Hebron's market had been closed by the army, supposedly to safeguard the Palestinians. No one had suggested that the Jewish settlers perpetrating these vicious attacks be arrested or removed.

As I ventured down one of the Old City's narrow alleys near the Noble Sanctuary, I saw stall owners hurriedly closing up their shops. One of them told me that a party of Jewish extremists was visiting the area and he thought it best to shut down. Near the entrance to the compound of mosques, I found the group. They were waiting at a barrier guarded by well-armed Israeli policemen; behind the barrier, yet more Palestinian stallholders were packing up. It was clear that the Jewish group was entirely composed of the religious-nationalist camp of settlers: the men wore knitted skullcaps, while the women were dressed in long skirts and had their heads covered. Most were trailing young children and pushing prams; many of the settlers view their mission to displace the Palestinians largely in terms of a battle of numbers, so they have huge families, the women regarding themselves as little more than Zionist incubators.

I spoke to one of the policemen, who told me that the group were holidaymakers who had come to visit the house of a long-dead rabbi overlooking the Temple Mount. Anyone was welcome to join them, he said. So I followed them inside, into the long covered alley that leads Muslim worshippers to the gate by which they reach the compound of mosques. A little before that entrance we turned left into a side alley and up a twisting flight of stone steps. Near the top we entered a narrow stone passageway, where I was hit by the nauseating smell of urine and faeces. Around me was rubbish and decaying food. No one else in the group seemed to notice.

The true shock came, however, as we stepped out of the passageway and into a small courtyard. There, standing impassively watching us, were several women wearing hijabs and an old man; at their feet, young children were playing with dolls and a battered old tricycle. We had burst uninvited into the homes and lives of these Palestinian families, though their faces showed that they knew they were powerless to prevent our entry. The Jewish group pushed past the children, who seemed hardly aware of their presence, and carried on up another short flight of steps.

At the top was an incredible sight. The floor above the Palestinian families had been taken over by armed Jewish settlers, who had built a watchtower from which they could train their guns on the families below. The "holidaymakers," I now realised, were there to show their support for this military outpost in the middle of the Muslim quarter. I was reminded of the incident a few years earlier when I had been in hospital, before the outbreak of the intifada. Then I had seen a settler brandishing his gun in the ward and saying that he had "requisitioned" an Arab home in Jerusalem. Now I knew precisely what he meant.

I left the settlers on their tour of this outpost and went back down the steps to talk to the families below. They told me that the settlers had taken over the top-floor home several years before and become their unwelcome neighbours. The settlers' purpose was to make these families' lives so unbearable that they would choose to leave and the settlers' control could be extended. The old man said that the settlers had never shot at them. Instead, these Jewish extremists were using methods that apparently neither the police nor the Israeli courts objected to. They were using the passageway as a toilet, so that the Palestinian families would find their homes pervaded by the revolting smell and would be frightened that their children might pick up a disease. The messianic Jews lived in the outpost in shifts, so they could make noise all night to keep their Palestinian neighbours awake.

"They think they can break us and make us leave," said one woman. She told me that the settlers had occupied another apartment near them two years before, after the owner, an old Palestinian woman, died; the settlers claimed it was also part of the rabbi's home. The families were currently trying to challenge the illegal occupation in the courts. "We will not be forced out," said the old man defiantly. "It is our home, and we have nowhere else to go."

I turned away from this demonstration of naked Jewish power feeling a mix of anger and revulsion. For me, it encapsulated everything that the modern state of Israel has come to represent: a compulsive, racist and colonial hunger for land and the control of resources in the face of opposition from a largely powerless but implacable Palestinian population. Although the methods vary in Tamra, Jerusalem and Hebron, the goal is always the same: the accumulation of land by whatever means possible for the exclusive use of Jews.

I remember once being asked by the Christian Peacemaker Teams, an organisation founded by American churches in the mid-1980s to promote interfaith nonviolent resistance, to go to Hebron, where one of their main tasks is escorting young Palestinian children to school, because the children are afraid to walk alone past the armed Jewish settlers, who threaten them. The Peacemaker Teams wanted me to visit because the children had never met an unarmed Jew. They wanted me to show these children that not all Jews hate them and want to harm them. Bar, whose jobs included accompanying the Hebron settlers to the synagogue, had told me of the settlers' brutal treatment of the local Palestinian population. The children were particularly violent; she would watch helplessly as Jewish youths cursed and spat at old Palestinian men or threw tomatoes at pregnant Palestinian women. She said it made her physically ill to see the way these Jewish children were being raised.

Today there is an almost universal commitment among world Jewry to the Zionist project. It is worth noting that it was not always thus. Many prominent Jews rejected the idea of a Jewish state in Palestine, both before and shortly after its creation. Sigmund Freud, for example, foresaw with uncanny prescience the danger that in settling Palestine, the Zionists would unleash a new form of Jewish fanaticism. In a letter in early 1930 to his friend Dr. Chaim Koffler, the head of the Jewish Agency, who was asking for Freud's signature on a petition condemning riots among the Palestinian population against the waves of Jewish immigrants, he wrote:

> It would have seemed more sensible to me to establish a Jewish homeland on a less historically burdened land. But I know that such a rational viewpoint would never have gained the enthusiasm of the masses and the financial support of the wealthy. I concede with sorrow that the baseless fanaticism of our people is in part to be blamed for the awakening of Arab distrust. I can raise no sympathy at all for the misdirected piety which transforms a piece of a Herodian wall into a national relic, thereby offending the feelings of the natives.

Unlike Freud, we do not have the luxury of wishing away the existing bitter conflict. In this intifada alone, hundreds of innocent people have died on both sides as the two national groups battle over the same piece of land. But everyone—apart, apparently, from our current leaders in Washington and Jerusalem and a few Islamic extremists—agrees that armed conflict can offer neither side a meaningful victory. At some level, ordinary Israelis understand that the Palestinian nation's desire for independence and freedom cannot be defeated with weapons; and most Palestinians accept that they cannot vanquish one of the most powerful armies in the world with their light arms and suicide bombers.

A Palestinian friend of mine, Dr. Said Zidane, a professor at al-Quds University in East Jerusalem, has observed of both sides' original hopes, "Neither were the Israeli Jews drowned in the sea, as the Palestinians wished, nor did the Palestinians disappear into the distance, as Israeli Jews wished." Rather than holding on to one of these absolutist positions, Dr. Zidane has been trying to devise a workable solution to settling the conflict, one he believes that in the right circumstances can be accepted by both sides. He is in an ideal position to make such an attempt. Born in Tamra (his mother is my next-door neighbour) and educated in a mixed Jewish and Arab school in Haifa, he understands the fears of Jews intimately. But also, as a resident of the West Bank for the past twenty years, teaching at Bir Zeit University, near Ramallah, as well as at al-Quds University, he knows first-hand how soul-destroying it is to live under occupation.

Said dismisses the oft-expressed idea that the conflict between Israel and the Palestinians is over either religious or moral rights. It is not, he says, a clash of civilisations or cultures, as popular opinion now casts it. Although religious and moral sentiments have polluted the debate about the need for a Jewish state and Palestinian counter-claims, he rightly points out that the essence of the conflict is rival political demands from two national groups for sovereignty over the same territory. "As soon as you start using religious or moral justifications for a Jewish state, you are in a logical minefield," he told me. "The idea that Jews have a moral or religious right to return to this land after the passage of more than two thousand years is plain crazy. Are these historic rights? And if so, what about the historic rights of Palestinians uprooted nearly forty and sixty years ago? Don't they have rights? Or are the Jews' superior rights based on the length of absence? Surely it should work the other way round." A viable solution, he says, must forgo such nonsensical debates and concentrate instead on the political realities.

Since Israel's occupation of East Jerusalem, the West Bank and Gaza in 1967, the debate about ending the conflict has swung between two incompatible positions, which have come to be known as the one-state and two-state solutions. The two-state solution is usually premised on the idea of two secular, democratic states living alongside each other, one Palestinian, based on 22 per cent of historic Palestine (East Jerusalem, the West

Bank and Gaza), the other a Jewish state based on the remaining 78 per cent, which is Israel. The problem for the Palestinians is that in practice their mini-state would be weak and over-crowded, and it would be living in the shadow of a very powerful neighbour. In any case, Israeli governments, whatever their declared intention, have never appeared even close to conceding such a state. Its creation would require the uprooting of more than 400,000 Jewish settlers, many of them armed and some of them holding fanatical messianic beliefs. It would also transfer to Palestinian control the large aquifers under the hills of the West Bank, Israel's main source of drinking water.

The one-state solution, in contrast, is usually based on the idea of a binational democratic secular state in which Jews and Palestinians live as equal citizens. Although it should appeal to both sides' notions of equality and justice, in practice it has very few takers. For the Palestinians it would mean abandoning their cherished dream of independent statehood and trying to merge their fledgling national institutions with those of the long-established Jewish state. For Israelis it would effectively mean the end of the Jewish state, both in the sense of a state controlled by Jews and in the sense of a state which ensures a strong Jewish majority. Within a few years the Palestinians would be a demographic majority in any binational state, provoking Jewish fears that such a country would not be democratic and that its Jewish citizens would have to surrender their privileges.

Said, however, believes it is a mistake to assume that possible solutions exist only at these two poles. "There is in fact a range of solutions between these two extremes," he says. "We should think in terms not of a just solution, by which I mean giving to everyone what is due to them, but rather of a solution that is reasonable and accommodative, one which people feel they have a stake in and which they can live with." He proposes a modified two-state solution, which involves elements of separation along the lines of the two-state solution and elements of sharing along the lines of the one-state solution. There would be one secular, democratic country, but it would be divided into two confederated states, one Palestinian and the other Jewish, each with its own political institutions. This plan would allow most of the two populations to remain in their present homes, including the problematic cases of the settlers in the West Bank and East Jerusalem and the Palestinian citizens who live in Israel. In the new country, each citizen could choose the place he or she wants to live; the Arab citizens could move to Palestine or remain in Israel, and the settlers could live under Palestinian rule or return to Israel. The security of each minority would be guaranteed by legal codes that banned discrimination and ensured equality of citizenship. Resources would have to be divided equitably between the two states and within each state. The Palestinian refugees would be able to return to the Palestinian state or to be compensated.

One of the advantages of Said's idea is that it makes the damaging ideology of Zionism redundant. It offers a way out of the mutual recriminations and the pervasive atmosphere of fear, allowing for confidence-building between Jews and Palestinians, and it could lead slowly to the sort of reconciliation achieved between whites and blacks in the new South Africa. As Said says, his solution is dynamic and does not preclude the possibility that the new joint country could evolve eventually into a binational state. However, neither he nor I is naïve enough to believe that his proposal is likely to be adopted by either side in the near future. The two-state solution is the one currently fashionable in Europe, America and increasingly among Israelis, even if the Israeli government's policies are fatally undermining the chance of its realisation by entrenching most of the settlers in the West Bank and East Jerusalem. The problem, says Said, is that the world is still blindly committed to the Zionist enterprise and believes that a simplistic two-state model is the only way to ensure a Jewish state in the long term.

"But what does everyone mean by a 'Jewish state'?" he asks. "There are many possible meanings, the least problematic of which is a state in which Jews are the numerical majority. But in fact the world is using the term 'Jewish state' in its most problematic sense: a state owned by Jews and which privileges Jews both inside the country and outside it in the Diaspora, through the Law of Return. A state designed to exclude Arabs from its resources and benefits.

"I remember a discussion with [left-wing law professor] Ruth Gavison at a pancl at Tel Aviv University. I said, 'OK, I am a liberal democrat and you proclaim yourself a liberal democrat. All I want is that both of us should be equal citizens within one state.' She agreed at the theoretical level, but then told me I had to appreciate the improvement in my situation over the past twenty or thirty years and said that the steps to end discrimination would have to be gradual. She and other Israelis are not ready for anything more than this, because it would mean the end of Zionism. If we had liberal democracy in Israel, that would mean the end of Jewish nationalism. Israel doesn't even want to change the personal-status laws [on marriage and conversion], because it worries that it would lead to the assimilation of Jews."

The main obstacle to reaching a peaceful solution to this conflict is not, as most commentators observe, age-old hatreds or religious wars. It is not even incompatible nationalisms. It is a psychological condition demonstrated by Israelis—and mirrored by Palestinians—that sociologists have termed "learned helplessness." In societies where people feel events are outside their control, either because they see themselves as effectively disenfranchised or because they believe powerful and uncontrollable forces are at work, they give up, refusing to take responsibility for their lives or their choices. Their response ranges from "Nothing will make any difference, so I won't bother trying" to uncritical support for strong, even fascistic leaders.

Mamphela Ramphele, a founding member of the Black Consciousness Movement and a former vice-chancellor of Cape Town University, describes the phenomenon in her book *Steering by the Stars* (2002), about growing up in South Africa: "How else can one explain why it took so long for the voting white public to realise that apartheid was not only bankrupt politically, socially and economically but also unsustainable in a modern world? The authoritarian culture that enveloped much of apartheid South Africa encouraged learned helplessness and an over-reliance on authority to make all the important political and social decisions." It is not just the whites who suffer from this legacy in South Africa. Following the fall of apartheid, after years of living in the shadow of white assumptions about their inferiority, many of the country's blacks, Ramphele says, have lost the sense of themselves as equals. Their lack of self-belief is compounded by despair resulting from exhausting, long years of struggle for liberation and the devastating impact of economic apartheid on their lives.

The parallels with the present psychological condition of Israelis and Palestinians hardly need pointing out. Israeli rule has truly ghettoised Palestinians in Israel and in the occupied territories, making it difficult for their intellectuals and leaders to organise and develop a vision of the future. There is no doubt in my mind that it is Israeli state policy to fragment Palestinian society, making it weak and ineffective—something I know well from my work with Mahapach. The tragedy is that because of this, too many Palestinians have started to believe the Israeli narrative which tells them that they are inferior and incapable of challenging Israeli domination. Once persuaded of this, they are more likely to abandon dialogue and moderate strategies of resistance, such as civil disobedience, and turn instead either to

the path of fatalism or to radical strategies such as suicide bombings, the ultimate weapon of the weak.

Too often I hear both Jews and Palestinians, even their leaders, asking, "Ma la'assot?" ("What to do?"), as though they have
no stake in their future or power to change events. For example,
when the Or Commission, investigating the shooting of thirteen
unarmed Arab citizens in the Galilee at the start of the intifada,
refused to identify the policemen and commanders who were responsible for ordering and carrying out the killings, I heard just
such a comment from the Arab Knesset member Issam Makhoul.
Justice Or had refused to allow Arab families to participate in the
proceedings or to cross-examine the witnesses. I told Makhoul
that the inquiry had chosen to make the political voice of the
Arab minority irrelevant. Makhoul tried to put a gloss on it: "This
is the best we have had so far." He was presumably referring to
the fact that the commission's report did at least admit that
there had been decades of discrimination against the Arab population. But his kind of attitude, which always resigns itself to second best, is not good enough.

Makhoul's comment reminded me of another statement I
had heard, this time by the architect Michael Mansfeld, a Jew,
who said that he could not speak out about the discrimination
against Arabs because the Shin Bet might make life very difficult
for him and his business. "My responsibility is to my family," he
told me. But do we not also have a responsibility to the health of
our society, including the values we raise our children with?

Although my friend Asad Ghanem does not use the term
"learned helplessness," he has strong views about how living in a
Jewish state has damaged the Arab minority. It has, he says, made
it impossible for them to identify with their country and so learn
the true meaning of citizenship; it has eroded their sense of their
Palestinian identity and the collective rights that flow from that
fact; and these two factors together have fragmented the Arab

political leadership, which has singularly failed to articulate a vision for the Arab minority, as citizens of either a future Palestinian state or a reformed Israeli state. "The one area of our lives where we have equality is our right to participate in elections," he told me. "But even that is not as it appears. As citizens, we expect to be able to influence the election result, but that is not what happens. Our electoral participation is completely symbolic; our parties are never allowed to join the government. Instead the state is mobilised entirely to its Jewishness, to its identification with the Jewish people and with its Jewish character. In this sense the key to the allocation of resources is derived not from citizenship, as it is in a normal democracy, but from ethnic belonging. Israel is what I call an ethnocracy, a state that depends on ethnic support, rather than a democracy, a state that needs the support of the demos [the body of citizens]. As Arabs, we can have no meaningful place or role inside such a state."

I knew what Asad meant. Israel has plenty of Jewish political parties in the Knesset, many of them small religious or extreme nationalist parties which sit in government coalitions making outrageous demands, such as passing more powers to the rabbis or expelling Palestinians and the Arab minority from the country. Such language is considered entirely acceptable and nowadays is echoed even by senior members of the country's biggest party, the Likud. By contrast, no Arab party has ever been allowed to sit in the government; instead, Arab Members of Knesset (MKs) are allowed only to shout from the sidelines of the parliamentary and public debate. The two small Arab parties, and the equally tiny Arab-Jewish Communist Party, are effectively outside the national consensus. Even the main platform of the Arab parties—that Israel should be transformed from a Jewish state into a state of all its citizens—contravenes basic legislation, which requires all candidates to the Knesset to swear allegiance to a "Jewish and democratic state." In the 2003 general election, three senior Arab MKs were disqualified by the Central Election Committee from standing on just such grounds, although the decision was overturned by the courts.

Televised parliamentary debates on controversial issues in which Arab MKs speak invariably make for dismal viewing. As soon as the MK stands up to speak, he finds himself being howled down by the Jewish Members around him. If he shouts back, as Arab MKs too often do, the Speaker ejects him from the chamber. Arab MKs are regularly punished by the Knesset's ethics committee or investigated for incitement by the attorney-general after delivering speeches in the Knesset; Jewish MKs never seem to face these sanctions. The Israeli media express widespread animosity for the Arab political parties, a hostility only too readily accepted by the public and the security officials. A report by the Arab Association for Human Rights in Nazareth in 2002 revealed that during the parliament, eight of the nine Arab MKs had been assaulted by the police or army at demonstrations, several on more than one occasion. In most cases the officers were fully aware of whom they were attacking.

According to Asad, however, the symbolic nature of citizenship for the Arab population has played a significant role in damaging their understanding of their wider rights to a collective Palestinian identity. As members of the Palestinian nation, they should be entitled to cultural, linguistic and social rights in Israel, just as Jews enjoy these rights. Recognition of these rights is vital in protecting Palestinian heritage and traditions and therefore also the Palestinian minority's national identity. "Although the courts safeguard some of our individual rights, which derive from our Israeli citizenship, they ignore other types of rights, most notably our collective or national rights," Asad says. "It is historically true that in countries founded on colonial occupation, such as the United States, Canada and Australia, the offer of full citizenship to the indigenous people, however magnanimous it sounded, was really another form of colonialism. The same is true in Israel. Here, for example, the authorities tell us we have to be 'fully Israeli'—that is, to make our heritage and our past subsidiary to our citizenship—before we can have the right to belong. As happened in the U.S. and Australia, we are expected to renounce our traditions and identity before we can become proper citizens. We must stop being Palestinian before we can be allowed to be Israeli. But I don't accept this in our case. So far Zionism has not succeeded like the white settlers of America and Australia. We still have the strength to believe we are a national group and that we deserve our rights both as a national group and as citizens."

I was reminded of the comments of a Palestinian political activist in Nazareth, Ziad, who had once believed strongly in coexistence but who told me that since the start of the intifada he had grown profoundly disillusioned. "Before we can coexist, we must first exist," he said. "The problem is that we don't exist for the Jews. It's about time we woke up to that fact."

Asad fears that the Palestinian minority's national identity is being increasingly undermined by the Arab leadership in Israel, a subject on which he is outspoken. He says that traditionally the minority's leaders fell into two camps: either they collaborated with the system, accepting that the Jews were a privileged group, or they rejected the system entirely, refusing to deal with it. Now, he says, the Israeli policy of divide and rule has found its ultimate partners among the Arab minority. "A third political group has emerged in the last fifteen years, from a generation which is more educated and more aware of the different aspects of our lives, but which is also far more opportunistic. The sole mission of these politicians is to keep their seat; they say whatever it takes to remain popular. One day they will criticise the Palestinian leadership in the occupied territories and the next day meet with it. This group of leaders is disconnected from the real needs of their electorate. They are what I call a TV phenomenon: they give soundbites, speak of the hardships they have endured, but only ever visit Arab areas like Tamra just before an election. Maybe they have adopted this strategy partly because they have seen that in the past, true leaders were usually jailed or deported by the Israelis. But because they are so opportunistic, there is no real coordination among them. They are not a collective leadership, they are not taking decisions together, they are not sitting down to formulate a common strategy. In fact, they don't meet or speak at all. But the precondition for success, however limited, in our struggle as a minority must be a collective vision.

"Undoubtedly, our leaders' political failure reflects a wider failure in our society. We, the public, have changed too. After the collapse of communism and Arab nationalism, individualism has become the dominant ideology. Most people see their duty on election day as putting a mark on the ballot paper rather than being part of a collective body. In the end, people will follow their politicians just because they have no one else to follow. But really this is a dangerous illusion. When you are a majority, such as the Jews here, you have the privilege of an institutionalised collective leadership called the government. But Arab citizens cannot allow themselves to behave like the Jewish majority when they are really a minority. Instead of our opportunistic and competing leaders, we need a single inspirational figure, like Nelson Mandela or Mahatma Gandhi."

Asad has been campaigning to abolish the main political institution in the Arab sector, a body known as the Higher Follow-Up Committee, which comprises dozens of Arab leaders, from the Knesset representatives to the local mayors. With all the leaders pulling in different directions, each championing his own causes, the committee has become little more than a talking shop, which few in the Arab community bother to listen to anymore. Asad has suggested creating a new supreme Arab political body, a sort of mini-parliament, which would be elected by direct national elections among the Arab citizens. As he says, "Discrimination and Jewish dominance are at the heart of the system. As a community, we long ago reached the conclusion that the system is incapable of offering us equality. And yet we keep struggling for equality. Instead we have to alter the debate, to talk about the real change that must happen both in our society and in the Jewish society to achieve some sort of equality. We must recognise that we are stuck in a dead end in the fight for equality, that the system will never allow us to be equals. Our new institutions must be ready to enter into a confrontation with the authorities. Only in this way can we move forward."

Asad understands how difficult and frightening such an option is. In the spring of 2003, Israel jailed the leader of the Islamic Movement, Sheikh Raed Salah, the nearest thing the Arab community has to a spiritual leader. Salah is a widely respected and uncompromising figure behind whom much of the community, religious and secular alike, had united. After his arrest, leaks in the Hebrew media suggested he would be charged with having links to terrorists in the occupied territories, but when the charges finally came, they referred only to financial irregularities regarding fund-raising activities and channeling a small amount of funds to humanitarian causes in the West Bank and Gaza. Even though the police have admitted that Salah is being held on charges of technical breaches of Israeli law, at the time of writing he has been refused bail and has spent more than eighteen months in jail during a lengthy trial.

"Of course people are afraid," says Asad. "We are a fragmented and disorganised community. If you enter into confrontation like Raed Salah, you are alone. Nowadays hardly anyone speaks of him—and he has a party and a town behind him. If I speak out, no one at all will notice. I will simply disappear. But if we are more organised, a person who is arrested can be sure that a lawyer will be sent to the jail, that a demonstration will be organised, that members of the community will be ready to make sacrifices. I need to know someone will take care of my wife and children if I am in prison. We have to start organising the society from the bottom upwards."

Today the same charge of disunity can be levelled, to a lesser degree, at the Palestinians in the West Bank and Gaza, where poverty and lengthy army-enforced curfews are undermining a strong tradition of solidarity. The "What to do?" philosophy is beginning to take hold there too. But it is important to keep these failings in perspective. They derive from the damaging experience of discrimination and occupation enforced by Israel. The Palestinian population is not in a position to help itself without winning allies in Jewish society, particularly from the left. Without Jewish partners and the support of the international community, the Palestinians can achieve little against the might of the Israeli army. But apart from some of the people mentioned in this book—Uri Davis, Eitan Bronstein, Daphna Golan—and a few hundred others who support their work, Israeli Jews are in deep denial. They are even more the victims of learned helplessness than the Palestinians.

Said Zidane accurately describes the intellectual complacency of Israeli left-wingers: "They know that they came from Europe, took a country that was not theirs and displaced and dispossessed hundreds of thousands of Palestinians and their descendants. And then they tell you, 'But we had no other choice. We had to rescue our people.' This is an argument that might convince the Americans, the French or the British, but do they really think that they can convince the Palestinians that they had no choice but to displace us, to disinherit us, to kill us? It is just an absolute evasion of responsibility."

His comments echo a similar discussion I had with Dr. Adel Manna of the Van Leer Institute in Jerusalem. Dr. Manna's work includes lecturing to Jewish audiences, often comprising senior academics, about an alternative, Palestinian narrative of the war of 1948. We discussed the reactions he typically gets. "Usually they respond either by simply refusing to hear the other narrative or by trying to tell me their narrative instead," he said. "As a historian, I can say this is natural when two peoples are in a bloody and continuous conflict—each side has its own story and portrays its camp as the victim and the other camp as the aggressor. But I think in the case of Jews, the response is complicated by the fact that because of their long history as victims all over the world, they are unusually convinced that they are the ultimate and eternal victim of everybody else. This makes them closed to the idea that a victim could be transformed into the victimiser or aggressor. They cannot accept it. So whatever I tell them, they always have an excuse for why their side has to behave in this way. If Palestinian civilians are killed, how else can Israeli soldiers respond to terrorism? If children are killed, it's the Palestinians' fault for sending their children to the street.

"Even outside the terms of the conflict, they refuse to think of the Palestinians as victims. I ask them to see it from a humanitarian point of view. I say, imagine you have a home that has been in your family for generations and a stranger comes along and says, 'I am poor and need refuge. Can you let me stay in one of your rooms?' Would you not tell this man, 'This is my house, I am the owner and you are a guest'? And they reply, 'But we cannot think of it in this way. This is Eretz Israel, this is our homeland.' And I say, 'Yes, but think about it from the other side, from the viewpoint of the Palestinians who lived here.' 'No, no, there were no Palestinian people,' they say. 'They are not a nation.' OK, I say, let's assume that they are not a nation, they are just a collection of people living in their homes. They still have rights in their homes. How would you feel if someone came along and said, 'Now we are the landlords, this is our house. Maybe we will keep you here as tenants, or maybe not'? What would your response be? But they refuse to discuss it. I talk in front of groups of doctoral students and professors, and almost none of them is able to think in this way. Even if they can understand what I am saying at a human level, they refuse to take responsibility for it. They admit it is tragic, that it is just cause against just cause, but still it's the Palestinian leadership to blame, or the Arab world—anyone but their people. In other words, they cannot take responsibility for what their people did to the Palestinians, even after they have understood the Palestinian tragedy of 1948. That makes me very pessimistic. If that is the response of the stronger side, where are we to go?"

I witnessed this absolute refusal to accept responsibility at the Van Leer Institute in the autumn of 2004, in an auditorium filled with left-wing Israelis who had come to hear a presentation by Arun Gandhi, the grandson of Mahatma Gandhi, on the philosophy of nonviolence. Most of the audience had been invited by the peace activist networks and were keen to hear about nonviolent strategies. Gandhi spoke of his childhood in South Africa with his grandfather, of the evils of apartheid and of the lessons the mahatma had taught him about the power of nonviolent resistance. He had learned from his grandfather, he said, that nonviolent resistance was possible only once one had let go of anger and found peace within oneself. He spoke calmly and gently, but I was struck by his failure to understand the depth of the anger and fear on both sides that stands in the way of nonviolence in Israel. I know of that fear myself, because I was raised with it: I once thought of Arabs as marauding savages whose only goal was to drive us Jews into the sea.

Gandhi was joined by a panel of academics and activists, who spoke about their practical experiences of trying to encourage the participants in this conflict to adopt nonviolent strategies. The best speakers were Lucy Nusseibeh, a British Palestinian, and Shai Carmeli, an Israeli film-maker. Lucy works for Middle East Nonviolence and Democracy (MEND), a project which specialises in teaching Palestinian children how to react nonviolently to the occupation. She said much of the organisation's time was spent explaining to youngsters that they should not throw stones, even when taunted by Israeli soldiers, and that she always found widespread support for nonviolent strategies inside Palestinian communities.

Shai, who is in his late twenties and is studying at Tel Aviv University, showed us a documentary he had just completed on the ways Palestinian villagers have been nonviolently resisting Israel's building of its security barrier on their land. It was a remarkable diary of the kinds of protests that are never given coverage by the Western media. We saw villagers chanting against the soldiers and children standing in line holding banners. And we saw the army's response too: soldiers firing tear gas and rubber bullets, and individuals entirely losing control as they beat children and old people. Shai had taken the film to the Israeli Broadcasting Authority and to international broadcasters, but none of them wanted to touch it. The reaction was always the same: "This didn't happen in Israel," they told him.

When the talks came to an end, the floor was thrown open to the audience. After a brief hushed pause, a sixty-year-old rabbi stood up and told us that he had been in the "business of peace" for a long time and that the speakers had entirely misrepresented the situation. "You have failed to understand the effects of the suicide bombings on Israelis," he said. Then someone else stood up and said the same thing. Another asked indignantly, "Is this a court of law? Are we Israelis being judged?" His comment reminded me of Harry's wife, who had asked me if I hated Jews; it was another example of the same persecuted psychology. Another member of the audience said, "We have the right to be afraid."

Lucy Nusseibeh bravely tried to respond to the barrage of comments, and began by saying that the issue of suicide bombings had been sensationalised. I had a pretty good idea of the point she was trying to make: that the issue of someone strapping on a suicide belt has become *the* issue, overshadowing everything else, including the occupation. But we never heard the rest of her reply, because at that point most of the audience became hysterical. The evening came to an abrupt halt.

Emerging from the hall, I bumped into Adel Manna's wife, who looked as disgusted as I felt by what had just taken place. I had raised my hand in the auditorium but had not had a chance to speak. I told her I had wanted to say that not once had I heard a Jew saying that we ought to be asking ourselves what makes people so desperate that they believe they need to blow themselves up. Even on the rare occasion the question is raised outside Israel, it is immediately made clear that such a line of thought is totally unacceptable. British prime minister Tony Blair's wife, Cherie, for example, found herself forced to apologise for the innocuous comment that Palestinian suicide bombers felt "no hope."

The Jewish refusal to listen to the Palestinian narrative, to understand the Other's feelings and to take responsibility for our role in his misfortune, was again demonstrated to me one summer afternoon when I was by the sea in Herziliya. The beaches were packed with French Jews on their vacations, making solidarity visits to Israel. I was talking to one group who were keen for me to know that they were first-generation French, their families having survived the Holocaust. Each had relatives who had been gassed in the concentration camps. They were fascinated by the idea of my living in an Arab town. "But the Arabs are primitive," one said. "They have a primitive mentality." How did he know that? I asked. "Because they want to push us into the sea," he said, parroting the Zionist propaganda I knew only too well.

These people asked me about life in an Arab community, so I explained the ways in which we as Jews oppress Arabs in Israel, how we discriminate against them and steal their land. They were interested in a dispassionate way that suggested they did not really see it as their problem. Then one of the men interrupted: "I want to ask you a question which I am sure you will know the answer to. Tell me: we hear stories that in 1948 we ethnically cleansed the Arabs from their villages. Is it really true?" I said yes. He looked at me blankly, then raised his hands helplessly, lost for a response and unable to come to terms with the gravity of my answer. Finally he said, "But after all we have been through, all the persecution, the Holocaust, why could they not just have opened their arms and let us in?"

From his condition of learned helplessness, his statement probably sounded perfectly reasonable. But to me it made about as much sense as asking, "Why did the Palestinians force us to kill and ethnically cleanse them?" It was a refusal to take responsibility for our past and for our crimes. It was like saying, "We are so persecuted, our history is so much worse than anyone else's, we don't have to take responsibility for what we do." That was the Zionist ideology I was raised with. I tried a different tack. "Can't you see the similarity between what happened to us in Europe and what we are doing here? Can you not see that the persecution is the same?" I asked.

What they could not accept was that the Palestinian story is essentially a Jewish story. That is what I have learned from living in Tamra, listening to my new family and my Palestinian friends. The tale of Adel Manna's parents taking a boat journey under cover of night to return to their village is a Jewish story. So why do most Jews close their minds when faced with the Palestinian narrative?

"I understand why the majority of Jews are afraid to open their eyes," Dr. Manna had said to me. "Psychologically speaking, if you see the reality and acknowledge the narrative of the other side as your victim, you have a problem. If you take responsibility for what your side did, you endanger your relations with your family, friends, colleagues, the whole society—with everything you have, in fact. You find yourself in a tiny, marginalised minority, facing a majority that sees you as a traitor. If you are strong enough, you can face it and fight against it, but most people are not strong enough. Most are not able to do it, and so they get depressed, emigrate, or suppress what they know. I understand that. It is a big sacrifice to make. Against the background of Jewish history and each individual's fear of opening his mind and accepting responsibility, Jews in Israel are in addition educated to believe that if they give something to the Palestinians, the Palestinians will want more and the Jews will lose everything. The fear is that if you are not strong in the way the Zionists tell you to be, you will weaken the collectivity, and then you may find yourself with nothing. You may end up the victim again. And that is the complexity of this case."

I do not think I truly appreciated those words until I made a trip to the town of Umm al-Fahm to visit Palestinians torn from their families by a combination of Israel's increasingly dismal human rights record and the wall that is being built to separate the Palestinian populations under Israeli rule. Umm al-Fahm lies in the Triangle, close to the Green Line which officially separates Israel from the West Bank. From the hill at the far end of the town, Jenin and its surrounding villages are visible.

Jihad, a portly, middle-aged Palestinian, took me to meet several families whose lives can only be described as horrific. Like many others now living in Israel, these families have been forced into hiding because of an outrageous piece of legislation passed by the Knesset in the summer of 2003. An amendment to the Citizenship Law has made it all but impossible for an Arab citizen of Israel to live legally inside Israel with a Palestinian spouse

from the occupied territories. The measure, universally con-
demned by international human rights organisations, has created a whole new class of "underground families," living in fear
of being discovered by the authorities. The Palestinian partner,
usually the husband, cannot work or claim benefits for fear of being discovered and then forcibly deported to the West Bank; the
wives must hide their marriages even from friends; and the children have to live with the ever-present fear of suddenly losing
their father if they say a wrong word. The fact that this law passed
in the Knesset with barely a murmur from anyone in Israel, including most of the left, is a sign of the society's complete loss of
moral direction. It is the ultimate proof of the extent to which
learned helplessness has gripped Israeli Jewish society.

Afterwards, Jihad took me to his home for lunch with his family. I had first met him during my peace walk in the West Bank
with David Lisbona's organisation, Middleway. I had not been
impressed by the peace walk or by the motives of the Jewish participants and had ended the trip wondering what Arabs like
Jihad gained from these encounters. I knew from Harry that
Jihad was the most active of the Arab members, even sitting on
the Middleway steering committee. Did he have a vision of a fair
and equal future for the Palestinian people? And if he did, did
he believe that the Jews on the peace walks shared this vision? Or
was there a more cynical motive behind his involvement?

On the peace walk, Jihad had seemed pushy and arrogant,
and I had viewed him suspiciously. But as I sat in his home I
started to reconsider. Although he was inarticulate about what
exactly he thought Middleway stood for, he did seem genuinely
and passionately loyal to it as an organisation. "I believe in
peace," he said repeatedly, "but I know I cannot get equality. So
I concentrate on peace instead." He spoke of David in more than
glowing terms, as though he were some sort of guru.

I was curious to know more about Jihad. I asked him about his family's history, and he told me that before the creation of Israel his father had been a wealthy resident of Umm al-Fahm, with a large house and forty dunums (ten acres) of land. During the war, however, his parents had been forced to leave the town and go to the Jenin refugee camp, a few kilometres away, on the other side of the Green Line. Born shortly afterwards, in 1951, Jihad had never known Umm al-Fahm; he grew up as a resident of the West Bank, then under Jordanian control, first in a tent and later in a small apartment provided for his family by the United Nations refugee agency. But he was determined to get out of the refugee camp. He lived and worked abroad for many years, slowly making a small fortune as an English translator in Saudi Arabia and later as the manager of a water and sewerage company in Jordan. After 1967, when Israel captured the West Bank and effectively erased the Green Line that until then had separated Palestinian families living in Israel and the occupied territories, Jihad met and married a woman from Umm al-Fahm. Unlike the families he had introduced me to that day, he had managed to get himself Israeli citizenship after a few years. With an Israeli ID card, he had the choice of raising his family on the Israeli side of the Green Line, in the squalor and overcrowding of Umm al-Fahm, or staying on the West Bank side. He chose the latter option, building a large home in the village of Taibe, not far from Jenin. There he could afford not only a good home but also three dunums of land, on which he planted an olive grove. Through hard work he had earned back a little of the quality of life and the self-respect stolen from his family in their dispossession in 1948.

Taibe was home to Jihad, his wife and their five children when the intifada erupted in late 2000. Then, in 2002, Israel began building the first sections of its security barrier, on the pretext that it needed to protect itself from suicide bombers. (That argument rings a little hollow, as Israel did not choose the Green Line for the route of the wall but instead let it cut into large sections of the West Bank, thereby justifying the effective mass annexation of Palestinian land, particularly land over the West Bank aquifers.) The first sections of the hundreds of kilometres of wall went up in the area between Umm al-Fahm and Jenin, effectively reestablishing the border between the neighbouring Palestinian populations that had been erased nearly forty years earlier. Jihad at least had a choice about where to live, unlike many others, who have been trapped on one side of the wall or the other, cut off from family and friends because they have the wrong ID card. But the choice facing his family was still a stark one. They could remain in Taibe, keeping everything they had built up over many years, but then watch their life slowly crumble under the weight of the Israeli army occupation of the West Bank and the collapse of an economy starving behind a wall of razor wire and concrete. Or they could pack up the things they could carry, take them to Umm al-Fahm and begin again from scratch. Jihad chose the second course, returning to Umm al-Fahm more than five decades after his family had been expelled. But he did not come back in some glorious right of Palestinian return, compensated with land or money by Israel for the years of his family's dispossession. No, he returned to Umm al-Fahm with his wife and children as a penniless itinerant. He had been made a refugee by Israel yet again.

Today Jihad and his family live in a run-down rented apartment, the seven of them squashed into a few small rooms with almost no furniture. Jihad, who damaged his back several years ago, has no savings left, cannot find someone to rent his home in Taibe and has paid no contributions to the Israeli welfare system. He has had to leave everything behind on the other side of the wall.

I asked him where he felt he was from. "From Jenin refugee camp," he said. But where do you want to be? I asked. "Back in my house in Taibe." And if there was a just peace tomorrow, where would you want to be? "Back in Umm al-Fahm with my forty dunums," he said decisively. "But only if I can return as an equal citizen with equal rights." "But that's not the kind of peace Middleway wants," I pointed out. "The peace they want is not the same as the peace you want. They want an end to the shooting and killing, but they also want the Jews to stay in control." He nodded, shrugged his shoulders and said, "What to do?"

There it was again: the cry of learned helplessness. Jihad, it was now clear to me, had no conception of himself as an equal citizen. He was happy to be with Middleway because all he had come to expect after years of dispossession and mistreatment was whatever scraps he could get from the Jews' table. His words confirmed my view that he was being exploited by Middleway, which needs Arabs like him to give it an air of inclusivity and legitimacy. But the group was using him as little more than a guide dog to the West Bank. It reminded me of a moment on our trip to Yabad when Harry had pulled out from his wallet a photograph of himself shaking Yasser Arafat's hand. "That's my protection if I ever get in trouble," he said proudly. Was that not also Jihad's role for the peace walkers?

What was really distressing was to see how Jihad was so dislocated from everything: his past, his nation, his natural surroundings, even his family. Middleway had become everything for him, like some sort of peace cult which promised nothing but allowed him the slim hope that one far-off day, a little of what was owed to him might be returned. After everything else had been taken from him, Middleway gave him back his sense of belonging, of being part of a community.

Jihad and the other families I met that day had each been made refugees several times over. The Palestinian people are overwhelmingly a refugee nation, and like many others, Jihad had been uprooted from the place he called home more than once. The fate of Palestinians like him so closely mirrors the fate of the Jewish people through the centuries that it strikes me as amazing that it is so rarely remarked upon. What makes Jihad's story so tragic is that those responsible for turning him and his people into eternal refugees are the Jews themselves. Israel was created precisely to enable the Jewish people to stop being a nation forever wandering, forever homeless. The price of creating such a homeland has been to inflict the Jewish story on another people, the Palestinians. It does not matter where in Israel or the occupied territories you go—Tamra, Jenin, Umm al-Fahm, Hebron, Rafah—you will find a Jewish story of dispossession and wandering; but the victims this time are the Palestinians.

Hearing Jihad's words about not knowing where he really belonged, I thought this must have been how the Jews felt after the Holocaust. I was also struck by another, frightening thought. Jihad's story sounded so like mine. Like Jihad, I too had never known my roots or where I belonged. My grandparents had been hounded from Lithuania to South Africa; my father had left South Africa, where he could not get the education he needed, to go to Europe; I had left Britain, where I felt few emotional attachments, to live in Israel; and finally, and most ironically, I had felt compelled to uproot myself from the Jewish side of Israel through my new understanding that my state was built on a lie. Just as Jihad was destined to be the wandering Palestinian, I was destined to be the wandering Jew.

Jihad's story made it clear to me that Zionism has forced upon Israeli Jews a terrible choice: they feel they must continue rooting themselves in someone else's soil—the Palestinians'—because otherwise they would have to uproot themselves yet again. This was why we Jews find the idea of facing up to the truth about Israel, about our past, so impossibly difficult. To live honestly inside Israel as a Jew is to plunge oneself once again into a state of rootlessness.

I remember attending a coexistence meeting in the Galilee at which Jews and Arabs discussed planning issues in the region. One Jewish woman, a recent Russian immigrant, asked in exasperation, "Why are the Arabs so attached to the land?" In Hebrew she used a word for "attached" that conveys the sense of being glued to it. But the Palestinians are no more glued to the land than the Jews are. The prospect for both peoples, if they are not deeply rooted to the land, is just too terrifying to contemplate. The cycle that has to be broken is not a cycle of violence but a cycle of lies we Jews tell ourselves to persuade us that we have a two-thousand-year-old title deed to this land.

Whereas Jihad had been forced by Israel to become an eternal refugee, I have chosen my fate of wandering, of being rootless, by questioning the very basis of the Jewish state. I cannot pretend it has been an easy choice. I have had to develop a new sense of belonging—to the struggle to help a new country emerge here, to which one day we all, Jews and Palestinians, will belong. I hope others will take the same path, because a true peace, a just reconciliation with the Palestinians, can never happen until Israelis and Jews accept that this was not their land; that they are, in Dr. Manna's words, living uninvited in someone else's house. But I do not want to disguise from anyone the fact that being honest with oneself, seeing the truth beneath the layers of lies and misinformation, is deeply disturbing.

After I had been living in Tamra for some time, my thirty-two-year-old son, Daniel, who at the time was working in Germany for a sportswear firm and planning his marriage to a Swedish woman, came to visit me. In one intensive day I took him on a similar journey to the one you have taken in this book. I showed him around Tamra and introduced him to my friends and neighbours. I explained the discrimination and the way the state steals land from Palestinians. I took him to the machsom, the checkpoints where Jewish youngsters humiliate Palestinians and control their lives. I showed him the wall where it cuts through the very centre of Bartaa, chopping a Palestinian community and its families in half. I must have explained it ten times to him, and still he could not make sense of the lunacy of it.

My son had a Zionist upbringing and spent much of his youth in Israel, working in summer camps or volunteering on kibbutzim. He is a very typical Diaspora Jew, and he found it a profoundly troubling day. "How do you think the Jews in the Diaspora will cope with this?" he asked me. "I can see that what you are showing me is not what I was brought up to believe—that there is a whole other story I never knew about. In one day you are trying to change my whole perspective. You are showing me that everything I believe is a falsehood."

I realise as I finish writing this book that my journey was not really about crossing a divide, but about a far harder journey, one in which I have learned that the divide is really an illusion. It is an artefact we have created in our imaginations—just as we have built a concrete wall in the West Bank—to protect us from the truth. It is not about living in Tamra or Tel Aviv, or for that matter Umm al-Fahm or Jenin. It is not about *where* we live but about *how* we live. It is about learning to look honestly at the places we inhabit and want to call ours, to understand the past and to face up to the crimes committed in our names. Then we Jews will be ready to apologise and to reach out a welcoming hand across that divide. To embrace the Other, who is really ourselves.

GLOSSARY

by Jonathan Cook

Terms in italic are explained in greater detail elsewhere in the glossary.

ALIYA   The Hebrew word (literally, "ascent") used to describe the immigration of *Diaspora Jews* to Israel. It has Biblical connotations, suggesting that Jews were ordained by God to return to the Promised Land. Nearly three million Jews have made aliya, brought to Israel by the *Jewish Agency* under the *Law of Return*, since the founding of the nation in 1948.

ASHKENAZIM   The Hebrew word, originally meaning "German," for Jews of northern and eastern European origin, distinguishing them from the *Sephardim*, Jews of Mediterranean or Arab origin. The Ashkenazi experience of persecution led many European Jews to become early and enthusiastic supporters of *Zionism*. Almost all leaders of the pre-state Jewish organisations in Palestine were Ashkenazi, and Ashkenazi political, cultural and religious dominance continues to this day in Israel.

BALFOUR DECLARATION   A letter written in November 1917 by the British foreign minister, Arthur Balfour, to the banking magnate Lord Rothschild, in which Britain officially declared its support for the goals of the Zionist movement, namely, to create a Jewish national homeland in Palestine: "His Majesty's Government views with favour the establishment in Palestine of a national home for the Jewish people and will use their best endeavours to facilitate the achievement of this object, it being clearly understood that nothing shall be done which may prejudice the civil and religious rights of the existing non-Jewish [i.e., Palestinian] communities in Palestine or the rights and political status enjoyed by Jews in any other country."

BEDOUIN Israel's 200,000 Bedouins comprise two separate populations: the majority, living in the *Negev,* originate from the Sinai Peninsula; a much smaller group, living in the *Galilee,* are descended from tribes that arrived from Syria and Lebanon. Most of the Bedouins, the poorest social group in Israel, live either in *unrecognised villages* or in state-planned urban reservations, although more privileged communities exist in the north, where the men volunteer to serve in the army, usually as trackers. The Bedouins are also well represented in the Arab neighbourhoods of the *mixed cities* of Ramle and Lod, in the centre of the country, to which they were forcibly relocated by the state after 1948 to provide a pool of cheap labour serving the construction industry in Tel Aviv.

BLUE LINES The Planning and Building Law (1965) established "blue lines" around every community in Israel. Development can occur only within these lines; all land outside the lines is considered agricultural. Many tens of thousands of Arab homes, particularly in the *unrecognised villages,* are located outside the blue lines and are therefore illegal and face demolition.

BRITISH MANDATE British and French officials carved up much of the Middle East empire of the defeated Ottomans according to the Sykes-Picot Agreement of 1916. Britain occupied Palestine in September 1918 and two years later secured a mandate for the region from the San Remo Peace Conference. The Mandate for Palestine, an area defined as running from the Mediterranean Sea to the River Jordan, was confirmed by the Council of the League of Nations in 1922. Under the *Balfour Declaration,* the British government promised the Zionist movement that it would assist in the creation of a Jewish national homeland in Palestine. The first British census in 1922 recorded 670,000 Palestinians and 80,000 Jews in Palestine. By 1946, on the eve of the establishment of the state of Israel, an Anglo-American commission estimated the population at nearly 1.3 million Palestinians and 600,000 Jews. The Mandate ended in May 1948.

CITIZENSHIP   Two pieces of legislation, the *Law of Return* of 1950 and the Nationality Law of 1952, define the ways in which Israeli citizenship can be acquired: by birth to Israeli parents, by residence, by naturalisation and, in the case of Jews, by return. These laws did not automatically apply to the country's Arab population: some 30,000 *present absentees* received citizenship belatedly when the Nationality Law was amended in 1980. Government officials have wide-ranging powers to prevent non-Jews from gaining Israeli citizenship, and in some cases even residency rights. A harshly critical report by the Association of Civil Rights in Israel (ACRI) in December 2004 observed that the Interior Ministry's rules for assigning citizenship to non-Jews are "shrouded in mist" and that the ministry has demonstrated "an endemic, systematic and pervasive bias against non-Jews." Often the children of marriages between an Israeli Jew and a non-Jew are also denied citizenship. Since 2002 it has been impossible for Palestinians from the occupied territories to acquire citizenship when they marry an Israeli, effectively forcing the couple to live apart. Conversion to Judaism—another possible route to citizenship—is exclusively controlled by the *Orthodox rabbinate,* which approves a tiny number of converts each year and demands that they become strictly observant. The relationship between citizenship and nationality is far more problematic in Israel than in other countries. Although the 6.5 million inhabitants of Israel all enjoy Israeli citizenship, none—Jew or Arab—is considered an Israeli national. The Interior Ministry has assigned 137 other nationalities to the country's citizens so that it can perpetuate the idea that Israel is identical to the Jewish nation. Registered nationalities include Jew, Georgian, Russian and Hebrew through to Arab, *Druse,* Abkhazi, Assyrian and Samaritan. The courts have rejected the claims of individuals seeking to be registered as Israeli.

CUSTODIAN OF ABSENTEE PROPERTY   An Israeli state official responsible for the confiscation of the homes, lands and bank accounts of all Palestinians made refugees in the *war of 1948* and their descendants, both 4 million Palestinians registered today as living in refugee camps across the Middle East and 250,000 internal refugees who live as Israeli citizens. Estimates put the value of confiscated movable property alone (bank accounts, shares, jewellery, farm equipment, etc.) at many tens of billions of dollars at today's prices. These assets were used to finance the immigration of Jews to Israel. Palestinian confiscated lands, worth far more, were used to settle Jewish immigrants. No compensation has been paid to the Palestinians by Israel.

DECLARATION OF INDEPENDENCE   A document published on 14 May 1948, at the expiry of the *British Mandate,* proclaiming "the establishment of a Jewish state in Palestine" and promising to "uphold the full social and political equality of all its citizens, without distinction of religion, race or sex." The declaration also promised to draw up a constitution "not later than the 1st October 1948." That obligation has never been honoured because of two major obstacles faced by Israeli legislators. First, a constitution would provide a set of legal principles by which Arab citizens could challenge the many state policies which discriminate in favour of Jews. Second, the privileging of secular law over *halakha* (rabbinical law) would break the fragile Jewish consensus with the *ultra-Orthodox Jews.* Instead Israel has relied on eleven Basic Laws, which include elements of a constitution. Two Basic Laws passed in 1992, Human Dignity and Freedom, and Freedom of Occupation, for the first time codified some key human rights. However, the rights to equality, freedom of expression and freedom from religious coercion, as well as social rights such as the rights to education, health care, work and welfare, are still not guaranteed in law.

DECLARATION OF PRINCIPLES   See *Oslo Accords.*

DESTROYED VILLAGES   Some 750,000 Palestinians were forced from their lands during the *war of 1948* which created Israel. The 400-plus villages they lived in (some estimates suggest more than 500 but are based on a looser definition of what constituted a village) were demolished by the Jewish state in the aftermath of the war to prevent the refugees' return. The *Jewish National Fund* was responsible for planting forest over many of the destroyed villages. The farmlands of the destroyed villages are usually leased by the state or the JNF to exclusive Jewish communities such as the *kibbutzim* or *moshavim.*

DIASPORA JEWS   The world's total Jewish population is estimated at a little over 13 million, with roughly 5 million living in Israel. A larger number, about 6.5 million, live in North America. About 1.5 million Jews live in Europe, the majority in Western Europe (particularly France and Britain), and a shrinking number in Eastern Europe and the Balkans. Zionist demographers are particularly concerned at the high rate of assimilation, mainly through intermarriage with non-Jews, among Diaspora Jews.

DRUSE   A secretive sect, originally from Egypt, that broke away from Islam in the eleventh century. Today more than half a million Druses live in the mountainous regions of Lebanon, Syria, Israel and Jordan. Inside Israel there are 100,000 Druses, the majority, who became Israeli citizens in 1948, living in the *Galilee,* and a smaller number who were captured along with the *Golan Heights* from Syria in the *war of 1967*. Before the creation of Israel, the Galilee Druses were an integral, if distinct, part of the Arab Palestinian population, and many still live in mixed communities alongside Muslims and Christians. However, during the *war of 1948* the Druse leadership reached a deal with the new Jewish state to fight on the Israeli side. The 1956 Compulsory Conscription Law formalised that relationship by obliging Druse youngsters (unlike those of the other Arab communities) to do military service. Today Israel treats the Druses as a separate nation, identifying them as Druse on their identity cards and educating them according to a separate school syllabus overseen by a Druse department in the Education Ministry. Despite their inhabitants' military service, many Druse villages are among the poorest in Israel. After conscription, Druse youngsters have few employment opportunities apart from joining the security services, often as low-paid policemen or prison wardens. The Druses have earned a reputation among Palestinians in the occupied territories and inside Israel for holding virulently anti-Arab attitudes and being quick to use violence. In recent years a fledgling anti-conscription movement has emerged among them.

DUNUM   One thousand square metres (e.g., an area measuring ten metres by one hundred metres), or a quarter of an acre. A traditional land measurement used in the Middle East.

GALILEE   The most northerly region of Israel, which is home to the country's largest number of Arabs, about 600,000. After decades of government *Judaisation* programmes, the region's population is now evenly split between Jews and Arabs.

GOLAN HEIGHTS   An area of land east of the *Galilee* belonging to Syria but occupied by Israel in the *war of 1967.* The Golan population of 250,000 was reduced to just 8,000, mainly *Druses,* by the fighting. Most of the Golan Druses remain loyal to Syria (and do not serve in the army), although a minority took *citizenship* when the region was annexed by Israel in violation of international law in 1981. Jewish settlement of the Golan Heights has been limited: about 18,000 Jews live among a similar number of Druses.

GREEN LINE   The armistice line agreed between Israel and Jordan in 1949, following the *war of 1948.* Until 1967 the Green Line separated Israel from the West Bank, which was under Jordanian occupation. After the *war of 1967,* when Israel occupied the West Bank, the Jewish state's leaders considered the Green Line effectively erased and even removed it from official maps. In violation of international law, Israel has moved large numbers of Jewish settlers into the West Bank and smaller numbers into Gaza. Outside Israel, the Green Line is widely considered to be the only feasible future border between Israel and a Palestinian state on the West Bank. The wall and fence that Israel is building to separate itself from the Palestinians deviate substantially from the Green Line, effectively annexing large parts of the West Bank.

HALAKHA   The legal system of Judaism based on the Torah and developed by later rabbinical interpretations. *Orthodox* and *ultra-Orthodox Jews,* unlike the Conservative and Reform streams, subscribe to a literalist reading of halakha. At the founding of the state, Israel's leaders reached a deal with the *Orthodox rabbinate,* giving it exclusive regulation of *personal-status laws* and the right to define who is a Jew for the purpose of public records. The rabbinate insists that official bodies observe the Sabbath and kosher (kashrut) laws governing food preparation and consumption. Halakhic law exists in uncomfortable parallel with secular laws passed by the *Knesset.*

HAMULA   Arab clan or extended family.

INTIFADA   Arabic word meaning "shaking off," as in the shaking off of the Israeli occupation. The word is used to refer to two popular uprisings by Palestinians in the occupied territories, the first between 1987 and 1993 and the second which began in September 2000, following a visit by Ariel Sharon to the sacred compound in the Old City of *Jerusalem* known to Muslims as the Noble Sanctuary (the Haram al-Sharif) and to Jews as the Temple Mount. Palestinians often refer to the second intifada as the Aqsa intifada, after the biggest mosque in the Noble Sanctuary compound.

ISRAEL DEFENCE FORCES (IDF)   The Israeli army. Muslim and Christian citizens are excluded from serving in the army and as a result lose the right to many benefits—grants, loans, mortgages, scholarships, jobs—which depend on military service (although most of these benefits arc still available to *ultra-Orthodox Jews*, who are also exempted from military service). Conscription was made compulsory for the small *Druse* community in 1956. The *Bedouins* can volunteer to serve in the IDF, usually as desert trackers. In practice, only a small minority do so.

ISRAEL LANDS AUTHORITY (ILA)   A government body which manages all land owned by the state and the *Jewish National Fund*, today some 93 per cent of all the territory inside the borders of Israel. Such land is generally used for the settlement of Jews only. Half the members of the ILA Council, which determines land policy in Israel, are nominated by the JNF.

ISRAELI ARABS   The term originally used by the government, state bodies, Israeli media and most Israeli Jews to describe those Palestinians who were not expelled from Israel during the *war of 1948*. However, since 1967, Israel has included the 230,000 Palestinians of East *Jerusalem* in its figures on Israeli Arabs (even though few East Jerusalemites have accepted Israeli *citizenship*). According to the Central Bureau of Statistics, there are nearly 1.3 million Israeli Arabs, making up 19 per cent of the Israeli population. The main Israeli Arab communities are Sunni Muslim (81 per cent), Christian (10 per cent) and *Druse* (9 per cent). Israel also often chooses to distinguish between its Muslim and *Bedouin* populations. Israeli Arabs live in 116 Arab-only communities and what are known as seven *mixed cities*. Israeli Arabs may also refer to themselves—or be referred to—as Palestinian citizens of Israel, Israel's Palestinian minority, Palestinians of '48.

JERUSALEM   East Jerusalem was occupied by Israel in the *war of 1967*, along with the Palestinian territories of the West Bank and Gaza, in what Israel hailed as the unification of the city's two halves. East Jerusalem was officially annexed, in violation of international law, a few weeks later. Israel has repeatedly expanded Jerusalem's municipal boundaries to increase the number of Jews considered resident in the city. There are now some 680,000 residents, roughly a third Palestinian, a third Jewish settlers in East Jerusalem, and a third Jews living in West Jerusalem. Israel has declared Jerusalem its "eternal capital," a change of status rejected by the UN. Most countries continue to regard Tel Aviv as the capital of Israel.

JEWISH AGENCY (JA)   A Zionist organisation established in 1929 to act as the political representative of the Jews in Palestine and to help in the creation of a Jewish national home through the "ingathering of the exiles," i.e., the encouragement of mass immigration by Jews in an attempt to change Palestine's demographic balance. Today the JA encourages *Diaspora Jews* to make *aliya*. The JA is regarded as a charity by most countries, and donations are tax-exempt.

JEWISH NATIONAL FUND (JNF)   Known in Hebrew as the Keren Kayemet LeIsrael (Perpetual Fund for Israel), the JNF was established in 1901 as an organ of the *World Zionist Organisation*. Its main task before the founding of Israel was to buy land on behalf of the Jewish people in Palestine. Although there is some dispute about how much land the JNF actually bought, it is known that before 1948 Jews owned no more than 7 per cent of what was to become Israel, much of that privately bought by wealthy Jews. Today, following a policy of land confiscation from the Arab population, the state and the JNF together own 93 per cent of the land (13 per cent is held by the JNF and 80 per cent by the state). According to its charter, the JNF can lease land only to Jews. It also oversees tree-planting operations and manages some forests, particularly on *destroyed villages* and land confiscated from Arab owners. The JNF is regarded as a charity by most countries, and donations are tax-exempt.

JUDAISATION   A long-standing government policy in the regions of the *Galilee, Negev* and *Triangle* to change the traditional demographic balance so that Jews outnumber Arabs. The purpose is to strengthen Jewish control and dominance of land in these traditional Arab heartlands. Jews are encouraged to move to these peripheral regions by incentives, usually cheap land and housing.

KIBBUTZ (PL. KIBBUTZIM) Collective rural Jewish communities originally intended as socialist communes. Inhabitants usually depend on farming to generate income. Traditionally, all property is communally owned. Today, when the kibbutzim are generally unprofitable, much of their land is being sold off to private developers.

KNESSET The Israeli parliament, with 120 members. Each party selects its Knesset members from its candidate list in strict proportion to its share of the national vote. The leader of the single largest party in the Knesset usually forms the government. For much of Israel's history, power has resided in the hands of the Labour Party, but since the late 1970s the more hawkish Likud Party has become dominant. To form a government, the biggest party needs a coalition of smaller parties to give it a majority of seats in the Knesset. The choice is usually between *ultra-Orthodox* parties demanding a more openly theocratic state and extremist right-wing parties demanding a harsher policy towards Palestinians in the occupied territories, and in some cases espousing the expulsion of *Israeli Arabs*. Currently there are two small Arab parties, one the nationalist Tajamu Party (known as Balad in Hebrew) and the other the United Arab List, an ad hoc alliance between an Islamic faction and a Bedouin leader. There is also a small joint Arab-Jewish Communist Party, known as Jebha in Arabic and Hadash in Hebrew. In most elections, the Labour and Likud parties each puts forward one or two Arab candidates, with Likud usually choosing former senior-ranking *Druse* soldiers. No Arab party has ever been allowed to sit in the government. Arab parties are regularly threatened with disqualification at election time through legislation which bans parties whose platforms "negate the existence of the state of Israel as the state of the Jewish people" or "the democratic character of the state." The demand for "a state of all its citizens," the platform of most Arab parliamentary candidates, is regarded as contravening the legislation because it opposes the idea of Israel as both Jewish and democratic.

LAW OF RETURN A piece of legislation passed by the Knesset in 1950 which guarantees every Jew in the world the right to come to Israel as an immigrant and receive citizenship. The law defines a Jew as anyone with one Jewish grandparent, as opposed to the stricter definition of *halakha* (rabbinical law) that a Jew must be born to a Jewish mother. Exceptions to the rights conferred by the Law of Return are made only for political dissidents and certain convicted criminals.

MILITARY GOVERNMENT   Israel established a military government to restrict the movement and rights of the 150,000 Palestinians it inherited after the *war of 1948*. No Arab citizen was allowed to leave his or her town or village without a permit from the local military governor. The regime was abolished in 1966.

MITZPE (PL. MITZPIM)   Literally, a "lookout" settlement. Exclusive Jewish settlements developed in the 1980s and 1990s as a way to attract middle-class Jews to live in Israel's rural Arab heartlands. The name "mitzpe" derives from the idea that the inhabitants should watch over their Arab neighbours to ensure they do not build and thereby try to reclaim land the state has confiscated from them.

MIXED CITIES   There are seven mixed cities inside Israel, although officials often include an eighth: annexed East *Jerusalem*. They are Tel Aviv–Jaffa, Ramle, Lod, Haifa, Acre, Upper Nazareth and Maalot-Tarshiha. The label "mixed city" is misleading, as in all these cases *Israeli Arabs* live in distinct, separate communities, usually poor ghetto neighbourhoods, attached to what is effectively a Jewish city. By the design of state planners, Arabs are never supposed to comprise more than 20 per cent of the population of a mixed city.

MIZRAHIM   See *Sephardim*.

MOSHAV (PL. MOSHAVIM)   A rural community similar to the *kibbutz*, but each family privately leases its own farmland and home and makes its own decisions. Only buying and selling is organized cooperatively.

NAKBA   Arabic word meaning "catastrophe," used by Palestinians to describe the defeat and mass dispossession of the Palestinians that occurred during and after the *war of 1948*.

NEGEV   The large southern desert region of Israel which has been inhabited by semi-nomadic *Bedouin* tribes for many generations. After mass expulsions during and after the *war of 1948*, the number of

Bedouins dropped precipitously. Today, after state-sponsored *Judaisation* programmes, the 145,000 Bedouins in the Negev make up a quarter of the population there, with half living in urban reservations created by the government and the other half living illegally in *unrecognised villages*. The Negev's Bedouins have one of the highest fertility rates in the world and are regarded as a "demographic time bomb" by most Israeli officials.

ORTHODOX JEWS   The name for Jews who observe *halakha*. Although there are several streams of Judaism, Orthodoxy is the only one with official standing in Israel. Since the creation of Israel, particularly following the *war of 1967*, a significant proportion of Orthodox Jews have adopted nationalist and messianic views, which encourage them to regard the settling of the *Palestinian occupied territories* as a religious duty.

ORTHODOX RABBINATE   The rabbinical authorities in Israel are drawn exclusively from the Orthodox stream of Judaism, ignoring the other major, and more liberal, streams, Conservative and Reform Judaism. Since the founding of the state, the Orthodox rabbinate has been given control over *personal-status laws* for Jews and over deciding who is a Jew for public records. Traditionally there have been two chief rabbis, one representing *Ashkenazi* Jews and the other representing *Sephardi* Jews. Nonetheless, Sephardi Jews often complain that Ashkenazi rabbis have greater powers, particularly in controlling religious education. Splits have developed in the rabbinate between those supporting the settlement project in the *Palestinian occupied territories* and those opposed to it.

OSLO ACCORDS   After secret talks in the summer of 1993 in Oslo, Israel and the *Palestine Liberation Organisation* signed accords at the White House on 13 September 1993. Called the Declaration of Principles, the accords provided for Palestinian self-rule in much of Gaza and in the small West Bank town of Jericho, followed by promises of Israeli troop withdrawals from the main Palestinian population centres. By 1999 the Palestinians had control of about 40 per cent of the West Bank and 70 per cent of Gaza. However, any chance of effective Palestinian sovereignty was severely eroded by the doubling of the Jewish settler population to 200,000 in the West Bank during the Oslo period. Progress made under the Oslo Accords was reversed following the failure of talks at Camp David in July 2000 and at Taba in February 2001 to reach a final-status agreement. A Palestinian *intifada* erupted in September 2000, and Israel subsequently reoccupied much of the West Bank.

PALESTINE LIBERATION ORGANISATION (PLO)   An umbrella organisation created in 1964 to represent the Palestinian people, which called for the establishment of a single democratic and secular state in the area of Mandatory Palestine (what is today Israel, the West Bank and Gaza). After Israel's occupation of the West Bank and Gaza in 1967, the PLO declared armed struggle as the only way to liberate Palestine, and two years later Yasser Arafat, the leader of the biggest Palestinian faction, Fatah, became chairman. In 1988 the PLO renounced violence and recognised the state of Israel. When Israel officially lifted its ban on contacts with the PLO in 1993, the path was laid for the signing of the *Oslo Accords,* in which Israel for the first time recognised the PLO as the representative of the Palestinian people. The creation of a Palestinian Authority, led by Arafat in the West Bank and Gaza in 1994, effectively marginalised the significance of the PLO.

PALESTINIAN OCCUPIED TERRITORIES   The West Bank, Gaza and East *Jerusalem,* occupied by Israel in the *war of 1967.* The West Bank has a population of 2.3 million Palestinians as well as 200,000 Jewish settlers living in communities that are illegal under international law. Israeli Jews often refer to the West Bank by its Biblical names, Judea and Samaria. The tiny Gaza Strip has 1.2 million Palestinians and a Jewish population of 7,000 settlers, who are due to be withdrawn by the Israeli government in 2005. The Palestinian areas of the Gaza Strip are some of the most densely populated places on earth. Unlike the *Israeli Arabs* and the Jewish settlers, both of whose rights and duties derive solely from Israeli law, the Palestinians in the occupied territories are affected by a web of overlapping legal systems, including local laws (based in the West Bank on Jordanian law that applied till 1967), Israeli laws, Israeli military decisions and international humanitarian law. Israeli military judges have wide-ranging powers to approve the detention of those arrested by the army and to sentence them, often on secret evidence. Adjudication in disputes over the application of laws in the occupied territories is overseen by the Israeli Supreme Court, which, according to the leading Israeli jurist David Kretzmer, has served to clothe "acts of military authorities in a cloak of legality."

PERSONAL-STATUS LAWS   Under Israeli law, issues relating to births, marriages and deaths are the exclusive preserve of the religious authorities of each religious community. Separate religious courts exist for Jews, Muslims, *Druses* and the Christian denominations, each having sole authority within its community to rule, for example, in cases of divorce. The only marriages permitted in Israel are religious ones, so that it is impossible for members of different faiths, say a Muslim and a Jew, to marry unless one converts (although Israel does recognise interfaith marriages performed in civil courts outside Israel). Jewish personal-status laws are particularly problematic in relation to defining who is a Jew. Since the founding of the state, exclusive control of personal-status laws has been invested in the *Orthodox rabbinate*. The world's two other major, more liberal Jewish streams, Conservative and Reform, have no official standing. This has led to the anomaly that Jews eligible for citizenship under the *Law of Return* (which defines a Jew as having one Jewish grandparent) are not considered Jews by the Israeli religious authorities (who use the halakhic definition of a Jew as someone born to a Jewish mother). Such Jews are effectively invisible in terms of their personal status: they cannot marry in Israel, they cannot be buried in Jewish cemeteries, they cannot be ascribed a Jewish nationality on their identity cards. A large number of such Jews arrived following the collapse of the Soviet Union; some estimates suggest half of these one million Russians, as they are called, are not Jewish according to halakha.

PRESENT ABSENTEE   The Israeli state's term for an internally displaced Palestinian citizen (expelled refugees are known simply as "absentees"). The present absentees were present in Israel after its founding (and therefore gained *citizenship*, although in many cases belatedly) but are considered by the state to have been absent, even if briefly, from their property during the *war of 1948*. Present absentees lost all rights to their homes, lands and bank accounts. These were passed to an official known as the *custodian of absentee property*. Today, a quarter of *Israeli Arabs*—250,000—live as present absentees.

SEPHARDIM   The descendants of Spanish and Portuguese Jews. After the Jews were expelled from Spain and Portugal in the fifteenth century, they settled mainly in North Africa, Turkey and Greece. The label Sephardi is often also applied to Oriental Jews, known in Israel as the Mizrahim, who have no ancestral ties to Spain. Descended from Jews who remained in the Middle East, their main population centres were in Yemen, Iraq and Iran. Many of the Sephardim and Mizrahim were late or unwilling converts to *Zionism*. Those living in Arab countries were often forced to leave after the creation of Israel strained relations with neighbouring Arab states.

SHIN BET   Officially known as the General Security Services, the Shin Bet is Israel's domestic security service and has various subdivisions monitoring *Israeli Arabs,* Jewish extremist organisations and foreign diplomats as well as protecting senior military and political figures. After 1967 the Shin Bet moved its intelligence-gathering operations into the *Palestinian occupied territories,* where it runs an extensive network of spies and collaborators. It sometimes cooperates overseas with Mossad, the foreign intelligence service.

SIX-DAY WAR   See *war of 1967.*

TRIANGLE   A thin, triangular strip of land in central Israel close to the northern West Bank which is populated by 150,000 Arabs. Government *Judaisation* programmes have largely failed to bring Jews into the area. In many places the wall being built by Israel runs directly through mixed *Israeli Arab* and Palestinian communities (e.g., Baqa and Bartaa) astride the *Green Line*, thereby splitting families in half. Several Israeli leaders, including Ariel Sharon, have raised the idea of a land swap with the Palestinians which would transfer the Triangle to a future Palestinian state in the West Bank.

ULTRA-ORTHODOX JEWS   Fundamentalist Jews, numbering about 700,000 in Israel, who refuse all modern innovations and subscribe to a literalist reading of the Scriptures. The ultra-Orthodox are strongly opposed to *Zionism*, mainly because the Talmud enjoins Jews not to immigrate en masse to the Promised Land until the coming of the Messiah. The ultra-Orthodox are exempted from serving in the army and enjoy special state subsidies to study in seminaries. After the *Bedouins*, they have the highest birthrate in Israel. Also known as the Haredim (the "God-fearing").

UNRECOGNISED VILLAGES   Several dozen Arab communities that Israel has refused to recognise since its creation in 1948. Some 100,000 Arab citizens live in these villages—one in ten of the Arab population. By law, the unrecognised villages cannot be supplied with services from the water, electricity, sewerage and telephone utility companies. The homes in unrecognised villages are all without licences and therefore subject to demolition. In the *Negev*, unrecognised villages usually comprise tin shacks and tents because anything more permanent would be demolished.

WAR OF 1948   Known by Israel as the War of Independence. A year-long war, following the end of the *British Mandate*, between the Israeli army and Jewish militias on one side and a combination of Palestinian militias and armies from neighbouring Arab states on the other. For many months before May 1948, when the Jewish leadership in Palestine issued the *Declaration of Independence* establishing Israel, there had been tit-for-tat killings, mainly of civilians, culminating in several well-planned and large-scale massacres by Jewish militias, including the most famous, Deir Yassin, on 9 April 1948. During the war Israel captured 78 per cent of Palestine (excluding the West Bank and Gaza) and expelled 750,000 Palestinians (or 80 per cent of the 900,000 Palestinians under its control). The refugees, most now in Lebanon, Syria, Jordan, the West Bank and Gaza, have never been allowed to return. During the war Israel declared a state of emergency, adopting emergency regulations drafted by the British during the Mandate, which has never been revoked. The emergency laws give the government draconian powers.

WAR OF 1967   Known by Israelis as the Six-Day War, when Israel captured the Palestinian areas of the West Bank and East *Jerusalem* from Jordan and the Gaza Strip from Egypt. Israel also occupied the Sinai Peninsula, which was returned to Egypt in a peace deal in 1982, and the *Golan Heights*, which Israel has yet to return to Syria.

WAR OF INDEPENDENCE   See *war of 1948.*

WORLD ZIONIST ORGANISATION (WZO)   A body established by the First Zionist Congress in Switzerland in 1897 to work towards the creation of a Jewish national home. It continued in existence after the founding of Israel in 1948 and today is active in financing settlement projects in the *Palestinian occupied territories.*

ZIONISM   An ideology which became a popular political movement, usually ascribed to Theodor Herzl, who articulated the idea of a state for the Jews in his book *Der Judenstaat* (1896). Critics of Zionism have observed that not only did it emerge in the context of growing nationalism in Europe, but it also shared the assumption of many anti-Semitic Europeans that the Jews were a separate nation who could not be integrated into the European nations and should therefore be forced to live apart. Zionism spawned a set of key institutions: the *World Zionist Organisation,* the *Jewish Agency* and the *Jewish National Fund.* Conceived of as a secular nationalist movement by Herzl, Zionism has developed several offshoots, including a strong religious movement inside Israel. Today secular Zionists often blur these distinctions by using Biblical justifications for the establishment of Israel in the Promised Land.

SOURCES

Interviews

Dr. Asad Ghanem, Tamra, 24 May 2004
Dr. Adel Manna, Van Leer Institute, Jerusalem, 13 June 2004
Dr. Daphna Golan, West Jerusalem, 13 June 2004
Eitan Bronstein, Kfar Shemaryahu, 5 July 2004
Dr. Uri Davis, Sharon Hotel, Herziliya, 13 August 2004
Dr. Said Zidane, American Colony Hotel, Jerusalem, 3 October 2004

References

1: THE ROAD TO TAMRA

Marwan Dwairy, lecture at the First Annual Conference of the Palestinian Arab Minority in Israel, Nazareth, 10 June 2004.

2: DEATH OF A LOVE AFFAIR

Sara Liebovitch-Dar, "Living with Them," *Ha'aretz*, 26 September 2003 (only in Hebrew).
Mufid Abdul Hadi, *The Other Side of the Coin*, PASSIA, 1998, p. 138.

3: SECOND-CLASS CITIZENS

Yair Ettinger, "Arab Editor Opts Out of Katsav Trip After Airport Flap," *Ha'aretz*, 17 February 2004.

Michal Aharoni, "Either Racism or Journalism," *Maariv online*, 13 June 2004.

Yossi Melman, "Even the Shin Bet Is Against Discrimination," *Ha'aretz* supplement "Arab Snapshots," 25 May 2004.

Anat Balint, "IBA Illegally Confiscated Papers of Arabs," *Ha'aretz*, 1 June 2004.

Sigal Shambiro, "IKEA Refuses to Deliver to Israeli Arab Town, Citing 'Danger,' " *Ha'aretz*, 23 July 2004.

"The Official Summation of the Or Commission Report," *Ha'aretz*, 2 September 2003, www.haaretz.com/hasen/pages/ShArt.jhtml?itemNo=335594.

Aryeh Dayan, "Teachers' Pests," *Ha'aretz*, 1 October 2004.

Shahar Ilan, "Report: Haredi School Spending Twice as Much per Pupil as State Schools," *Ha'aretz*, 6 August 2004.

David Ratner, "MK Urges Debate on Arab Schools After *Ha'aretz* Exposé," *Ha'aretz*, 16 July 2004.

Yuli Khromchenko, "Ministry of Education Scuttles Plan to Open Jewish-Arab School in Kafr Kara," *Ha'aretz*, 2 July 2004.

Aviad Kleinberg, "Numerus Clausus," *Ha'aretz*, 16 December 2003.

Omar Barghouti, "On Dance, Identity and War," *Al-Ahram Weekly*, 13–19 June 2002.

Yair Ettinger, "Survey Finds Few Arabs in Top Echelons of Civil Service," *Ha'aretz*, 11 November 2004.

Shlomo Swirski and Etty Konor-Attias, "Israel: A Social Report 2003," Adva Centre, February 2004, www.adva.org/ISRAEL_2003_ENG.pdf.

Moshe Gorali, "Second-Class Status and a Fear of a Fifth Column," *Ha'aretz*, 24 May 2004.

Ramit Plushnik-Masti, "Israel Marked Helmets of Arab Workers," Associated Press, 9 March 2004.

Jonathan Cook, "McDonald's Manager Admits Arabic Led to Firing," *Electronic Intifada*, 10 March 2004, www.electronicIntifada.net/v2/article2492.shtml.

4: ECHOES OF APARTHEID

Ein Hod artists' village homepage, www.ein-hod.israel.net

Jan C. Smuts, "Address to the Jewish Community of South Africa," 3 November 1919, Johannesburg Town Hall.

Jewish National Fund website, www.jnf.org/site/PageServer?page name=Trees.

Jewish National Fund website, www.jnf.org/site/PageServer?page name=PR_UN_NGO_ Status.

Uri Davis, *Apartheid Israel*, Zed Books, 2003.

Will Hutton, "How the Zealots Are Killing a Dream," *Observer*, 25 July 2004.

5: THE MISSING LEFT

Jonathan Cook, "A Jew Among 25,000 Muslims," *Guardian*, 27 August 2003.

Sara Liebovitch-Dar, "Living with Them," *Ha'aretz*, 26 September 2003 (only in Hebrew).

Daphna Baram, "A Sham at the Heart of Israel," *Guardian*, 1 September 2004.

Motti Bassok, "Klein: Central Bank Favors Hiring Arabs," *Ha'aretz*, 31 May 2004.

Vered Levy-Barzilai, "Know Thy Neighbour—But Don't Hire Him," *Ha'aretz*, 12 July 2001.

Paul Eisen, "Speaking the Truth to Jews," in *Speaking the Truth About Zionism and Israel*, ed. Michael Prior, Melisende (London), 2004.

6: A TRAUMATISED SOCIETY

Amir Rapoport, "Suicide No. 1 Cause of Death in IDF," *Maariv online*, 15 July 2004.

Gideon Alon, "30–40 Per Cent of Conscripts Request Psychological Help," *Ha'aretz*, 18 August 2004.

Rabbi Jon-Jay Tilsen, "Conscientious Objection to Military Service in Israel," Beth El-Keser Israel website, undated, www.beki.org/conscientious.html.

Zvi Harel, "The Defendant Was an 'Impressive Officer,'" *Ha'aretz*, 9 September 2004.

Jonathan Lis, "IDF Questions Reservists Who Organised Hebron Photo Exhibit," *Ha'aretz*, 23 June 2004.

Molly Moore, "Breaking the Silence on West Bank Abuse," *Washington Post*, 24 June 2004.

Yitzhak Laor, "In Hebron," *London Review of Books*, 22 July 2004.

Anonymous, "A Soldier in Nablus," Znet, 5 September 2004, www.zmag.org/content/showarticle.cfm?SectionID=22%20&ItemID=6172.

Chris McGreal, "Israeli Officer: I Was Right to Shoot 13-Year-Old Child," *Guardian*, 24 November 2004.

Amir Buhbut, "Elite Soldiers Contend Razing Palestinian Houses Is 'Immoral,'" *Maariv online*, 27 September 2004.

"The Official Summation of the Or Commission Report," *Ha'aretz*, 2 September 2003, www.haaretz.com/hasen/pages/ShArt.jhtml?itemNo=335594.

Neve Shalom/Wahat al-Salam website, Frequently Asked Questions, www.nswas.com/article278.html.

Yoav Keren, "Hamas Among Us," *Maariv*, 11 July 2004 (only in Hebrew).

7: WHERE NEXT?

Sigmund Freud, "Letter to Dr. Chaim Koffler," 26 February 1930, www.freud.org.uk/arab-israeli.html.

Said Zidane, "Palestinians and Israeli Jews: Divide and Share the Land," personal position paper, August 2003 (unpublished).

Mamphela Ramphele, *Steering by the Stars*, Tafelberg, 2002, p. 109.

Jonathan Cook and Alexander Key, *Silencing Dissent*, Arab Association for Human Rights, 22 October 2002.

Useful Websites

The following reliable websites have English pages dealing with issues related to the Arab citizens of Israel.

ARAB

Adalah

www.adalah.org/eng/index.php

Established in 1996, Adalah ("Justice" in Arabic) is a legal organisation dedicated to protecting the human rights of Israel's Arab minority, mainly through legal challenges in the courts. It publishes an informative monthly newsletter on its website as well as its annual *Review* in Arabic, Hebrew and English, which carries articles by leading lawyers and academics on key issues facing the minority.

Arab Association of Human Rights (HRA)

www.arabhra.org

The HRA was founded in 1988 to promote the political, social, economic and cultural rights of the Arab minority inside Israel by lobbying major international bodies such as the United Nations. It also runs programmes in schools to educate Arab children in their rights. It has published a series of six comprehensive fact sheets on its website and regularly issues reports on aspects of Israeli discrimination against the Arab minority. Each week it publishes a digest of reports from the local Arab media.

Arab Centre for Alternative Planning

www.ac-ap.org

The centre was created in 2000 in response to the huge pressures on the Arab minority in terms of land, planning, housing and development. In 2004, ACAP became the first independent Arab organisation ever to win the right to file objections on local and national planning procedures. The website includes a newsletter and articles on planning and land matters.

Association of Forty

www.assoc40.org

The website of the lobby group begun by Mohammed Abu Hayja (see Chapter 4) to win recognition for those Arab communities the Israeli state refuses to recognise, commonly known as the unrecognised villages. Some 100,000 Arab citizens live in such communities, including 75,000 Bedouins in the Negev. The website includes historical and statistical information on the unrecognised villages.

Galilee Society

www.gal-soc.org

Established by health-care professionals in 1981, the Galilee Society campaigns for equality for Arab citizens in their health, environmental and socio-economic conditions. Much of its work concentrates on training programmes and compiling data and surveys. Its Rikaz database, which includes a great deal of demographic information on the minority, can be found at http://www.rikaz.org/en/index.php.

I'lam

www.ilamcenter.org

I'lam was founded in 2000 as the minority's first media centre to try to open up the Israeli media to little-heard Arab perspectives, combat bias in the Hebrew media and improve standards in the local Arab media. It was one of the key organisations documenting police violence towards the minority during the October 2000 events. The website includes useful information about discriminatory policies in the Israeli media.

Ittijah

www.ittijah.org

Ittijah is the umbrella organisation for all the nonprofit groups working for the Arab minority, helping to coordinate their activities. The website includes several fact sheets and a regular newsletter providing details of forthcoming activities by its members.

Mada

www.mada-research.org

Established in 2000, Mada is an Arab-run research institute developing public policy proposals advancing the national rights of Arab citizens. It also organises conferences and seminars exploring issues of citizenship, national identity and democracy models in multiethnic states. It has published a detailed book on the situation of Arab citizens in Israel, *Citizens Without Citizenship*. In 2005 it will publish the first edition of a new journal, *Palestinian Review*.

Mossawa

www.mossawacenter.org

Mossawa, an advocacy centre for Arab citizens founded in 1997, works both locally and internationally to raise the profile of the minority. It specialises in compiling comparative data on social and economic discrimination against the Arab minority. The website includes some short reports in English and press releases.

JOINT ARAB AND JEWISH

Alternative Information Centre

www.alternativenews.org

A well-established anti-Zionist website run from Jerusalem and Bethlehem by Israelis and Palestinians. Although its main focus is on the occupied territories, it does also publish informed fact sheets and articles on the Arab minority. The AIC publishes a monthly magazine, *News from Within*; some of the articles are available from its separate website, http://www.newsfrom within.org/.

Sikkuy

www.sikkuy.org.il/english/home.html

Founded in 1991, Sikkuy is jointly managed by an Arab and a Jewish director. The Jewish branch has established three civil action groups in Jewish areas to lobby for equal rights for their Arab neighbours. Sikkuy is also behind an initiative to encourage Jewish and Arab muncipalities to increase levels of cooperation. The website publishes an important annual report monitoring equality in government programmes, budgets and resources.

JEWISH

Adva

www.adva.org/indexe.html

An organisation dedicated to analysis of Israeli policy towards marginalised communities, including women, Mizrahi Jews and Arab citizens. The website includes comparative data in the Social Gaps section, as well as analysis reports.

Association for Civil Rights in Israel

www.acri.org.il/english-acri/engine/index.asp

Founded in 1972, ACRI is dedicated to protecting human rights inside Israel and the occupied territories, mainly through legal challenges in the courts. The website has useful information on discrimination inside Israel, particularly against the Bedouins.

Zochrot

www.nakbainhebrew.org/index.php?id=49&search_word=english

Most of the "Nakba in Hebrew" website, as its name suggests, is in Hebrew, but a few articles and reports on Zochrot events can be found on this page.

INTERNATIONAL

Palestine Remembered

www.palestineremembered.com

An invaluable website with a great deal of relevant material about the hundreds of Arab villages destroyed in 1948. The best feature is a geographically listed guide to each of the villages, with information on the date of its ethnic cleansing, the Israeli army operation in which it was attacked, the amount of land owned by the village and its population, where the survivors are now and which Israeli settlements have been built over the village. Refugees also have a noticeboard on which they can leave stories, messages and photographs.

INDEX

A NOTE ABOUT THE AUTHOR

SUSAN NATHAN was born in England and when young visited family and friends in apartheid-era South Africa, the country of her father's birth. There she had several deep encounters with the social and political situation of that country. She became an AIDS counselor in London, and after she was divorced and her children were grown up, following the Jewish Law of Return, she moved to Israel.

A NOTE ABOUT THE TYPE

The text of this book is set in ITC New Baskerville®. This version of the font was designed by Matthew Carter and John Quaranda in 1978 for the International Typeface Corporation. Legible and eminently dignified, New Baskerville is based on a typeface designed by British printer and typographer John Baskerville (1706–1775). With the delicacy and grace that come from a long elegant serif and the subtle transfer of stroke weight from thick to very thin, New Baskerville makes an ideal text typeface.